The Procrastinator's Guide to Financial Security

The Procrastinator's Guide to Financial Security

How Anyone over 40 Can Still
Build a Strong Portfolio—and
Retire Comfortably

David F. Teitelbaum

AMACOM

American Management Association

New York • Atlanta • Boston • Chicago • Kansas City • San Francisco • Washington, D. C.
Brussels • Mexico City • Tokyo • Toronto

This publication is designed to provide accurate and authoritative information in regard to the subject matter covered. It is sold with the understanding that the publisher is not engaged in rendering legal, accounting, or other professional service. If legal advice or other expert assistance is required, the services of a competent professional person should be sought.

Library of Congress Cataloging-in-Publication Data

Teitelbaum, David F.
    The procrastinator's guide to financial security: how anyone over 40 can still build a strong portfolio—and retire comfortably / David F. Teitelbaum.
       p.   cm.
    Includes index.
    ISBN 0-8144-0621-1
    1. Baby boom generation—Finance, Personal.   2. Retirement income—United   States—Planning.   3. Investments—United States.
I. Title.

HG179 .T395   2001
332.024′01—dc21   00-045126

Printing number

10 9 8 7 6 5 4 3 2 1

This book is dedicated to
my late grandfather,
Philip Ringel,
who taught me many things about life,
including spirituality and money
management.

CONTENTS

ACKNOWLEDGMENTS

First, I'd like to thank my late father, Perry Teitelbaum; my mother, Miriam Korenblatt; my brother, Daniel Teitelbaum; and my stepfather, Martin Korenblatt, for their support and their positive influences.

I'd like to thank my friend and stockbroker, Rick Malone, for teaching me some of the concepts I discuss in this book.

I'd also like to thank the friends who suggested that I write this book and those who gave me such positive support. There are too many to name, but I would particularly like to recognize Erica Clary, Thomas Clary, Lewis Fisher, Noreen Hannigan, David Kerr, Chris Mallder, Kris Mason, Julie Murdoch, and Bryan Weinert.

Chapter 1

THE BABY BOOMERS' RETIREMENT CONUNDRUM

One of the most important events affecting the U.S. economy in the second half of the twentieth century was the baby boom. The sudden surge of births starting in 1946, after World War II, and continuing through 1964 has helped to define the history, culture, and economy of the United States. The baby boom generation, totaling 77 million people, includes almost one-third of the current U.S. population.

The generation that once listened to phrases such as "Don't trust anyone over 30" and lyrics such as "I hope I die before I get old" is well over 30 and getting older. Starting in January 1996, the first baby boomer turned 50, and many more reach that age every day.

Baby boomers are waking up to the fact that retirement is not some far-off dream or idea but a reality that will arrive soon. They are also waking up to the realization that many of them have little or no retirement savings, that the ground rules for retirement have been changing, and that many do not have enough money for a comfortable retirement. Although a majority (72 percent) of baby boomers have given some thought to their retirement years,[1] a recent study has shown the average boomer's net worth at less than $50,000; for many, a large portion of this amount is in their home and not liquid.[2] Thus, the average boomer will not have enough to retire and live on unless he or she starts saving and investing now. One study concluded that on average, boomers should be saving three times as much as they are currently to avoid a sharp decline in their standard of living.[3]

Large numbers of American workers are concerned about their retirement, and this trend is driving many changes, including a desire to learn about investing and a shift toward starting to invest. To find evidence of the former, consider the amount of coverage of financial matters in print and on the radio, Internet, and TV today;[4] the media are simply reflecting this growing desire to learn about and stay informed about the

---

1. Source: "Baby Boomers Envision Their Retirement: An AARP Segmentation Analysis," American Association of Retired Persons (AARP), www.aarp.org, February 1999.

2. In 1994, the typical boomer's net worth was a little more than $40,000. Older boomers' net worth was about $58,000, and younger boomers' net worth was about $23,000. Without counting home equity, the net worth for these two groups was about $18,000 and $7,000, respectively. (Note: All figures are in 1994 dollars.) Source: John R. Gist, Ke Bin Wu, and Charles Ford, "Do Baby Boomers Save and, if So, What For? Executive Summary," AARP, www.aarp.org, June 1999.

3. Stanford University professor Douglas Bernheim performed this study for Merrill Lynch. Source: Betsy Morris and Erin M. Davies, "The Future of Retirement," Fortune, August 19, 1996, www.fortune.com.

4. In 1998, the Oxbridge Communications Study counted 187 financial publications, 5 financial television stations, and 162 financial Internet sites. Source: Peter Lynch, "Fidelity's Guide to Investing Responsibly," www.fidelity.com.

financial world. To find evidence of the latter, compare the number of households with money in stocks or mutual funds twenty years ago with the number of such households today: It has skyrocketed, going from 4.6 million in 1980 to 48.4 million in 1999.[5]

Baby boomers are in their peak earning years. Demographic models usually assume that people in their forties and fifties are at the top of their game in terms of skills, earnings, and earning potential.[6] The late 1990s were characterized by a booming economy with low unemployment. This low unemployment means that there has been high demand for skilled employees, which translates into higher salaries and generous benefit packages. Even though many baby boomers have additional financial burdens, such as college tuition for their children, this is clearly the time for boomers to be putting away money for retirement.

Unfortunately, this doesn't seem to be happening. The level of knowledge and sophistication about financial matters among baby boomers has not risen with the increase in financial information. Many baby boomers still approach investing as if it were a foreign language, something they know little about and are not very comfortable with. The reason is quite simple: They have never learned the fundamentals of money management, which include budgeting, saving, and investing. These fundamentals are not taught in school, nor are they taught once a person graduates college and enters society. In the last thirty years, baby boomers have heard much more about spending than about saving and investing. American society resonates with the ideas of instant gratification, debt, and spending. The easy availability of credit cards, installment

---

5. *Mutual Funds Magazine,* May 2000.
6. Harry S. Dent Jr., *The Great Boom Ahead* (New York: Hyperion, 1993), p. 27.

plans, and layaway plans promotes buying today with little thought for tomorrow. As long as boomers think about spending and not saving, about borrowing and not investing, about today and not tomorrow, few will have the money to retire successfully.

About half of the baby boomers do not take savings and investing seriously.[7] They must learn fundamental concepts and grow in experience to become wise investors. Like other disciplines, investing and finance have their own rhythm and their own vocabulary. To get their financial lives in order, boomers will have to study, experience, and learn about these disciplines.

Learning to curb impulse spending, invest, formulate a financial plan, and stick to that plan can help to ensure a comfortable retirement. However, most people grow up without having learned money management skills and habits. Savings and the miracle of compound interest are rarely taught, and the need to be disciplined is rarely emphasized. By the time people are earning money, bad habits and patterns have become ingrained and are very difficult to break.

All too often, investments are based on a hot tip, magazine article, tape series, or radio talk show discussion. Many people expect to get rich from these tidbits of information, in part because of the common belief that investing is a crapshoot, similar to playing the lottery, and there are no underlying principles involved. Nothing is further from the truth.

Imagine trying to fix your car, fly an airplane, perform brain surgery, or ski competitively based on a hot tip, magazine article, tape series, or radio talk show discussion. To do

---

7. About 46 percent of boomers save regularly for retirement, but about 24 percent don't save at all, and the rest save only occasionally. Source: Gist, Wu, and Ford, "Do Baby Boomers Save?" AARP, www.aarp. org, June 1999.

any of these sophisticated activities based on such skimpy information seems ludicrous. Yet this is what many baby boomers do when they make major financial decisions.

Securing a comfortable retirement will not occur overnight and will not occur without some work. To learn financial material, boomers need to be learning constantly; this includes reading appropriate financial materials, attending seminars, and listening to financial programs. For most boomers, the need to take money management seriously cannot be emphasized enough; they need to devote more time and energy.

Why is this so important? Because people have only a finite amount of time to earn the money they need to live the rest of their lives comfortably. A major fear of many Americans is running out of money during retirement. This can happen for any number of reasons, including poor planning and unexpected expenses, such as health-related expenses. Imagine suddenly realizing, well into retirement, that you do not have enough money and will have to find a new job. There is a good chance that it will not be the high-paying job you have today but a low-paying, low-skill job that will do little to ease your long-term financial worries. Do you think your employer (or a competitor) will welcome you back if you have been out of your field for fifteen or twenty years? Not only will you not be current in your field, but your work skills will be rusty, your command of the new technology will be lacking, and you would be hard pressed to keep up with your fellow workers.

Alternatively, imagine that you are running out of money but cannot hold down a job because of illness or disability. Or imagine that you simply can't afford to retire. You will soon find yourself dependent on the generosity of others. Social Security will almost certainly be there in some form and will act as a safety net, but it was never intended to be a major source of income during retirement. Unfortunately, Social Security may be the only retirement program some boomers will have.[8]

How can you ensure that any of these things do not happen to you? The best way to make sure that you have the money you need is to take steps now to make it happen. That way, you are in charge of your own fate and will not have to depend on anyone else. Your decisions and actions today will determine your retirement lifestyle.

There are no guarantees, for certainly a medical emergency or other type of emergency can wipe out the results of many years of saving, investing, and planning. However, you can take steps to help prevent catastrophe. It is important to start planning and investing now; the earlier you start, the larger the nest egg you will have when you retire.

We can't change the past, but we can change the future. If you, as a boomer, have piled up a huge debt and live paycheck to paycheck or have never gotten around to investing for the future, you can't change the circumstances that got you to the present. If your financial situation is not what you want it to be, you can't go back in time and adjust how you managed your money. But you can take matters into your own hands today and work toward a better tomorrow.

To secure a better tomorrow, you need to take specific steps:

1. First, define your short-, medium-, and long-term goals. Determine what is important during each of these time frames. Short-term goals include those in the next six to twelve months and might include buying new clothes or taking a vacation. Medium-term goals might include buying a home, re-

---

8. Fifteen percent of boomers expect to rely on Social Security for most or all of their retirement needs. Source: "Baby Boomers Envision Their Retirement," AARP, www.aarp.org, February 1999.

placing your car, or funding your children's college education. Long-term goals include retirement, funding your children's college education, and helping your parents. Intertwined with each of these goals are your family's life and health insurance needs.

2. Next, look at your current assets and liabilities. Liabilities can be divided between short term (such as credit card debt), medium term (such as college loans), and long term (such as mortgage payments). If your short-term debts exceed your available assets, your first priority should be reducing this debt. There is no point in considering investing in stocks, which have averaged about 11 percent annually, when you are paying credit card interest of 18 percent.

3. Next, establish a monthly budget. Learn to control spending and see what is essential and what is not; one way to do this is to review spending patterns over the last six months. If you are spending more than you are taking in, you must reduce your spending or increase your income.

4. Next, from this new budget, start earmarking money to be saved. The common inclination is to buy whatever you need during the month and then bank the rest. This approach almost ensures that you will save very little, for money has a habit of being spent. A better strategy is to set aside a certain amount of money, such as 10 percent of take-home or gross pay, and live off the remaining amount of money; this ensures that you will pay yourself before paying anyone else.

5. Along with paying off short-term debt, establish a savings account for emergencies. Most financial planners recommend having an amount equal to three to six months' worth of normal living expenses. This money is intended to carry you through situations such as medical emergencies or layoffs and

keep you from dipping into your long-term savings and investments or taking on more debt.

6. Once this emergency account has been established and is being funded, earmark money for different types of investments. Your first investment priority should be to fund your retirement; you are far more likely to find people and institutions that will lend you money for a car or a house or to pay off debts today than for living expenses during retirement. Therefore, it is up to you to provide your own resources for retirement. If your employer offers a 401(k) or 403(b) plan, you should immediately take full advantage of this opportunity; often your employer will match all or part of your contributions, making these plans even more valuable to you. Another easy way to fund retirement is an Individual Retirement Account (IRA); anyone who earns income can contribute to these. If you are self-employed or run your own company, you can set up and contribute to a Simplified Employee Pension (SEP) IRA, Savings Incentive Matching Plan for Employees (SIMPLE), or Keogh plan. In each of these account types, your money grows on a tax-deferred basis, which allows it to grow faster than if the money were being taxed annually. When considering these and other investments, you need to figure out your risk tolerance: How much can the value of your money drop, in the short and medium term, without causing you undue concern?

7. Concurrent with the preceding steps are decisions about your home. The decisions you make today about choosing and paying off mortgages and refinancing can have major effects on your cash flow and the growth of your net worth.

8. After paying off your debts, establishing an emergency fund, and contributing to your retirement accounts, you

should consider making other investments. You should invest this money in ways that complement your retirement investments, support your goals, and are consistent with your risk tolerance levels.

As with any other new skill, people will make mistakes in learning to invest and manage money. It is never easy or comfortable losing money through a poor investment decision or other mistake. Beginning investors who can admit their mistakes, pick up the pieces, and move on can make a lot of money; people who quit after one bad experience will not. By being willing to make mistakes and learn from these mistakes, boomers will gain confidence in their ability to control their financial future.

Along with taking the aforementioned steps, boomers must continue their financial education. Reading a few books or magazines is a good introduction, but it cannot be the sum of one's research into the world of finance. The world is changing constantly, new ideas and strategies appear, and yesterday's winning investment trend may become tomorrow's losing trend. New products and services and changes in consumer spending trends mean that an investor cannot simply buy stock in a company or invest in a mutual fund and then forget about it. On the other hand, it is important to develop the discipline not to change plans constantly, following the latest craze. The wise investor stays focused, reviews investment selections and strategies periodically, and educates himself or herself about finance and investing.

Historically, stocks have provided the best returns and probably would be appropriate for long-term and often medium-term goals. Given fluctuations in the stock market, you should set aside cash to fund the shorter-term goals. Bonds are appropriate for someone with a low risk tolerance, for short-to medium-term goals, for safer money, and as part of a portfolio held during retirement. The bulk of stock and bond investments probably are best made in stable, growing companies, and it is best to hold rather than trade in and out of these investments.

This book is designed to assist the baby boomer who is worried about the state of his or her finances and the prospects for a comfortable retirement. The rest of the book fills in many of the details from the eight steps just listed. Chapters 2 and 3 focus on the problems of relying on the traditional programs of funding retirement—pensions and Social Security—and look at current retirement funding options. Chapters 4 and 5 concentrate on getting out of debt, establishing a budget, and watching out for deals that sound too good to be true. Chapter 6 focuses on real estate; bad decisions about refinancing or paying off a mortgage early can limit one's ability to get out of debt and accumulate wealth. Chapter 7 deals with college tuition; wrong decisions about saving and investing to meet tuition and other college-related expenses can have major financial consequences. Chapter 8 looks at family-related concerns; poor life insurance decisions and bad health-related and wealth transfer planning for boomers' parents can also cause major financial problems.

Chapters 9 to 15 concentrate on developing an investment philosophy; without knowing how to invest, how the different securities markets work, and what stocks, bonds, and mutual funds are, it will be difficult to develop a successful investment program. Chapter 16 talks about a number of investment strategies designed to help boomers increase their wealth.

Some of the material in these chapters will seem familiar because the amount of financial knowledge available has grown. The average baby boomer almost certainly knows something about mutual funds. But there is a big difference between having a passing knowledge of such a topic and knowing how to use this knowledge wisely. The majority of people underperform the market; as will be seen in Chapter 10, from 1984 to 1998 the average investor's appreciation in the stock market was only 63 percent of the market's appreciation. Thus, without a thorough understanding of how the securities markets work and how to best use the investment options available, you probably will have to put off retirement for several years beyond your preference. Even those who feel that this material is already familiar should study it and use it to build up their knowledge.

Each chapter is made up of many short sections; breaking the material up into small pieces makes it easier for the reader to understand. Important material discussed in one section is repeated in later sections or chapters to help the reader understand these concepts. Web sites, which can help uncover additional information, are listed throughout the book. Major themes such as the exceptional long-term historical record of stocks, the need to take saving and investing seriously, and the importance of letting time work in your favor are key to understanding the fundamentals of investing and ensuring a secure and comfortable retirement.

Chapter 2

TRADITIONAL RETIREMENT PLANNING

Pensions

Retirement means different things to different people. These can include travel, a more leisurely pace, and the chance to do things you can't do while working in a full-time job. Whatever the meaning, it is the goal of many people; indeed, it is one of the main reasons why people invest. As baby boomers age, retirement has become a topic of talk shows, newspaper and magazine articles, and legislation. Over the last twenty years, Congress has been paying more attention to people's desire to have a comfortable retirement. The number of retirement investment vehicles has increased in recent years to include different types of Individual Retirement Accounts (IRAs), employee-funded accounts (such as the 401(k) and 403(b)), and variable annuities.

These new retirement vehicles are important as the trend toward corporations not providing guaranteed pensions is accelerating and the viability of consistent long-term benefits from the Social Security system is uncertain. According to the Social Security Administration (SSA), Social Security and pensions won't even make up half of the money needed to live on during retirement.[1] Before learning about IRAs, 401(k)s, and annuities (covered in Chapter 3), it is important to understand pensions and Social Security and their limitations.

Guaranteed pensions started off as a way for corporate owners to reward selected employees for time spent with a company. Labor unions gradually influenced companies to provide pensions for workers who spent a specific number of years at that firm. However, some companies fired employees only months away from qualifying for a pension. Other companies did not fully fund their pensions or used funds set aside for pensions for other purposes. Other companies went bankrupt without having segregated the money to fund their pension liabilities, leaving long-term employees without recourse. Enough outrageous practices occurred for Congress to pass the 1974 Employee Retirement Income Security Act (ERISA) to try to stop these practices. Although the situation has improved, occasional stories surface about companies that have underfunded their pensions.

Many pension plans are based on a combination of the number of years the employee worked, his or her age, and the average of his or her highest three, four, or five salaries. So if you worked for twenty-five years and this average was $58,000, your first year's pension might be worth $29,000.

---

1. This assumes that the money needed to live on is 60 to 80 percent of one's preretirement salary. Source: Peter Lynch, "Fidelity's Guide to Investing Responsibly," www.fidelity.com.

Often, you cannot receive your first pension payment until age 55 or 60, regardless of when you retire.

Although the idea of $29,000 coming in year after year may sound enticing, you must compare this amount with your current salary. How easily could you live on roughly 50 percent of your current income? What would you cut back on? Although you will not have the same expenses that you had when you were working, if you rely primarily on your pension for retirement income, your standard of living will drop. In addition, if you choose any of the survivor benefits options, so that your spouse will still receive money after you die, these monthly pension payments will be lower.

Not all pensions are tied to inflation. This was perceived as more of a problem in the 1970s into the early 1980s, when inflation reached double digits. Still, even with an average inflation rate of 3 percent, the cost of goods doubles every twenty-four years. So, you could start retirement at age 62, and by age 86 your non–inflation-indexed pension would buy approximately half as much.

To qualify for a pension, an employee must remain employed at that firm for a set number of years. Given the increased mobility of the American workforce, many workers have not spent enough time at any job to meet the criteria. These workers will not receive any pension, limiting their ability to fund their retirement. If you believe that you are not getting the correct payments based on your time on the job, a Web site that can provide invaluable assistance is www. dol.gov/dol/pwba.

Companies have been moving away from a guaranteed pension program for a number of years, and this trend is expected to continue. Whereas pensions make up 8 percent of total income today, by 2029 they will make up only 4 percent.[2] It is far cheaper and easier for companies to provide a qualified defined contribution retirement plan, such as a 401(k) or 403(b), than to fund and manage a pension plan; currently, more full-time employees are enrolled in a 401(k) plan than a pension plan.[3] The slow decline in the number of pension programs puts more of the retirement responsibility on the employee's shoulders.

In sum, people whose employers offer pension plans should be meticulous in researching how much money they will receive and under what conditions. Otherwise, they will be in for some rude surprises.

Social Security: Background

Since its introduction in the 1930s, Social Security has formed the bedrock of retirement planning for most Americans. The concept seemed very simple: Working Americans would pay into a system that would help take care of them when they retired. Although this system has helped millions of Americans, it is not clear that this arrangement can or will continue to help Americans as much in the future.

Social Security was originally set up in 1933 as part of a safety net but was not intended to be the majority of someone's income during retirement. Unfortunately, that is not what has happened. Millions of retired people depend solely or to a large extent on their monthly check. They have little

---

2. Betsy Morris and Erin M. Davies, "The Future of Retirement," *Fortune,* August 19, 1996, www.fortune.com.

3. The Bureau of Labor Statistics reports that in 1997, about half of all employees at medium and large private companies were enrolled in pension plans, whereas 55 percent of full-time employees were contributing to a 401(k) plan. Source: "Taking Inflation into Account," American Association of Retired Persons, www.aarp.org.

other income; without this monthly check, they would have major problems surviving.

The system is funded by a flat tax that has increased over the years. This tax is levied on all salaries up to a specific cap, and this cap has grown over time based on increases in the Consumer Price Index (CPI). Originally, the tax was set at 2 percent of the first $3,000 earned; in 2000, it is 6.2 percent of the first $76,200 earned (with an additional 1.45 percent going to pay for Medicare with no salary cap). Since 1972, the annual increase in monthly benefits has also been tied to increases in the CPI. The first benefits were paid out in 1939, and today, millions of people receive Social Security benefit checks.

To tell people what they can expect in terms of benefits, the SSA started sending a Personal Earnings and Benefit Estimate Statement in October 1999 to everyone who is over age 25 and is not yet receiving Social Security benefits. The SSA will continue to send out these statements annually. Each statement shows an estimate of monthly benefits, based on receiving benefits at ages 62, 65 to 67 (depending on the year born), and 70. If your projected benefits seem inadequate, check the history of your payments shown on the statement; mistakes can happen. If a mistake has occurred and you do not catch it within seven years, the SSA is not required to fix it.

These statements are based on generalized income and inflation scenarios. You can customize these scenarios by going to www.ssa.gov and requesting a new statement. Within two to three weeks, you will receive this statement, which will show projected monthly benefits based on your specific information.

The SSA projects that the average worker probably will get about 40 percent of his or her preretirement income from

Social Security benefits.[4] One way to think of these benefits is to imagine that you have a large amount of money in a certificate of deposit (CD) or a bond that is yielding a certain monthly dividend. Because this money will come in every month, you can think of that CD or bond as part of your overall retirement portfolio. Because this is part of the safe part of their portfolios, many investors might feel more comfortable putting other portions of their portfolios into more aggressive investments, such as stocks.

The money that is taken out of your paycheck for Social Security taxes does not go into a separate account, under your name, to grow and to be available when you retire. Instead, money that is flowing in now goes to pay the current retirees who are eligible for benefits. This arrangement is known as a pay-as-you-go system. Benefit checks depend on money flowing in. And this is where some of the problem comes in. In 1960, there were more than 5.1 workers per beneficiary. In 1999, the ratio was 3.4 to 1. By 2030, when all the boomers have retired, there will be about 2 workers for each beneficiary.[5]

Originally, the benefits were not tied to the CPI, but they have been indexed to inflation since the early 1970s. Because of the continuing drop in the worker-to-beneficiary ratio and the annual increase in benefit payments, money flowing out began to exceed the money flowing in. In both the 1970s and 1980s, solutions were implemented to compensate, resulting in increases in the tax rate, the salary cap, and, starting in 2000, the age at which full retirement benefits can be collected. Unfortunately, these fixes have proved only temporary,

4. Susan Dziubinski, "How to Know if You'll Have Enough," November 24, 1999, www.morningstar.com.

5. The Concord Coalition, Social Security, Facts and Figures, Part II, Demographics Is Destiny, Chart 25, pp. 52–53, www.concordcoalition.org.

for insolvency threatens the Social Security system some time before 2050. Although the booming economy of the 1990s has poured more money into the system than was originally anticipated, at some point the sheer number of baby boomers collecting Social Security payments will exceed the amount of money in the Social Security Trust Fund.

Therefore, one of the most contentious issues in America today is the future of Social Security and its funding sources. Social Security is a political sacred cow; any politician who hints at reducing benefits or touching it in any way comes close to committing political suicide. This is unfortunate because changes must be made to ensure that the money needed to pay benefits in the future will be available. What can be done to correct the situation? The next section looks at more traditional approaches, and the following section examines some nontraditional approaches.

Saving Social Security: Traditional Solutions

One of the most common solutions to increasing funding for the Social Security Trust Fund has been to raise the payroll tax. Recall that it started out at 2 percent and has grown to 6.2 percent. (It is actually twice this because employers match this 6.2 percent, and self-employed people pay 12.4 percent of their net income, up to the salary cap.) Given the national desire to hold the line on taxes and reduce the size of the federal government, there may not be enough political support to raise the tax. One reason is that this tax actually has a higher impact on people earning lower salaries than on those earning higher salaries. For example, in 2000, the most that a salaried employee will pay is $4,724.40 (0.062 × $76,200). Therefore, someone earning $76,200 or less will have 6.2 percent of his or her salary deducted. On the other hand, someone making $120,000 will have 3.9 percent ($4,724.40/$120,000) of his or her salary deducted. Therefore, raising the tax rate would hurt the nonwealthy the most.

Another solution would be to eliminate the salary cap. However, given the low percentage of Americans earning more than $76,200, this solution would not bring in a large amount of additional money.

A third solution would be to raise the age at which one is eligible to draw on benefits. Back in the 1930s, this age was set at 65, which was the traditional age that people retired. (People can start drawing before age 65 but get a lower benefit.) The problem is that people are living longer than they were sixty years ago. Therefore, the average person will draw benefits longer. Current law mandates a slow change in the age at which one can draw benefits; starting in 2000, the retirement age for receiving full benefits will rise gradually from age 65 to 67.[6] Speeding up this increase or increasing the eligibility age to 68 years or more could mean additional savings.

A fourth solution would involve reducing the annual benefit increase. Originally, increases in benefit checks were not linked to inflation, although benefits increased periodically. In the early 1970s, because of increasing inflation and political pressure, annual increases were tied to the CPI. The CPI is a measure of a basket of goods and services that the typical American purchases. Monthly price increases in any of these goods and services reflect, in theory, price increases that the typical American would pay each month.

---

6. Starting with people born in 1938, the normal Social Security eligibility age will rise by two months for each year until it reaches 66 for those born in 1943 through 1954. After that, the two-month-a-year increase in the retirement age starts again, until it is finally capped at age 67 for those born in 1960 or later.

However, the CPI has flaws, and using it to calculate monthly increases for retired people may not be appropriate. One flaw in the CPI stems from the fact that there is no way to measure productivity increases resulting from new technology; a new computer today costs about the same as it did five years ago, but it has much more capability. Another flaw is that the index does not recognize that the average consumer might switch from a more expensive item to a cheaper substitute. One large component of the CPI is the price of a home; because many retirees rent apartments or have paid off their mortgages, increases in the price of a home would not affect all retirees. Thus, it may not make sense to use the full CPI to calculate increases in Social Security checks. One option for modifying the payments is to apply only a portion of the annual CPI increase to annual benefit increases, decreasing the annual percentage increase by one percentage point, for example.

Saving Social Security:
Nontraditional Solutions

Given the size and complexity of the problems facing Social Security, some innovative, nontraditional ideas have been circulating in attempts to solve these problems.

One idea that has gained currency since the federal government started running a budget surplus is to dedicate most or all of the surplus to saving Social Security. Surpluses of more than $3 billion have been projected for the next ten years. Adding this money to the Social Security Trust Fund would stave off insolvency for decades. However, a large portion of this surplus consists of payments into Social Security and Medicare. When politicians claim that they are saving the bulk of this surplus for Social Security and Medicare, all they are doing is making sure that these transfer payments are being earmarked for their original purpose. They are being good bookkeepers, not good Samaritans.

Another idea that has been gaining prominence in recent years involves the privatization or partial privatization of the Social Security system. There are many variations of this idea; most revolve around the idea that instead of people paying into the current large pool of money, which then funds recipients, everyone would pay into special accounts set up for them. The money in these accounts could be invested in various ways. Several mutual fund–like vehicles would be set up, and these might include stock funds, bond funds, and money market funds. Each person would be able to choose the investments that fit his or her investment objectives, risk, and age. This approach would give people more freedom of choice and a potentially larger amount of money to draw on for their benefits.[7] Because stocks have returned, on average, about 11 percent per year over the last sixty years,[8] these returns could exceed the return that current recipients are getting on their money.

This is similar to the current system in Chile, where it has worked well. Chile's system originally was somewhat similar to that of the United States but was converted to a new system in 1981. All employed people pay a fixed percentage of their income into this mandatory pension system. Most of the

---

7. A variation on this idea is for the SSA to invest this money in the stock and bond markets rather than allow people to make investment choices themselves.

8. From 1926 to 1998, stocks have had an average annual return of 11.2 percent. Source: Ibbotson Associates, *Stocks, Bonds, Bills, and Inflation,* 1999 Yearbook TM, Ibbotson Associates, Chicago (annually updates work by Roger C. Ibbotson, et al.). However, this is not the same as saying that you are guaranteed to earn this long-term average.

money is invested, by law, in the domestic stock market; the contributors have a choice of several different investing options. A number of other countries have followed Chile's lead in creating a private, individual investment account system. In the first few years, there were major transition costs, largely to make sure that people who had contributed to the original system would still get benefit payments.

This concern has led to criticism, which has helped to keep the United States from adopting such a system. Someone who has not paid much into the system yet would not have much to lose, and someone who is young would have plenty of time for the money to grow. However, someone who has paid a lot of money into the system would lose out, and someone who is close to retirement would not have the time for his or her contributions to compound. Programs would be needed to ensure the viability of the system for people who have already paid in large sums of money, and these programs would be costly.

One solution would be to phase in a privatized program over a number of years, ensuring that those who have paid in will continue to get their fair share. Another would be to start diverting some percentage, say 2 percent, of the money going into the Social Security Trust Fund to allow people some flexibility in how their money is invested, with the rest going to maintain the current system.

Another concern with privatization is that there is no guarantee that the stock market will continue to grow. Critics point to the time period from 1966 to the early 1980s, when the stock market went through several bear markets; the Dow Jones Industrial Average (DJIA) hit 1,000 in 1966 and, but for one short interval, didn't hit 1,000 again until 1983. In the bear market of 1973 and 1974, the DJIA declined more than 40 percent. Given the wrong choice of funds or a precipitous decline in the market, a person could wind up with a flat or negative growth rate, thus endangering his or her retirement. If this were to happen, there would be political pressure for the federal government to support such people.

Many Americans do not understand the intricacies of the stock and bond market and might fall prey to bad or inaccurate advice. Many investors panic at the first whiff of a market decline or sell at the wrong time. Many are buying high and selling low, certainly not the recipe for maximizing one's net worth. Therefore, there is legitimate concern that people would make poor investment choices. However, some do not believe that it is right to allow people to invest in stocks and bonds in their IRAs and other retirement plans and then say that people can't be trusted to invest their Social Security money prudently.

Other good ideas take very different approaches to solving the Social Security problem. For example, every student who graduates from high school would have $2,000 put into a special IRA that the person could not touch until age 65. This IRA could be invested in some sort of stock mutual fund. Assuming the historic appreciation rate of 11 percent per year, this initial sum would grow to almost $300,000 by age 65 and $500,000 by age 70. A major advantage would be that people in this program would know that they will have a large sum of money available to them when they retire. Another major advantage is that this money would not have to come out of the Social Security Trust Fund, which might reduce the pressure for annual benefit increases.

Probably no single solution will solve the Social Security problem. It is clear that there will be tremendous pressure to ensure that people who have paid into the system will continue to get some benefits. In addition, today's wage earners must begin to learn about investments; the return from these investments will determine whether they can retire in comfort.

When to Receive Social Security Payments

If you qualify to receive Social Security payments, you can choose when to start receiving payments. You can start receiving your regular benefit checks at age 65 (which will gradually increase to age 67). If you are willing to accept smaller payments, you can start receiving them by age 62. If you take payments early, your Social Security check is permanently reduced; this reduction can be as much as 30 percent.[9]

If you start collecting the checks at age 62, you will be receiving benefits longer, which for a time will offset the larger checks you'd receive at your normal retirement age (which varies, depending on your year of birth). Generally, it will take until age 77 or 78 for the cumulative value of the larger checks to exceed the value of the reduced ones received at age 62. Therefore, if you live past age 77 or 78, it would be better not to have started receiving checks at 62. Because no one can predict the future, you need to base such a decision on any continued employment, your risk tolerance, and other money sources. This decision also affects your spouse; if your spouse will collect payments based on your entitlements, delaying when you receive your benefits leads to a larger survivor's benefit.[10]

If you continue to work after you start drawing benefits and are currently under age 65, your benefits will be reduced if you

---

9. For those born before 1938, the reduction is 20 percent; for those born between 1943 and 1954, the reduction is 25 percent; and for those born in 1960 and after, the reduction is 30 percent. For those born between 1938 and 1942 or 1955 and 1959, the amount of the reduction is prorated.

10. If you were married for at least ten years, you may be eligible for Social Security benefits based on your ex-spouse's earnings. You would be eligible for 50 percent of your ex-spouse's benefits or 100 percent of your own benefit, whichever is higher. You do not lose this option if your ex-spouse remarries. However, if you remarry, you forfeit your right to base your benefits on your ex-spouse's earnings.

earn above a certain amount.[11] Currently, people under 65 lose 50 percent of their Social Security benefits for income earned above a certain threshold (which is indexed to inflation).

In deciding when to start receiving Social Security benefits, you need to examine your other sources of money. It does not make sense for you to sell tax-deferred investments, such as an IRA, Keogh, or 401(k), to pay for retirement expenses and lose years of tax-deferred growth if you can collect these benefits. On the other hand, if you have significant nonretirement assets and can afford to live off of this money, it may make sense to delay your Social Security benefits.

Another important consideration is your investment style and risk tolerance. If you're knowledgeable about investing and feel comfortable having a significant portion of your portfolio in stocks, it is probably to your advantage to take early benefits. The alternative would be to sell your securities, resulting in capital gains tax and the loss of future appreciation. On the other hand, if you are a conservative investor and invest mainly in bonds or CDs, it probably makes more sense to delay your benefits until you reach ages 65 to 67. The dividends you'll receive from these investments, given taxes and inflation, probably will not equal the benefit increase you would get by waiting until ages 65 to 67. In addition, there is a tax advantage in depending on Social Security benefits rather than depending on dividend income from stocks and bonds. Although some of the Social Security benefits may be taxed (the exact amount depends on the total amount of money you receive from different sources), all the stock and bond dividends will be taxed (unless they are from municipal bonds).

---

11. Until 2000, people between ages 65 and 69 who received Social Security and also worked lost a portion of their income if they earned above a certain threshold. Given the low unemployment in the late 1990s and employers' increasing difficulty in finding skilled employees, Congress and the president worked together to remove this earnings penalty.

Chapter 3

CURRENT RETIREMENT PLANNING

Chapter 2 showed that the traditional means of funding retirement are not as secure as they once were. These days, those who do not plan for and fund their own retirement will not have the money they need for a comfortable retirement and will become dependent on contributions from family and friends. Thus, boomers should take an active role in planning their own retirement, leading to the following questions and answers.

How much will boomers need for retirement? It depends. The standard answer is that a person needs about 70 to 80 percent of their annual needs before they retired, adjusted for inflation.[1] If you earn $50,000 per year, when you retire you

1. In a study by Kenn Tacchino and Cynthia Saltzman at Widener University, people 75 and up spend an average of 27 percent less than people 65 to 74 do. Most retirees don't buy as much new stuff and often

will need $35,000 to $40,000, adjusted for inflation, in retirement. Most people find that they need less than their preretirement salary because they no longer have expenses related to work such as work clothes, dry cleaning, and commuting. In addition, many expenses, such as putting children through college or mortgage payments, are no longer present. However, because some retirees plan to travel extensively or anticipate other expenses, 70 to 80 percent might be too low.

How should boomers plan for their retirement? They should be diverting a portion of their current income for retirement. This can be done using qualified retirement plans, such as individual retirement accounts (IRAs) and 401(k)s, as well as other investments outside of retirement plans, such as stocks, bonds, and mutual funds. The advantage to the qualified retirement plans is that the money grows tax deferred;[2] boomers should take advantage of this tax-deferred growth. You might be better off putting investments that generate a lot of dividends in a retirement plan because the taxes on these dividends are deferred. You should put investments that pay few

---

have paid off their mortgages. Of course, their health care costs are higher. Source: Jane Bryant Quinn, "Capital Gains—Planning: the Next Stage," Newsweek, April 3, 2000, www.newsweek.com. Because some people 65 to 74 are still working, it seems reasonable to use the 70 to 80 percent level as representative of what retirees need.

2. Most investments generate payments each year, often in the form of interest or dividends or, for mutual funds, capital gain distributions. In non–tax-deferred investments, you must pay taxes each year on these payments, leaving less money in the account and less money to compound in the future. In addition, in these types of investments, you must pay taxes if you sell an investment that has appreciated in value. In tax-deferred investments, you do not pay taxes on these distributions or this appreciation until you withdraw the money from the account, ideally during retirement, when most people are in a lower tax bracket. The disadvantage of tax-deferred plans, with the exception of the Roth IRA, is that when you take money out of these plans, the growth is taxed as income rather than as capital gains.

dividends and generate a lot of capital gains outside a retirement plan to take advantage of the lower capital gains rate.[3] The top two priorities of investing in qualified retirement plans should be to fully fund a 401(k) plan (and, if applicable, a Simplified Employee Pension [SEP] IRA, Keogh, or Savings Incentive Matching Plan for Employees [SIMPLE]) as well as an IRA.

When should boomers plan for their retirement? The sooner the better! It is important to start investing now and not put it off. One of the most important factors in accumulating money for retirement is to use time wisely and take advantage of compound interest. Assume that you are 40 and you start putting $8,000 a year into an investment that returns an average of 11 percent a year. By the time you are 65, you will have accumulated about $1.14 million. Simply delaying this program for two years and starting at age 42, you will have about $907,000 by age 65. Delaying two years means that you will have about $230,000 less!

Many mutual funds, brokerage houses, organizations, and financial publications have Web sites with sections devoted to many of the retirement planning options that are discussed in this chapter. Ones to look at include www. 401kafe.com, www.americanexpress.com, www.benefitslink. com, www.fidelity.com, www.financenter.com, www.money central.com, www.myprimetime.com, www.prudential.com, www.quicken.com, www.schwab.com, www.smartmoney.com, www.strongfunds.com, www.troweprice.com, and www.van guard.com. Many of these also have retirement worksheet calculators to help you figure out how much money you'll need for retirement and the proper asset allocation for your money

---

3. Short-term gains are taxed at the investor's marginal tax rate, which can be as high as 39.6 percent. Long-term gains are capped at 20 percent.

in retirement. In addition, you can estimate your life expectancy at www.northwesternmutual.com/games/longevity.

Traditional Individual Retirement Accounts

In the current environment of corporate downsizing, career relocation, and the changing economy, the average employee switches jobs frequently, often not qualifying for each company's retirement plan.[4] In addition, as discussed in Chapter 2, a growing number of companies are eliminating their pension programs. Thus, employees must start funding their own retirement by contributing to IRAs. IRAs were invented in the 1970s for people whose employers did not offer corporate retirement accounts. They became popular in the early 1980s when legislation allowed everyone who earned income to set up and contribute to one.

The main reason IRAs are such good investment vehicles is that the money grows tax deferred while in the account. Because you generally cannot withdraw the money until at least age 59$\frac{1}{2}$ without a penalty (but must start to withdraw the money by age 70$\frac{1}{2}$), money put into an IRA ordinarily has a lot of time to grow and take advantage of the tax-deferred growth.

A numerical example is useful. Assume two investors, A and B, each put $1,000 into a mutual fund that pays a 10

---

4. On average, women change jobs every 4.7 years, and men change jobs every 5.3 years. Because many companies require 5 years of service before you are eligible for the company's retirement plan match or profit sharing, by changing jobs frequently, you will miss out on such retirement programs. Source: Martha Priddy Patterson, *The New Working Woman's Guide to Retirement Planning: Saving and Investing Now for a Secure Future,* as referenced in Kathryn Haines Allyn, "Remember Retirement When You Job-Hunt," May 2, 2000, www.morningstar.com.

percent distribution each year and that both investors reinvest this distribution. A has this mutual fund in an IRA, and B does not. At the end of the first year, B will owe taxes on the $100 distributed that year; assuming that B is in the 28 percent tax bracket, there would only be $72 ($100 − $28) worth of growth left after paying these taxes. Therefore, A will have $1,100 in the account, and B will have $1,072. At the end of the second year, the difference widens, with A's investment being worth $1,210 and B's worth $1,149. After twenty-five years, A's investment (approximately $10,800) is worth about 90 percent more than B's (about $5,700).

Many people fund their IRAs each year. Another way to see the advantages of a tax-deferred investment is by looking at two other investors, C and D, who each invest the maximum of $2,000 a year for twenty-five years in the same mutual fund. C's investment is in an IRA, and D's is not. D will owe tax each year on the appreciation of the investment. At the end of twenty-five years, C's investment is worth approximately $216,400, whereas D's is worth about $139,600.

Investing in IRAs originally entitled investors to two tax-related benefits. The immediate tax benefit was the ability to deduct $2,000 of earned income from taxable income, thus lowering taxes. For someone in the 28 percent bracket, this deduction was worth $560. The second, much more important benefit was the tax-deferred growth of the money in the account.

After 1986, the first benefit was scaled back. Only people not covered by any sort of retirement plan at work or earning below a certain income level were eligible to deduct their contribution and get a tax break. This change gave rise to the notion that many people could not or should not contribute to an IRA. However, this is not correct, for anyone who earns income can and should contribute to an IRA. Many people who have contributed to their IRAs since 1986 have not been able to deduct their contributions. These contributors are required to file a Form 8806 with the Internal Revenue Service (IRS) to keep track of their nondeductible contributions.

The importance of recording and filing this form cannot be emphasized strongly enough. Not only is this requirement part of the current tax code, but when you begin to withdraw money from your IRAs, you do not have to pay tax on a percentage of this money. This percentage is calculated based on the ratio of nondeductible contributions to the total worth of the IRA. By not recording and filing this form, a taxpayer will end up paying tax on the same money twice.

There are many investment vehicles for IRAs, including stocks, bonds, mutual funds, and certificates of deposit (CDs).

Roth IRAs

The Taxpayer's Relief Act of 1997 provided several new options for taxpayers who want to save and invest money in a tax-deferred account. Among these are expanded deductibility thresholds for the traditional IRA, additional penalty-free ways to withdraw the money before age $59\frac{1}{2}$, new spousal IRA eligibility rules, and a new IRA, called the Roth IRA. This IRA, named for its sponsor, Senator William Roth, has exciting features that all taxpayers should be aware of.

The major ways in which a Roth IRA differs from a traditional IRA are as follows:

- No contribution can be tax deductible.

- No taxes will be owed on any distributions after age $59\frac{1}{2}$ given certain conditions (for example, the money must have been in the IRA for at least 5 years).

- There are no required distributions (as opposed to the requirement that distributions from a traditional IRA must start by age 70$\frac{1}{2}$). This allows money to grow tax deferred for a longer period of time.

- Specific adjusted gross income (AGI) limits determine eligibility for a Roth IRA.

- If beneficiaries inherit these accounts, they will owe no taxes on distributions.

Someone who is not eligible to deduct his or her IRA contribution but wants to contribute to an IRA should choose the Roth IRA. With the former, distributions must always start by age 70$\frac{1}{2}$, and taxes are owed on the growth of these contributions; neither is true with the latter.

Someone who is eligible to deduct his or her contribution still is probably better off with a Roth IRA. It is better to avoid owing taxes when the money is withdrawn than to take a $300 refund ($2,000 in the 15 percent tax bracket) or $560 refund ($2,000 in the 28 percent tax bracket) now. The major advantage of the Roth IRA is the tax-free aspect of the distributions. The only reason a person should contribute to the deductible traditional IRA is if he or she cannot afford to contribute to the IRA without this deduction.

Roth IRAs also are great estate planning tools. When you contribute to a Roth, you are reducing your estate taxes and the income taxes your heirs must pay. Because you are contributing to a Roth with after-tax dollars, the tax has already been paid on the money going in, so no tax is owed when the money is withdrawn. You are basically prepaying your heirs' income taxes without using up any of your estate tax exemption ($675,000 for 2000 and 2001) or owing any gift taxes. Because your heirs won't owe income tax on their withdrawals from this Roth account, in effect you are using a Roth IRA to make tax-free allocations to your heirs.

Unfortunately, not everyone can fund a Roth IRA. A single person can contribute if his or her AGI is less than $95,000, and the eligibility phases out as one's AGI reaches $110,000. A married couple can contribute if their AGI is less than $150,000, and the eligibility phases out as their AGI reaches $160,000. These AGI threshold levels are not indexed to inflation. Married couples filing separately are not eligible to contribute to a Roth IRA.

If your AGI is less than $100,000, regardless of whether you are filing as single or married, you can convert a traditional IRA to a Roth IRA. You will have to pay taxes on any of the traditional IRA's accumulated earnings and on any tax-deductible contributions; these taxes are owed for the calendar year in which you make the conversion. As discussed earlier, the growth within an IRA is not taxed. In addition, some of the money you contributed to the IRA was pretax money. Because you did not pay taxes on most (or all) of this money and because rolling this money into a Roth IRA means that you will not pay taxes when they are withdrawn, the IRS wants its share, so you must pay taxes when the money is rolled into a Roth IRA. Conversion may make sense for you; it is a function of how long you have until retirement, what your current tax rate is now, and what you expect it to be when you retire. Some Web sites, such as www.vanguard.com, www.strong funds.com, www.smartmoney.com, and www.quicken.com, have online calculators to help you determine whether conversion is right for you. However, it almost never makes sense to convert if you have to use some of the money in the traditional IRA to pay these taxes.

401(k) Plans

A very popular retirement planning option is known by its tax code name: the 401(k). This type of plan shifts the retirement planning focus from the employer to the employee; instead of a guaranteed pension, based on salary and longevity, the 401(k) depends on specific proactive actions by the employee. Therefore, the employee assumes a greater responsibility for his or her own retirement.

In a 401(k) plan, an employee contributes pretax money into specific investments, and the employer often matches this contribution. (Nonprofit companies have a similar plan, called a 403(b). Most of the details of the 401(k) also apply to the 403(b) plan.) By contributing pretax money, the employee reduces the amount of tax he or she owes. For example, assume that an employee in the 28 percent tax bracket contributes $1,000 of his or her salary to a 401(k) plan. Otherwise, 72 percent, or $720, would be paid to the employee as salary and 28 percent, or $280, would go to pay taxes. By contributing $1,000, the employee gives up only $720 of take-home pay and reduces his or her tax bill by $280.

The specific amount of money or percentage of salary that employees can contribute depends on how the 401(k) plan is set up; total employee contributions in 2000 are capped at $10,500. These contributions grow tax deferred. As with traditional IRAs, employees cannot withdraw money before age $59\frac{1}{2}$ and do not have to begin making withdrawals until age $70\frac{1}{2}$. Therefore, contributions have a lot of time to grow tax deferred.

Depending on how the employer has set up the plan, employees usually have several investment options. In most cases, the choices in 401(k) plans are specific mutual funds that are part of one or several fund families. Typically, there are stock and bond funds along with a money market fund. Employees should make their 401(k) fund allocation decisions as part of their overall portfolio asset allocation.

Many employers either fully or partially match their employees' contributions. In a typical plan the employer might contribute 50 cents for every dollar the employee contributes. So if an employee contributes 10 percent of his or her salary to a 401(k) plan, the employer's match would make this, in effect, a 15 percent contribution. Another way to think of this contribution is that it is an immediate 50 percent return on the contribution. Because this matching provision gives employees an immediate return on their money, some people see matching funds as a guaranteed cushion and use this money for more aggressive investments, such as stock mutual funds, rather than keeping it in a money market fund. In most plans, employees have to work a certain number of years for this matched money to belong to them; becoming qualified for this money is known as being vested.

This combination of tax-deferred growth and matching contributions makes 401(k) plans one of the best investment vehicles available. All employees whose employers match their contributions should fund their 401(k) plans to at least the level of matching, and more, if they can afford it.

You can borrow money from your 401(k) plan. Unfortunately, many participants see this as an easy way to get cash, for when you repay the loan, you are basically paying yourself back. Don't borrow unless it is an extreme emergency. As long as the money is not in the 401(k), you are losing its ability to work for you.

When an employee changes jobs, he or she must decide what to do with the money in the 401(k) plan. The choices include the following:

- Leaving the money in the existing plan.
- Rolling the money into the subsequent job's 401(k) plan.
  - Rolling the money into a traditional IRA.
  - Taking a partial or full distribution.

There are pros and cons to each of these options, including potential tax consequences. For instance, if you take a distribution before age 59½, you will owe income taxes and a 10 percent penalty along with having 20 percent of the money withheld. By law, the company sends 20 percent to the IRS. This helps ensure that the employee will pay income taxes on the distribution. If the recipient decides to then roll the money into an IRA, he or she must make up that 20 percent with funds on hand. Otherwise the IRS will consider that money to be distributed. If money is left in a 401(k) when you die, it must be distributed immediately, whereas money in an IRA does not. Accordingly, many financial planners recommend rolling 401(k) funds into a traditional IRA when changing jobs rather than leaving it in the existing 401(k) or transferring it into the next job's 401(k). A wise employee should seek professional advice to help determine which option is best.

As mentioned earlier, most of the details of 401(k) plans also apply to 403(b) plans. Money in a 401(k) plan cannot be rolled over into a 403(b) plan and vice versa. Neither of these should be confused with a 457 plan; this type of plan has a lower contribution ceiling, and money in this plan cannot be rolled into an IRA when an employee changes jobs.

Annuities

Another popular retirement planning option that many people choose is an annuity. Annuities are insurance contracts that work like nondeductible traditional IRAs; contributions are not tax deductible, and taxes on earnings are deferred until the money is withdrawn. Similarly, if the money is withdrawn before age 59½, the IRS charges a penalty. However, there is no limit on how much money one can put into an annuity, and annuity withdrawals do not have to begin by age 70½.

Annuities come in two types: fixed and variable. Fixed annuities let you lock in a particular rate of return for a certain number of years. Variable annuities give you a choice of mutual fund–like investments called subaccounts. As with any other mutual fund, your return depends on the performance of your particular funds. You can switch between the mutual funds in the annuity without worrying about capital gains taxes. In addition, you can switch the money from one annuity custodian to another. A variable annuity gives you a number of withdrawal options, including guaranteed payments for the rest of your life.

The insurance portion of the variable annuity guarantees that if you die before you start withdrawing money, your beneficiaries will receive all the money you put in or the accumulated value, whichever is greater. This is a fairly useless and expensive feature.[5]

Annuity custodians charge several types of fees, including insurance charges and mutual fund fees. Most annuity custodians charge annual administrative fees and a surrender fee if you withdraw money before a certain number of years have gone by. Therefore, annuities have higher overall annual fees than most other investment vehicles, and these higher fees can

---

5. Only 4 out of every 1,000 variable annuities are surrendered because of death or disabilities. This is largely because in a rising market, this guarantee becomes almost worthless. In addition, according to Morningstar, Inc., the annual cost of this provision is 1.11 percent. Source: Limra International, an insurance industry research group, as referenced in "What's Wrong with Variable Annuities," www.smartmoney.com.

easily outweigh the benefits of tax deferral. The annual expenses for subaccounts alone average about three-quarters of a percent more than those of a mutual fund.[6]

As in traditional IRAs and 401(k) plans, the money grows tax deferred. However, because the top capital gains tax rate has been lowered to a maximum of 20 percent, some of the advantages of investing money in variable annuities (as opposed to non–tax-deferred investments) have decreased. This is because when you withdraw money from an annuity, the earnings are taxed as regular income (which can be as high as 39.6 percent in federal taxes), not as capital gains. The higher annual costs of annuities coupled with the fact that withdrawals are taxed as regular income often outweigh the tax-deferred advantages over the short and medium term. A good rule is that you should plan to leave the money in an annuity for at least fifteen years; otherwise the higher annual costs will outweigh the benefits.[7] Many retirees end up paying more in taxes on an annuity than they would have paid in capital gains if the same money had been invested in a taxable mutual fund. Some financial consultants believe that you'll do better to find a mutual fund that has a low portfolio turnover rate; a low turnover rate usually indicates low annual capital gains distributions, leading to low annual taxes on these funds and better performance.

Another disadvantage is that if you die with money left in

6. The average annual expense on variable annuity subaccounts is 2.08 percent of assets, according to Morningstar. The average mutual fund charges just 1.34 percent. Source: "What's Wrong with Variable Annuities," www.smartmoney.com.

7. This point is emphasized by both Certified Financial Planner (CFP) Dee Lee of Harvard, Mass., as referenced in "What's Wrong with Variable Annuities," www.smartmoney.com, and Patrick Reinkemeyer of Morningstar, Inc., as referenced in "Who Should Buy Variable Annuities" at www.smartmoney.com.

the annuity, your beneficiary will owe all the taxes that have been deferred. Mutual funds, on the other hand, have a stepped-up basis at your death, so your beneficiary will owe no taxes.

It is probably wise to fully fund your IRA and 401(k) accounts before you invest in an annuity. Not only does the annuity have higher fees, but you have more flexibility with your IRA (which may be deductible and which usually has a greater variety of investments to choose from) and your 401(k) plan (which often has matching employer contributions).

Self-Employment Retirement Options

Self-employed people participating in a sole proprietorship or partnership have additional options for funding their retirement. In addition to the regular IRA (which is available to anyone with earned income), several types of retirement vehicles have been designed specifically for self-employed people. These include the SEP-IRA, SIMPLE plan, and Keogh plan.

All three of these plans are tax deductible (unlike regular IRAs for many people) and grow in a tax-deferred manner (like all other qualified retirement plans). Taxes are not paid until the person begins withdrawing funds from the plan. These plans are subject to the same age-related distribution restrictions as traditional IRAs. A person who has a full-time job as an employee as well as self-employment income can still fund any of these plans even if he or she is covered under an employer's retirement plan; only money earned from self-employment can be used to fund these plans.

If you are a participant in any of these plans and you receive a lump sum distribution, you must roll the money into a traditional IRA within sixty days or pay taxes on it. If you are under 59½ when you receive this distribution and don't roll it over into an IRA within sixty days, you will be subject to a 10 percent premature distribution penalty.

Both you and your business stand to benefit with any of these plans: You, the owner, can take advantage of another tax-deferred account, and your business pays lower taxes and offers a perk that many other businesses don't. Any of these plans could be offered to employees in lieu of a salary increase because the employees gain a tax-deferred retirement account and lower their current taxes.

All three plans have advantages, and the best choice depends on several factors. Those who own a business with employees can use any of these plans; benefits must be extended to all employees who meet certain criteria. Self-employed people who have no employees cannot choose the SIMPLE. A tax specialist or financial planner can help you analyze the numbers and see which would give you the greatest investment and tax benefits.

■ SEP-IRA: You, as the owner, can set aside up to 15 percent of your net income in an IRA, up to $25,500 in 2000.[8] Your business must contribute the same percentage that you set aside for yourself to employees who meet the following three criteria and who elect to participate in the plan:

They have worked for this business for three of the last five years (including partial years).
They are at least 21 years of age.
They earned at least $400 a year from this business.

---

8. Net income includes the total income from the business minus certain deductible costs incurred while running the business, including contributions to the SEP-IRA.

■ SIMPLE: This plan, enacted by Congress in 1996, is similar to a 401(k) plan. Employees (including the owner) can set aside up to $6,000 of gross income into a SIMPLE if they meet two criteria:

> They earned at least $5,000 a year from this business.
> They have worked for this business for at least part of the last two years.

The business would contribute money for employees who elect to participate in the plan based on one of the following two scenarios:

> For at least three of the next five years, the matching amount is 3 percent, whereas in the other two years, it can be less than 3 percent.
> Every year, the matching contribution is 2 percent.

■ Keogh: The main difference between a Keogh and a SEP-IRA is the contribution limit and paperwork requirements. Although exact contribution limits depend on the type of Keogh plan selected, a participant can contribute much more to this type of a plan than to a SEP-IRA. There are three types of Keogh plans:

> Profit-sharing Keogh: A profit-sharing plan has a limit of 15 percent of the total payroll of the plan participants, including a compensation limit ($150,000) and a contribution limit ($25,500). These contributions are flexible and can be as low as zero in any given year. Because the 15 percent limit is the same as for a SEP-IRA, it would not make sense to set up only a profit-sharing Keogh.
> Money purchase Keogh: A money purchase

plan allows contributions from 1 percent to 25 percent of compensation; for 2000, the contributions are capped at $30,000. Once the contribution percentage has been set, it cannot be changed for the life of the plan; these contributions are mandatory for every year the plan is in existence.

Paired Keogh: This is a combination of the two plans, which allows more flexibility. Annual contributions are limited to 25 percent but can be as low as 3 percent. The amount contributed to the money purchase part is fixed for the life of the plan, but the amount contributed to the profit-sharing part (still subject to the 15 percent limit) can change every year.

Setting up a Keogh plan is significantly more involved than establishing a SEP-IRA. Most mutual fund companies or brokerage houses should be able to help you fill out the extensive paperwork. This paperwork must be completed before the end of the tax year for which the contribution will be made, but the money does not have to be invested until the following April 15 (or later, if you have filed the appropriate tax extension paperwork). In exchange for this initial hurdle, the contribution limits are higher than those of the other plans, so self-employed individuals should consider a Keogh plan seriously.

Investing Your Retirement Money

How should you invest your retirement money?

One popular approach is to put your most aggressive investments into your retirement accounts. Aggressive stocks and aggressive mutual funds tend to be among the most volatile investments, but they have the potential for tremendous returns. Investing in smaller companies may be risky in the near term, but they may become the next IBM, Intel, or Microsoft. The thinking behind this investment strategy is that because you can't touch this money for years, maybe decades, you should let this volatility and this potential for explosive growth work for you.

Unfortunately, when you look at the way in which retirement accounts and nonretirement accounts are structured, putting your most aggressive investments in a tax-deferred account may not be the wisest choice. Let's examine why not. In a tax-deferred account, you pay no taxes until you withdraw the money (except for the Roth IRA, for which you pay no taxes at all). When you take the money out, you pay taxes at your marginal tax rate because this money is treated as current income. Therefore, you can never take advantage of the preferential long-term capital gains tax rate with retirement account investments.

In nonretirement accounts, not only can you take advantage of these long-term capital gains tax rates (currently capped at 20 percent), but you can use the tax code to shelter some of your capital losses. If you lose $1,000 on an investment held for 12 months or less, and are in, say, the 31 percent tax bracket, you wind up with tax savings of up to $310. If you lost the $1,000 in an investment held for more than 12 months, you would still wind up with tax savings of up to $200. However, in a retirement account, you would have to absorb the entire loss.

In addition, in a nonretirement account, you don't have to pay taxes on any investments, such as growth stocks, until you sell them, so by not selling them, in effect you are deferring taxes on the gains. So why waste the tax-deferral aspect of a retirement account on an investment that has the potential to grow in a tax-deferred mode?

Let's look at a more conservative investment, such as bonds or high-dividend stocks such as utilities or Real Estate Investment Trusts (REITs). The main attraction of these investments is their regular dividends. If you hold these investments in a nonretirement account, you would have to pay taxes on these dividends annually. However, if you have these investments in a retirement account, you would be able to put off paying taxes on the dividends until you withdraw the money. In both cases, you would have to pay taxes at your marginal tax rate, but with the money in a tax-deferred retirement account, you would be able to put off paying these taxes for a number of years. In addition, when you retire, you may be in a lower tax bracket than you are now.

To sum up, because aggressive stocks and mutual funds have the largest potential for loss, putting them in a retirement account robs you of the possibility of getting the federal and state governments to shoulder part of this loss (through deductions on your tax forms). If these investments do pan out and are in a retirement account, you lose the possibility of paying the taxes at the lower capital gains tax rate. Conversely, if these aggressive investments are not in a retirement account, you pay less tax if you make money and you have less of a loss if you lose money. In addition, holding more conservative investments in a retirement account allows you to put off paying the taxes that you would otherwise have to pay annually.

There is another, non–tax-related reason to strongly consider putting your more conservative investments into a retirement account: You don't want to gamble with your retirement. If the money in these accounts were to take a big loss, your retirement, or the age at which you plan on retiring, could be in jeopardy.

Comparing 401(k) with Roth IRA Contributions

Many investors wonder how to best maximize their retirement funding options. Given many options and a limited amount of income, what is the best thing to do? The two best choices are the 401(k) plan (or 403(b) plan for nonprofit organizations) and the IRA, preferably the Roth if you qualify for it. But which of these should you choose?

Many employers match their employees' 401(k) plan contributions. In a typical plan, the employer might contribute 50 cents for every dollar the employee contributes. If you contribute 10 percent of your salary to a 401(k) plan, your employer's match would make this, in effect, a 15 percent contribution. In such cases, the preferred vehicle for retirement funds should be a 401(k) plan. After contributing to your 401(k), you should contribute to your IRA; the IRA of choice is the Roth IRA, if you qualify, because you will owe no tax on the money when you withdraw it.

Deciding where to put retirement money becomes murkier for those whose employers match little or none of the contribution. In some plans, employees can contribute up to 10 percent of their salaries, but the employer matches only the first 5 percent. In this case, is it better to contribute to the nonmatched portion of the 401(k) plan or to a Roth IRA?

The best strategy is to contribute as much money to the 401(k) plan as your employer will match, then fund the Roth IRA, and then, with any remaining money, fund the nonmatched portion of the 401(k) plan. Why? The nonmatched portion of the 401(k) is almost the same as a deductible IRA. The principal advantage of an IRA is not the initial deduction but the tax-deferred growth of the money. However, the Roth IRA, in addition to having the same tax-deferred growth, also has tax-free distributions. So if you are in the 28 percent tax bracket, you would need to have $13,900 in a 401(k) to give you the same spending power in retirement as $10,000 in a Roth. Thus, if the decision comes down to getting a possible tax break now for the 401(k) or traditional IRA or owing no taxes when you take the money out of the Roth IRA, the latter is the better deal.

Withdrawing Money from Your Retirement Plans

If you have money in a traditional IRA, 401(k), or any of the self-employed plans discussed earlier in this chapter, the IRS has established specific withdrawal methods. For all these plans, you must start taking distributions by April 1 of the year after the year in which you turn 70½. You must take an additional distribution by December 31 of that year and continue taking distributions every year after that. If you don't, or if you don't take a large enough distribution, you will owe a penalty to the IRS. The penalty for failing to take a minimum distribution is 50 percent of the shortfall. You can always take more than the minimum, but you can't take less.

There are several approved methods for calculating these distributions, and you should choose your method based on your goals. One goal is to maximize retirement income, stretching the balance out as far as possible. Another goal might be to meet the minimum requirements so as to pass as much as possible to your heirs. It is vital to realize what your goals are, for once you choose your calculation and distribution methods, you can't change them.

You can choose either single life expectancy, based on your age, or joint life expectancy, based on your age and the age of your primary beneficiary. Life expectancy is based on government actuarial tables. Choosing joint life expectancy when your beneficiary is younger than you means lower minimum withdrawals. If you have designated someone other than your spouse as the IRA beneficiary and that person is more than ten years younger, the joint life expectancy is calculated as if the other person were ten years younger. Two Web sites that have calculators to help compute your minimum distributions are www.founders.com and www.interest.com/hugh/calc.

Whichever you choose, you need to pick one of three distribution methods: recalculation, term certain, or hybrid. Once you've started taking distributions, your heirs must continue the same method. If you do not choose before your first distribution is due, your IRA custodian will choose for you. These three methods are as follows:

■ Recalculation: Each year, the amount you're required to withdraw is recalculated based on your life expectancy at your current age. If you are a single man age 70, your life expectancy is 16 more years, so you would divide your total IRA value of that year by 16. The next year, at age 71, your life expectancy is 15.3 more years, so you would divide your total IRA value at that time by 15.3. This method tends to defer taxes for you but results in higher minimum withdrawals for those who inherit your IRA. A downside to this method is that if you elect a joint life expectancy and your spouse dies, the amount you must take annually goes up dramatically.

■ Term certain: Every year, you subtract 1 from the previous year's life expectancy. So, using the preceding example, if your life expectancy is 16, it becomes 15 the next year. This results in larger distributions than recalculation, and you risk running out of IRA money if you outlive your life expectancy. However, your heirs are saddled with less of a tax burden.

■ Hybrid: This method is a combination of the other two distribution methods. For example, you might choose recalculation, and your beneficiary could choose term certain.

If you have different beneficiaries for your different plans, you must make separate minimum withdrawal calculations for each account. But you can then choose to take the required amount from just one account or from any combination of your accounts.

Because these distribution laws are complicated, it is easy to make the wrong choice. Because you are stuck with the choices you make, it pays to look at the alternatives carefully and not leave anything to chance.

How Much Money Do You Need to Retire?

Although more people are recognizing the need to save and invest for retirement, most are not sure how much they will need. This amount varies, but as discussed in the first section of this chapter, a standard answer is that people need, on average, about 70 to 80 percent of their annual needs before they retire, adjusted for inflation. This section and the next two describe how to determine how much money you will need in retirement. If you believe that you need more or less money at retirement than is shown in the following example, simply adjust the numbers to your specifications.

To determine the amount of money you will need to have available to generate your retirement income,

■ Calculate your required retirement income, adjusted for inflation.

- Determine how much of that money will be supplied by Social Security and any pension and annuity plans, both adjusted annually for inflation.

- You must make up the difference between these two figures through your investments.

The following examples flesh out this approach. To simplify the calculations, all dollars are rounded to their nearest $100, and these computations ignore the effects of taxes on retirement income.

Assume that you are earning $50,000 a year, have 20 years before retirement, and expect to need 80 percent of your current salary for your retirement. If inflation remains at around 3 percent,[9] when you retire you would need to earn about $90,300 to match the purchasing power of your current salary. So you would need to generate $72,200 (80 percent of $90,300) to finance your retirement in your first year.[10] How will you generate $72,200 the year you retire, and how can you maintain your purchasing power?

Let's consider the second question first. What is important to remember is that this $72,200 is not a static number. It will grow with inflation, so to maintain your purchasing power, you will need more income each year. Assume that you will live for an additional 20 years after you retire. Using the same 3 percent annual inflation rate, in your tenth year of retirement,

---

9. According to data from Ibbotson Associates, the annualized inflation rate for the past 72 years (1926–1997) is 3.1 percent. Source: David Harrell, ''The Time Value of Money,'' May 29, 1998, www.morning star.com.

10. At a lower inflation rate of 2 percent, these two numbers become $59,400 and $74,300, respectively, and at a higher inflation rate of 4 percent, they are $87,700 and $109,600, respectively. Thus, inflation can play a major role in determining how much you will need; even a 1 percent change in the annual inflation rate can make a major difference.

you will need to generate $97,000 to maintain your same standard of living, and in your twentieth year of retirement, you will need $130,400 to maintain the same purchasing power.

Assuming that you can obtain an investment return of 6 percent on your money, you will need $1.2 million available to generate the $72,200 needed in your first year of retirement. You will need almost twice as much, $2.2 million by your twentieth year of retirement, to generate $130,400 and allow you to maintain your purchasing power. Table 3-1 sums up this information.

The Critical Role of Investments

The last section discussed the amounts of money you will need to have generated at retirement and into retirement, given inflation. You may get some of this money from other sources. However, let's first suppose that you don't qualify for any of these plans so that we can understand the critical role of investments in retirement planning. We look at how you will generate the original $1.2 million in this section and discuss the importance of this 6 percent return in the next section.

If you had no savings and investments today and needed to have $1.2 million in 20 years, you would need to get to work immediately. One possible investment would be in com-

Table 3-1   Monetary Needs Now and during Retirement

	Now	At Retirement	Retirement + 10 Years	Retirement + 20 Years
Salary	$50,000	$ 90,300		
Retirement income		72,200	$ 97,000	$ 130,400
Money needed in retirement		1,203,000	1,617,000	2,179,000

mon stocks; assuming the historical annual rate of return of 11 percent, $16,800 invested every year for a 20-year period would yield $1.2 million. What if you believe that stocks are too risky and want a more stable investment? Bonds have averaged about 5.3 percent from 1926 to 1997;[11] assuming this annual return, you would have to invest more than twice as much, $33,400 each year, to reach $1.2 million.

Whatever investment vehicle you use, the earlier you start, the easier it will be to reach your goal. The preceding example assumed that you had no savings or investments today. If you already had $100,000 in your investment of choice today, you would have to save and invest less each year to reach this goal; you would need to invest $5,500 a year using stocks and $25,600 a year using bonds to reach your goals. Or, if you had $250,000 today, you would not need to invest anything more using stocks and $14,000 a year using bonds, hence the need to start investing and saving early.

If you have guaranteed payments from Social Security or pension and annuity plans, the amount you need to save and invest diminishes. Let's assume that of the $72,200 you would need when you retire, guaranteed payments make up $24,000, or about one-third of your needs. To obtain the additional $48,200, you would need about one-third less in assets when you retire, or about $800,000 (6% × $800,000 = $48,000). So let's see what you need to invest to reach $800,000.

If you were starting from scratch, the amounts you would need to invest would also be cut by one-third. So if you had no savings and needed to generate $800,000 over a twenty-year period, using stocks, you would need to invest $11,200

---

11. Susan Dziubinski, ''How to Know if You'll Have Enough,'' November 24, 1999, www.morningstar.com.

a year, and using bonds, you would need to invest $22,300 a year over this time period.

However, if you do have savings, the amounts you would still need to invest are cut by more than a third. Given a guaranteed stream of money, if you had $100,000 in your investment of choice today, you would not need to invest anything more if your money was invested in stocks, and you would need to invest $14,500 a year using bonds to reach $800,000. Or, if you had $250,000 today, you would still not need to invest any more if your money was in stocks, and would need to invest $2,700 per year using bonds to reach this same goal. Both these examples once again illustrate the need to start investing and saving early.

Table 3-2 sums up how much you need to invest annually to reach your goals.

Growing Your Money While in Retirement

The preceding examples looked at calculating the amount of money you would need in retirement. Here, we will look at increasing your money while in retirement. Again we will use the example of having $1.2 million when you reach retirement and look at how it can grow to $2.2 million over the twenty-year retirement period.

Table 3-2   Annual Investments Needed to Reach Goals

Current Net Worth	Guaranteed Payments = $0 per Year		Guaranteed Payments = $24,000 per Year	
	Stocks	Bonds	Stocks	Bonds
$ 0	$16,800	$33,400	$11,200	$22,300
100,000	5,500	25,600	0	14,500
250,000	0	14,000	0	2,700

Why do you need to increase your investment to $2.2 million; why can't you just draw down on your principal each year? You can certainly do so, but you do it at the risk of living longer than twenty years (remember that twenty years is simply an assumption) and running out of money. If both you and your spouse are age 63 and in good health, there is a more than 50 percent chance that at least one of you will live past 85.[12] One of the biggest fears Americans have is running out of money. If you were absolutely certain that you would need money for only twenty years of retirement and if you had no beneficiaries, you could certainly draw down your principal and die broke. Because you don't know how long you are going to live and what emergencies might occur, it is not wise to draw down your principal too much. Otherwise, you might be in the position of having been retired for a number of years and suddenly needing to go back to work. A possible compromise might be to draw it down slowly, making sure that you have a good buffer, but even this might be risky.

The goal of accumulating $1.2 million to generate $72,200 per year assumed a 6 percent return on your money. But if stocks have returned 11 percent a year and have done so well in recent years, why assume only 6 percent? This 11 percent return is a historical average, not a guarantee; the market goes through periods in which it averages far less.[13] Suppose your withdrawal rate was 11 percent a year and the

---

12. Source: 1983a Individual Annuitant Mortality Table, as referenced in Peter Lynch, "Fidelity's Guide to Investing Responsibly," www.fidelity.com.

13. Assume that you started retirement with $500,000 and decided to withdraw 10 percent per year. Had you started retirement in 1980, this amount would have grown to $4.35 million by the end of 1999. But had you started retirement in 1969, you would have run out of money by 1984. Source: J. & W. Seligman & Co. as referenced in Gerri Willis, "A Fixed Income Plan for Bond Cynics," at www.smartmoney.com.

market fell 10 percent a year for three straight years. This would be devastating for your principal; your $1.2 million would be chopped in half. Suddenly, you would have only about $600,000 to live on for the rest of retirement; you would have to consider reemployment because it would be difficult to make up so much lost ground. Given the possibility of market downturns, a 6 percent assumption is more cautious. In addition, a major study has shown that, given how the market has actually performed, 6 percent is the maximum safe rate of withdrawal.[14]

To be able to withdraw 6 percent and keep up with inflation, you need to keep a portion of your money in stocks during retirement.[15] If you withdraw 6 percent of your principal, given inflation and the historical return of just over 5 percent on bonds, your principal will shrink. With an inflation rate of 3 percent, your retirement income must grow by at least that amount to prevent your purchasing power from falling; your $1.2 million must grow to $2.2 million over the twenty-year period.

---

14. Philip Cooley, Carl Hubbard, and Daniel Walz, "Retirement Savings: Choosing a Withdrawal Rate That Is Sustainable," *AAII Journal,* as cited in "Retirement Planning: Making It Last Forever" by Frank Armstrong, January 8, 1999, www.morningstar.com. This work is popularly known as the "Trinity study" because the three authors are professors of finance at Trinity University in San Antonio, Texas.

15. Data from the Trinity study and *Stocks for the Long Run,* by Jeremy J. Siegel (New York: McGraw-Hill, 1998), show problems with the conventional wisdom that retirees should invest only in bonds and savings accounts. "For investors with 25 or 30 year payout periods, portfolios with more than 30 percent bonds have more volatility and lower total returns than more stock heavy asset allocations. Portfolios with a substantial allocation of stocks are more likely to 'survive.' " The key words here are *payout period.* Whereas a person who is 60 may have a payout period of twenty-five years, an older person, wanting to leave money for his or her grandchildren, may actually have a longer payout period. Source: John P. Greaney, "Asset Allocation for the Ages," September 1, 1998, www.geocities.com.

Consider a portfolio made up of 65 percent stocks and 35 percent bonds. Based on historical growth returns, such a portfolio would grow at an average of about 9 percent annually.[16] If you are withdrawing 6 percent a year, this leaves about 3 percent, similar to the long-term level of inflation. Therefore, this mix of stocks and bonds could allow you to maintain your standard of living, keep up with inflation, and increase your principal.

The proper combination of stocks and bonds in your retirement portfolio depends, in part, on your tolerance for risk and your need for an income stream. People in retirement can select a combination of stocks and bonds or stock and bond mutual funds. Another alternative is a balanced mutual fund; the portfolios of many balanced funds are made up of approximately 60 to 65 percent stocks and 35 to 40 percent bonds. These mutual funds may be a prudent investment choice for retired people.

16. From 1926 to 1998, a portfolio of 60 percent stocks and 40 percent bonds had an average annual return of 9.4 percent. These examples use the S&P 500 as a proxy for stocks and long-term U.S. corporate bonds as a proxy for bonds. Source: "Plain Talk: Realistic Expectations for Stock Market Returns," The Vanguard Group, www.vanguard.com, 1999.

Chapter 4

REDUCING DEBT

American consumers have amassed a large amount of personal debt and continue to run up this debt. How and why do people get into debt?

Some debt may be unavoidable. Anyone who buys a home by using a mortgage incurs debt. This is considered long-term debt. (The different mortgage options are covered in Chapter 6.) People often incur debt when they start up a new business, purchase an existing business, or expand an existing business. It is important to have sufficient capital or secure lines of credit in such situations; insufficient capital is a major reason why businesses fail. Thus, taking on debt may be the best way to ensure your business's success.

Another form of debt is education loans, whether for undergraduate, graduate, or professional school. Such debt can be thought of as a cost of doing business, for without such education, career advancement and earning potential often are seriously limited. Educational loans may be considered medium-term debt because the borrower usually has several years to pay them off.

Most short-term debt comes from credit cards. It is usually simple to get credit cards; people are showered with credit card invitations in the mail, banks invite you to apply when you open an account with them, and agencies abound dedicated to finding you a credit card even if you have a bad credit history. (You can look at your credit rating for free at www.freecreditreport.com.) Credit cards do not come with instructions on how to use them properly and sensibly. To make things worse, the credit limits on credit cards often can be increased very easily.

For college students, the ease of acquiring credit and raising credit limits can be disastrous. As teenagers go off to college, they are inundated with societal pressures to purchase more expensive items. In the teenage and college years, they become familiar with credit cards as a way to satisfy their desires for more goods and services. Unfortunately, the connection between being able to charge an item and having to pay for it is not always straightforward. Credit cards can be made to seem like magic money that allows one to obtain things without having to pay for them. Often, parents give a son or daughter a credit card that is in the parents' name, to be used in case of emergency; however, what constitutes an emergency for the kids may not be the same as for the parents. Without firm instructions, a desire to purchase clothing or stereo equipment or to finance a trip may seem like legitimate emergencies.

College students are bombarded with various card offers each semester. Without proper training, they can find it easy to sign up for these credit cards and start using them, never fully realizing that they are responsible for all payments. A 1998 study showed that the average undergraduate student has an outstanding balance of $1,843, and 14 percent have a balance of more than $3,000.[1] Credit card companies often extend credit to these students and graduates knowing that many will act irresponsibly and that many parents will wind up paying for their children's excesses.

Not only students act this irresponsibly. People who have never learned to live within a budget, compulsive spenders, and people seeking or needing instant gratification often do not think about the future consequences of their spending actions. Because it is so easy to use a credit card, goods and services are bought regardless of whether they are really needed; it's easy to accumulate thousands of dollars in debt. One spouse's spending and debt patterns can affect the other spouse even after they are parted by divorce or death.

The solution is to learn to use credit cards responsibly. Having a credit card for emergencies can be prudent financial management, but building up credit card debt is not. Paying off your credit card every month is prudent; paying only the minimum each month is not. Using and then paying off a credit card monthly so that you can keep your money in the bank earning interest can be prudent; spending without a budget, constantly spending up to your credit limit, and paying only the minimum monthly payment certainly is not.

Credit cards can be useful if they are used as part of an overall financial and budgetary plan, but they can be dangerous when they are not.

Paying Off Credit Cards

With the possible exception of contributing to retirement accounts, it is important to get rid of all short-term debt before

---

1. Lee Clifford, "The Semester of Living Dangerously," *Smart Money,* May 2000, p. 148.

implementing any investment strategies. Most short-term debt carries high interest rates; credit card interest typically ranges from 14 to 21 percent, compounded, depending on the card and the plan. No investment consistently averages this sort of return. Therefore, in most cases it is smarter to pay off the debt than to invest. It does not make sense to pay 18 percent on money owed on a credit card and use the money to earn 6, 9, or even 12 percent in an investment. In addition, you cannot deduct the credit card interest, and your investment gains are taxed. When you pay off your credit card interest, in effect you are earning 14 to 21 percent because you won't have to pay out this amount.

If you owe money on your credit cards and are paying finance charges, you are paying extra for all new purchases. It is important to cut back on your credit card charges, for they simply will add to your overall debt and accumulated finance charges. If you do not have an outstanding balance, you generally have a grace period to pay off the debt before finance charges kick in. However, if you have an outstanding balance, finance charges accrue to both your balance and new purchases. If you have a balance on your credit card and you buy something on sale that you just can't resist, you are really paying that sale price plus 14 to 21 percent. Usually, you are paying more for this item than if you bought it at regular price with cash. It will take longer to pay everything off, increasing your total finance charges even more. Cut up your credit cards, put them under the mattress, carry one only for emergencies—do whatever it takes not to use them.

At these high interest rates, finance charges add up quickly. It is important to pay much more than the minimum balance. By paying only the minimum balance, you will wind up paying more in total finance charges than you did for the items you originally purchased. For example, if you owe

$1,100 on an account charging 18½ percent per year and only pay the monthly minimum amount, you will pay nearly $2,500 in interest charges during the twelve years needed to pay it off. Paying $10 a month above the monthly minimum will reduce the amount of time needed to pay off the debt to about six years and will reduce the cumulative interest by about $600. Just think what might happen if you pay an additional $25 or even $50 a month. Clearly, it is in your best interest to pay more than the minimum and to pay it off as quickly as possible.

Another important way to reduce your credit card debt is to pay off the card with the highest interest rate first. If you have two credit cards, one charging 18 percent per year and the other 21 percent per year, your priority should be to focus your additional payments on the credit card with the higher interest rate.

A third course of action would be to transfer the balances on the cards with higher interest to cards with lower interests. Most credit card companies charge a fee to transfer existing credit card debt, but this fee generally is modest, especially compared to the amount of higher interest charges you would no longer have to pay. Often, these lower interest rate cards have annual fees. Annual fees generally make no sense for people who pay off their balance in full every month, but they may make sense for people with major credit card debts if the rate is low enough. One source of low-interest credit cards is www.ilife.com.

Another strategy would be to try to reduce the interest on your credit card. Consumers can do this because of the high demand by credit card issuers for new clients. Currently, because so many credit card companies want your business, it is a buyer's market for credit card consumers; in a buyer's market, the consumers have the clout. Savvy consumers know that credit card issuers do not want to lose existing customers. So you can call your credit card company and request a lower interest rate. State that you are tired of paying the current rate of 18 percent (or whatever) and would like them to lower it to 12 percent. If they don't, tell them that you will be happy to transfer your balance to a credit card that offers a lower rate. This puts the credit card company in a dilemma: Should they accept a lower interest rate on your money or risk losing all the interest on your money? Some credit card issuers would rather get part of your money than none of your money. This strategy doesn't always work, particularly if you have bad credit and may not be able to get a credit card from another issuer, but it is certainly worth a try.

Credit Card Company Come-Ons

Credit card companies have some wonderful ploys to enrich themselves at your expense.

The first and most obvious ploy is raising your credit limit. Almost every card holder has received a letter saying, "Congratulations. Because of your good credit history, we are raising the limit on your credit card." What this really means is that you can now buy more stuff and take on more debt. But how many people really need a credit limit of $5,000 or $10,000? Do you spend that much every month? Yes, it is nice to have such a high limit in an emergency, but the net effect usually is to increase the amount of debt people accumulate. And higher debt means more and higher interest payments and a longer wait until you are debt free. Some people claim that they don't have and can't live within a budget. Wrong: They are living within a budget, only it is a budget set by the credit card companies, not by them. The bottom line is be very wary about applying for, accepting, or using this increase in credit.

The second ploy is sending you those checks in the mail that let you draw against your credit limit as a cash advance. As they tell you, you can spend this money on anything, including a vacation, new furniture, or part of the down payment on a car. Isn't that nice of them? Unfortunately, the reality isn't so nice. Whenever you take a cash advance on your credit card, not only do interest charges start applying to this cash advance, but they also start applying to everything on your current balance! Suppose that you regularly pay off your credit cards every month so you normally don't pay interest charges. Then, one month, you write one of these checks for $500 at the beginning of your monthly credit cycle and also charge $1,000 worth of merchandise during the month. On an 18 percent annual interest charge (1.5 percent monthly interest charge), you will now owe $22.50 for that month (1.5 percent × [$1,000 + $500]). That's a pretty stiff fee for this extra $500. Be very wary about using these checks.

The third ploy is a message on your monthly bill telling you that because of your good credit record, you don't have to make a minimum payment this month, so you won't be charged a penalty. Normally, when you forget a monthly payment, both interest charges and a set penalty are charged. Eliminating the penalty for the month does not eliminate the accumulation of the interest charges for that month. So, taking their "gift" will cost you more in the long run. Be very wary about accepting their offer to waive the penalty for a month.

The fourth ploy is different: On your monthly statement, you get a message from the credit card company encouraging you to pay more than what you owe, to prepay the next month's minimum payment. Isn't that a nice thing for them to allow you to do? While you are at it, why not prepay all your normal monthly bills, such as your telephone and other utility bills? You have better things to do with any extra cash, such as paying off other credit cards, paying off other debt, saving it (and getting interest), or investing it. Prepaying is like giving the credit card company an interest-free loan. The only reason to do something like this is if you know that you'll be away for an extended period of time (such as several months), and you want to maintain your good credit rating.

Debt Consolidation Loans

Sometimes people who are in debt are tempted to take out a loan in an attempt to consolidate all their debts and monthly payments into one single monthly payment. This is certainly a seductive notion: No longer are there bills flying in at all times of the month, making you feel as if your finances are out of control. Suddenly, instead of writing three, five, or ten checks at different times a month, you write only one or two checks each month. It may be enticing, but is it right for you?

Debt consolidation loans can include getting an unsecured loan from a bank or some other lending institution or writing a check against your credit limit on a credit card. In addition, certain institutions that lend money send letters to people advising them of their "good credit history" and invite them to apply for a line of credit to draw from for unexpected emergencies. Evaluate all such offers with caution.

This need for caution stems from the interest rate charged and the other terms of these loans. Unsecured bank loans (i.e., loans that are not based on collateral) and other such lines of credit usually carry double-digit interest rates.

Let's look at the mathematics of such a loan. Consider a $20,000 loan at 14 percent over fifteen years; this loan would result in monthly payments of $266. This certainly looks attractive: You can pay off large amounts of debt, and $266 seems manageable. What is not apparent is the total amount of interest. Cumulative interest over the fifteen-year period equals almost $28,000. If you took out such a loan, you would be paying more in interest than in principal over this fifteen-year period. A shorter loan period would result in less interest but higher monthly payments. The same loan over a five-year period would result in monthly payments of $465 and cumulative interest of nearly $8,000. As with credit cards, this interest is not deductible on your taxes.

The interest on such a loan may be greater or less than the cumulative interest from gradually paying off the credit cards. However, what tends to happen is that as some people pay off credit card balances with this loan, they tend to start using them again. Such people often end up with both credit card debt and a debt consolidation loan to pay off.

Many lending institutions make home equity loans available. These are loans based on the amount of equity you have in your home. As discussed in Chapter 6, the major problem with such a loan is that if you default on the loan, you can lose your home.

The bottom line is that you should be very careful before taking on any type of loan to retire your debts.

Lesson from the Bible

A familiar story in Genesis has investment and financial themes that can be applied to modern life. In Chapter 25 of Genesis, Esau sells his birthright for some lentil stew. Jacob is cooking this stew when Esau shows up, famished. When Jacob demands the birthright for the food, Esau figures that he is close to death, so the birthright would do him no good, anyway.

Jacob is being a shrewd trader. He knows that Esau is no-where near death, but Esau doesn't seem to realize this, so Jacob is dealing in the marketplace with superior knowledge. Meanwhile, Esau has a credit card mentality. He wants everything today, he doesn't want to wait for it, and he doesn't seem to want to take into account the cost of this impatience. Thus, he seems to deal strictly in the short term while ignoring the long term.

In this transaction, Esau got exactly what he wanted: stew. Jacob got what he wanted: the birthright. Esau put such a low value on the future that he was willing to forgo the special blessing of the birthright to fill up his stomach. Esau, the action-oriented hunter, was no match for Jacob, the fellow with a vision of the future.

This story illustrates the tradeoffs between consuming goods today and consuming goods in the future. Each economic entity, whether a person or a country, decides whether to consume goods and resources today or to invest such goods and resources so as to have even more in the future. By reallocating and delaying our preferences, we can wind up with more at a future date and with a better and more favorable distribution.

In general, people tend to prefer enjoying the use of a good or a service in the present rather than in the future. Given the opportunity to choose between receiving something today or a year from now, people will select today. People discount the value of future goods. They want to be compensated for forfeiting the use of the money or good now. Indeed, this is where the idea of interest comes from: It is compensation for not using money today. Accordingly, the more present oriented a person is, the less he or she values the future. In the case of this story, Esau, who is present oriented, will have more in the short-term present and much less in the future. Jacob gives up very little in the present to get much more in the future.

The credit-card mentality referred to above can be applied here. Many people are impulse spenders and buy without thinking. Such people never seem to have money when they really need it. Emergencies happen, special occasions happen, and the money is not there.

Others are not impulse buyers. They do not spend money haphazardly; they use it as part of an overall plan. Often they invest this money to increase its overall utility. Such people have the necessary resources when they are needed.

There is another economic principle behind this story. Each economic entity, whether a person, a nation, or the entire planet, has only a fixed amount of resources available at any given time. Resources are the factors of production, and they can include money, land, knowledge, and time. Resources are traded in the marketplace; the more perceptive the trader, the better he or she will come out. Clearly, Jacob was the more perceptive trader because he used time and knowledge to his advantage. Esau used his resources very poorly.

Time Is Money

Time is money. This phrase has been used in so many contexts that it has almost become hackneyed. This section explores how you can use this concept in your life.

Everyone who works is paid a salary, a certain amount of money per unit of time. It could be expressed as an annual salary (say, $50,000 per year) or an hourly salary (say, $10 per hour). However it is expressed, it captures the idea that working people trade one commodity (time) for another commodity (money). If you are earning $10 per hour (after taxes) and buy a suit worth $320, you have determined, in effect, that this suit is worth thirty-two hours, or four days' worth of work to you. A corollary to this concept is that each hour, day, week, and year is worth something to you. If you are working and earning $10 per hour, how much is an hour of leisure worth to you? Generally, the marketplace has determined that it is worth more than $10 per hour, hence the notion of time and a half for overtime. In effect, you have to be paid more than your normal wage to give up your free time to work beyond your normal work week.

When you use a credit card and build up debt, you are mortgaging your present satisfaction into the future. As discussed earlier in this chapter, if you have a credit card balance of $1,100 on an account charging 18½ percent interest per year and pay only the monthly minimum amount, you will pay nearly $2,500 in interest. So let's look at this in terms of working time at the after-tax wage of $10 per hour. To pay for $1,100 worth of goods and services, you will have to work 110 hours, or about 2¾ weeks. To pay off the interest of $2,500, you will have to work an additional 250 hours, or about 1½ months. Just think, you'll spend 1½ months' worth of your future wages just to pay off the interest.

If you are earning $20 per hour after taxes, the amount of time to pay off $1,100 would be about 1½ weeks and to pay off the interest would be about 3 weeks. The higher the salary, the more goods and services you can afford, and vice versa; a higher salary means that the interest "penalty" is less severe (in terms of the future time needed to pay it off). You should equate time and money when thinking about all your purchases. This is particularly true when you are running up credit card debt and paying the monthly minimum: Is this particular purchase really worth that many hours, days, or weeks of your earning life?

The average person works thirty to forty years. Because there are roughly 2,000 working hours in a year, the average person has 60,000 to 80,000 hours of lifetime earning time. Although it seems like a lot, the preceding example shows how easy it is to fritter away large portions of this earning time. This 60,000 to 80,000 hours can be thought of as your time to earn the money you need to buy certain necessities, support you through emergencies, and save and invest for retirement. If you spend them paying off debt, you will have less time for these other needs. It also means that you will need to work many more hours before you can retire.

Save It, Don't Spend It

One way to get wealthy is to spend less money. That's obvious, isn't it? But how many Americans really understand or follow this?

Too many people look at only one side of the equation when it comes to getting wealthy: how much they earn. They reason that if only they could make more money, they would be wealthy. Often, however, the more they make, the more they spend or feel obligated to spend; an increase in salary often is accompanied by a corresponding increase in the standard of living. Having "the good life" tends to be oriented much more toward immediate consumption than future investment goals and satisfaction. After you spend this money, it's doubtful, six months or two years later, that you'll remember where that money went, and there's a good chance that you'll wish that you had put the money aside for your future.

Thus, to create wealth and future satisfaction, you need to moderate your current spending.

If both earning and spending go up, savings, investment, and wealth creation often do not.[2] A major reason that it is so hard to save money is that items you buy cost you a lot more than you think. Consider the real cost of eating a meal at a restaurant. Assume that the meal is priced at $8. Adding tax and tip increases the cost to around $10. But to have this $10, given federal and state income taxes, as well as Social Security and Medicare taxes, you might have to earn as much as twice the price of the meal. And if you charge this meal and you are paying finance charges, the actual cost can be even higher.

You might consider an $8 meal chump change, but apply this same reasoning to a major purchase, such as a television, refrigerator, suit, or automobile, and you can begin to see the real cost of this commodity; it costs much more than the purchase price to buy something. To have an additional $1,000 to spend, you have to earn much more than $1,000. Assuming that you are in the 28 percent federal tax bracket and a 5 percent state tax bracket and are paying Social Security (6.2 percent) and Medicare (1.45 percent) taxes, you need to earn nearly $1,700 ($1,000/[1 − {0.28 + 0.05 + 0.062 + 0.0145}]) to have that extra $1,000 available. If you are self-employed, the Social Security and Medicare taxes are doubled, so you might need to earn nearly $2,000 to net an additional $1,000. In addition, by spending now, you are depriving yourself of money to invest, to finance your future. No wonder it seems so hard to get ahead.

On the other hand, if you save or invest the $1,000, you have that amount (plus dividends or interest) in the future to

2. In a typical year, about two-thirds of U.S. households do not save money. Source: Paul A. Merriman, "17 Steps to Improve Your 401(k) Returns," October 1999, as found at www.brill.com.

spend; in addition, there are no taxes on money not spent (although there may be taxes on the dividends or interest). Living a little below your means can ultimately lead to a much more comfortable life than living at or above your means. A penny saved is equal to much more than a penny earned.

This is the key: By making purchases today, you are cutting into your ability to save, invest, and, most important, build up the money needed to ensure financial security. The money you spend today can never grow to help ensure your future. A good way to think of this is that you are planting seeds. By diverting some of your current money into these seeds, you will reap much more when the plants grown from these seeds come to fruition.

Ask yourself why you are making this particular purchase today. People buy for myriad reasons, some of which are to satisfy necessities such as food, clothing, and shelter. Everyone has these same basic needs; it is how we go about satisfying them and what we spend beyond these basic needs that makes the difference. Learning to curb impulse or emotional buying, which also means learning to plan for today and tomorrow, will allow you to increase your savings and investment and grow your wealth. Ideas to help you establish a budget are discussed in the next three sections of this chapter.

Establishing a Budget

Unless you win the $100 million lottery or find a magic genie who can grant all your wishes, it is axiomatic that all your purchases and other expenses are subject to a budget. Even independently wealthy people are subject to a budget, only theirs is much larger than most.

Economics sometimes is defined as the study of the allocation of scarce resources. This could also serve as a definition of most people's budgetary dilemmas: There are many things they would like to buy, but they simply do not have the resources to do so. What to do?

Establishing and following a monthly budget can be challenging if you've never done it before. It can be difficult if you always seem to be short on cash the last few days before a paycheck. People who are in such a position never seem to be able to save, and they feel that they are on a never-ending treadmill.

To establish a budget and determine your limitations, you first need to separate your income from your outflows or expenditures. One of the easiest ways to do this is to take a sheet of paper and draw a line down the middle. On the left, list your monthly income; on the right, list your monthly expenses. Several Web sites have sections devoted to budgeting, such as www.quicken.com, www.smartmoney.com, and www.finan center.com, which can help you with this exercise.

Monthly income is the sum of all money that flows to you in a typical month. It can include your monthly paycheck; interest from bank accounts; dividends from stocks, bonds, and mutual funds; Social Security and pension checks; and alimony. If you normally get bonuses during the year, add them up and divide by twelve to get the average bonus income for a month. If some of your stock, bond, or mutual fund dividends or other payments do not come in monthly, add up all these dividends over the course of a year and divide by twelve.

Expenditures are the sum of what you spend in a typical month. Some expenditures are common to just about everyone: food, clothing, and shelter. Food includes the amount you spend on groceries and a monthly average of your normal dining-out expenses. You probably don't buy clothing on a monthly basis, so it is best to add up the amount you normally spend each year on clothing and then divide by twelve to get a monthly average. Shelter includes rent or mortgage, along with things such as utility bills and a monthly average of normal maintenance bills. The key here is to use the amount you normally spend.

On top of these expenditures come a variety of additional expenses, which can include commuting costs, haircuts, gas and auto maintenance, doctor visits, vacations, and recreation. This category can be quite broad and includes things such as music, computer expenses, sports, trips to an amusement park, and movies. Again, many of these do not occur on a regular monthly basis, so it is important to estimate them, add them up over the course of a year, and divide by twelve.

After making up these lists, add them up and compare your total monthly income with total monthly expenses. If your expenses exceed your income, you have some serious work to do. If your income exceeds your expenses, you have a surplus. It is important to remember that this list of monthly expenses establishes your ordinary expenditures. Unfortunately, everyone has extraordinary expenses, such as emergency health problems, car repairs, or an appliance breaking down at the wrong time. You need to find money for these, too, and this can eat up your surplus.

Reining in Excessive Spending

Many Americans are never taught to budget their money or to think about the consequences of their actions. Therefore, they have no plan and no budget. If you ask most people to list what they spent money on over the last two weeks or the last month, they would probably have a hard time remembering one-fourth of their purchases. In a sense, that is okay, because many everyday details are insignificant. But in another sense it is not, especially if that person constantly seems to be short on cash.

Ironically, paying cash for almost everything is a key way to help reduce spending. There is a big psychological difference between paying for lunch with a $20 bill and paying with a credit card. In the former case, you will immediately see a much smaller amount returned and a smaller amount in your wallet, so you will feel that you have really spent money and that you have less left over. In the latter case, it is as if no money was spent as you won't have to pay until much later; the actual amount of money you are carrying in your wallet remains the same. When paying with a credit card, you can make many major purchases without seeing the cumulative effect for several weeks. Unfortunately, when you get the bill, this cumulative effect can take a major bite out of your savings and any potential savings and investment program.

When you write a check or use a credit card, you will have a record of your purchase, but cash transactions are very easy to overlook and ignore. To get a handle on this type of spending, try one of these two strategies. One is to carry around a small notebook and record every purchase in it and review it monthly. Another strategy is to ask for a receipt for everything you purchase, put all these receipts into a specially designated jar or container on a daily basis, and review them monthly. Either way, you'll begin to see what you spend your money on. You'll be amazed how much you spend simply to satisfy a momentary desire and how much you fritter away. Between newspapers, sodas, and snacks, you can spend several dollars each day without realizing it. Over time, this adds up.

It is very helpful to look at all your expenditures over the last three to six months because in any one month, extraordinary expenses can arise. When you look at this multimonth period, patterns will begin to emerge. Copy down the information from this list into categories such as groceries, rent or mortgage, clothing, entertainment, auto expenses, and household maintenance.[3] There will always be some expense items that don't fall into these basic categories, so you will need to expand your category list.

These lists give you many of the tools you need to get your expenses under control. By looking at the individual items listed in each category, you can begin to understand which of them are essential and which are not. If this is the first time you have done this, it is fairly certain that you will find a lot of extra fat in your weekly and monthly spending. Learning to cut out this fat, especially in the context of establishing a monthly budget, and learning to live within your means will become a priority and, over time, a more comfortable thing to do.

Adjusting the Budget

Dividing your normal monthly expenses into appropriate categories is the first step in establishing a budget and reining in excessive spending. Once you have done this, you need to take a serious look at what you are spending within each category to cut out what may be superfluous.

In making these decisions, you need to be as objective as possible. Think of your current and future goals as well as your

---

3. Much of this can be done with a computer checkbook software program such as Quicken or Microsoft Money. These software packages allow you to set up whatever categories you like and assign these categories to checks, credit card bills, and cash. These programs generate reports that show you how much you have spent each month in each category.

current and anticipated future lifestyles and try to see what is and is not important. For instance, how important is it to eat lunch out every work day, when this costs you at least an extra $1,000 a year?[4] Maybe you give generously to charity, which is a worthwhile activity. However, if you have little or no savings for your children's college education or your own retirement, you may decide that providing for your family's security is your most important charity. Maybe you have a small surplus each month but little savings. It is still important to cut back so you can build up three to six months' worth of savings to handle emergencies.

If your expenses outstrip your income, you have two basic choices: Cut back on your expenditures or increase your income. Most of the time, cutting back may be easier to do, at least in the short run. This is where the tough decisions come in, and given certain constants in the short run, such as rent or mortgage and doctor's bills, this could affect what you have left to spend on food, clothing, and entertainment. In the long run, this could also affect where you live, what kind of car you can afford, and, ultimately, your ability to retire.

---

4. People who eat out for lunch every business day probably spend, on average, $6 to $7 a day. People who bring their own lunches may spend, on average, $2 to $3 a day, maybe buying a drink or dessert. This $4-a-day difference becomes a $20-a-week difference. Over the course of a year, this difference equals about $1,000 a year of after-tax money.

Chapter 5

BUYER BEWARE

Cold Calls

It is easy to get taken by offers over the telephone. You are unprepared, but the person on the other end is very prepared. Your mind is not on specifics and details, but the person on the other end is focused on them. You are often in a relaxed or low-stress mood, but the person on the other end is very direct and intense. Your inclination might be to hang up, but often you don't want to be rude, you listen, and you wind up agreeing with whatever the person on the other end is selling or recommending. After all, it sounds so good, so plausible, and you don't want to think through all the ramifications. Yet this can get you into a lot of trouble. Unfortunately, the person at the other end usually is not giving you the whole story.

Here is one scenario. The phone rings. The voice at the other end says, "My name is [fill in the name]. You probably don't remember that I called you three months ago. Back then,

I recommended a stock, but you weren't ready to invest then. That stock has tripled in price. But don't worry, I have another one that has the same potential. My management is limiting me to 1,000 shares per client; can I sign you up for this amount now?" or "My name is [fill in the name]. I work for XYZ, Inc., a stock brokerage firm specializing in small up-and-coming companies with high growth potential. I am just calling today to introduce myself and to get permission to call you back when I have a promising recommendation."

We've all had calls like these. Some actually are legitimate, because some stockbrokers get new clients by cold calling. Too often, however, such calls play on our greed and get-rich-quick fantasies.

What actually happens in such cases is that people lose money. Much more often than not, in the first example, this person never called you three months before and is counting on your imperfect memory to help lure you in to the promise of another stock that will triple in a short period of time. In the second example, XYZ, Inc., specializes in buying up the stock of unknown companies and hiring people to work the phones. In that initial call, most of us expect the broker to try to pressure us into buying a stock. When this pressure is not applied, we relax and then are more amenable when this person calls a second time. The thinking is that he or she didn't try to pressure us last time, so he or she isn't one of those high-pressure salespeople. We let our guard down for this second call, and the broker recommends stock in these unknown companies.

In both cases, as more people buy the stock through these phone calls, the price gradually moves up. At a certain point, after the stock has moved up enough, the people at these firms sell their shares for a large profit. The price then plummets, rendering the remaining shares, those purchased over the phone, next to worthless.

The odds of striking it rich from being called by an unknown person peddling an unknown stock or commodity are essentially zero. If it is such a great deal, why is this stranger calling you? Why isn't this person buying up as many shares as he or she can? And why is this person pressuring you to buy a stock before you have done any research into it? Yet people continue to hope, don't ask questions, and throw caution to the wind.

Another example goes something like this: The phone rings, and it is someone from a long-distance phone company, asking you to switch to their service. As added incentive, they will add 10,000 miles to your frequent flier mileage with a specific airline: 5,000 after the first three months and the other 5,000 three months later. They will pay all switching fees now and, if you are dissatisfied with them in the first six months, they will pay to switch you back to your current long-distance provider.

Too many consumers, blinded by the 10,000 free frequent flier miles, jump onto such an opportunity. They do not find out how the long-distance rates of this new company compare with those of their current company or whether there are any conditions on usage over the six-month period. Often there is a monthly fee to set comparable rates. Are these "free" 10,000 miles worth paying this additional fee each month? Maybe they are and maybe they aren't, but these conditions are very different from the original proposition offered.

Consumers should avoid the desire to say "yes" just to get off the phone quickly and should take the time they need to analyze these offers from strangers. It is the consumer, not the stranger on the phone, who will have to live with these decisions.

Commodity and Natural Resource Promotions

You are listening to the radio. Suddenly you hear an ad that says, "For seventeen of the past nineteen years, this commodity has moved up in price by at least 42 cents in the middle three months of the year. A $2,000 contract on this commodity, given such a price move, would yield you a profit of $12,500. Of course, past performance is no guarantee of future results, and you could lose some or all of your money, but past results have been promising and this year looks like a repeat of past years."

Or you attend a free seminar on the profit potential of exploration for a particular mineral. The speaker says something like, "According to our geologic estimates, there is an excellent chance of finding this mineral in the areas where we are looking. This map of the region we're exploring shows proven reserves in blue, probable reserves in red, and possible reserves in green. Notice how much of the map is covered."

Given such sales pitches, why not invest? It all seems so simple, it seems to have worked before, and the chances seem high. You are already spending the profits.

Not so fast! If it was so simple, everyone would do it and everyone would be a millionaire. Trading in commodity futures and investing in natural resource exploration is quite complex, and most people who try to make money in these areas usually fail. Let's explore the reasons why.

The market for commodity futures exists to help smooth out day-to-day and seasonal fluctuations in the price and availability of certain commodities. The prices of these commodity futures can vary wildly because of factors such as politics and the weather. Being able to lock in a price to either supply or purchase a certain commodity (such as wheat) helps both the suppliers (such as the farmer) and the buyers (such as bread and cereal manufacturers) to plan and budget their expenditures. To some investors and traders, these fluctuations in price present a potential profit opportunity. Some traders believe that they can forecast overall trends in commodity prices and day-to-day or week-to-week price changes and, using sophisticated trading models, try to profit from such changes.

To profit from such changes, one needs an incredible amount of knowledge. The professionals who do this for a living often lose money. Unlike with many other investments, for every winner there is always a loser. Although there may be some truth in pitches such as the one mentioned earlier, many variables that affect the results are not discussed. Amateur investors, seduced by such ads or mesmerized by tales of people making large sums of money, walk blindly into these markets and almost always lose. It takes years of experience and knowledge to do most things well; consider what you do for a living and think how ludicrous it would be for someone without your training and skill to believe that they can do what you are doing and do it well. Yet this is what happens when someone thinks that he or she can make large profits with little knowledge. It just doesn't work that easily. Don't waste your money.

Natural resource exploration is a similar case. Each industry area has a unique vocabulary and dynamics. The terms *proven, probable,* and *possible reserves* have specific meanings in each industry; a neophyte investor cannot hope to understand these concepts without a lot of research. Someone who knows very little about a particular mineral industry does not understand all the details of these possible investments. People lose a lot of money this way.

Magazine Articles

You are looking through the magazines at your local store and come across the financial magazines. Some of the cover headlines scream out at you: "Eight Mutual Funds That Never Lose Money," "Seven Stocks to Buy Now for Retirement," or "Is Now the Time to Buy Bonds?" What should you do?

Over the last several years, the number of magazines devoted solely to finance and investing and the amount of space devoted to these topics by other magazines and newspapers have grown. This growth correlates roughly with the increased attention that the media have been devoting to money matters. The supply of financial information has been rising to meet the increasing demand for such information.

Given the increasing supply of such information, each publication must do something to get your attention and thus increase sales. The stories behind these headlines sometimes have very useful information and can be used as the basis for additional learning or research. But remember that these magazines need to keep supplying a reason for people to continue to buy them. Headlines about the "best" mutual funds, the perfect retirement vehicle, or the need to sell certain stocks are designed to generate more sales. A magazine that claims to have found the five best mutual funds one month may run another story a few months later on the six best mutual funds. Many times, there is little correlation between these two lists of mutual funds.[1]

---

1. For example, none of the 1998 *Mutual Funds Magazine* leaders made that list for 1999. Source: Doug Fabian, "Top 5 Reasons to Ignore Top 10 Lists," August 1999, www.fabian.com.

A little bit of knowledge is dangerous. Many beginning investors, flush with some knowledge or a few initial successes in the stock market, believe that they know the ropes and can evaluate the risks. Such people often willingly dive headfirst into these "surefire" ways of investing and making money, committing most or all of their savings to these strategies, only to lose some or most of their money. At best, advice that you get from magazines (as well as other sources) should be considered as potentially educational information but certainly not the only basis for an investment decision. It is important to do additional research and not take any of these recommendations blindly.

Newsletters and Information Advertisements

You are going through your mail, and suddenly you see the following words: "Stock Market Will Be Very Bumpy Ahead, Buy Only These Selected Stocks," "Global Disaster Ahead— Buy Gold," "Two Unknown Stocks Have Major Upside Potential," or words to this effect. Or you are surfing the Internet when you suddenly get information about some hot new stock tip. According to your new source, this stock is poised to move in just a matter of days or weeks.

Dozens of newsletters and Web sites claim to offer specialized information about what will be happening in the investment world. Some newsletters are reputable and deliver good investment advice. In addition, many Web sites are reputable and deliver good investment advice; a number of these are mentioned throughout this book.

However, this is not true about all newsletters and Web sites. In an effort to capture your subscription or investment money, these newsletters and Web sites imply that they know of investments that will make you large sums of money and that only they know of these wonderful opportunities. They are playing on fear and greed: the fear of being left behind and the greed that comes from hoping to buy the one investment that triples in just weeks or months.

Given the claims that accompany the newsletter or Web site teasers, it is hard to know which are worth your money and which are not. To complicate things, many of these teasers and promotions provide examples from the past in which their predictions came true, with the clear implication that they have a crystal ball, sometimes the only crystal ball. To complicate things further, many newsletters offer money-back guarantees if you are not satisfied. This allays many people's suspicions about the newsletters; however, although you can get some or all of your subscription money back, you cannot get back the money you put into bad investments.

That is one of the problems. These sources trumpet their triumphs, but they certainly do not say anything about their failures. Certain newsletters claim that their model portfolio has risen by a certain percentage over the last few months; these results may not include recommendations that were highly touted that may have done poorly but were outside their model portfolio.

A larger concern is based on the advertised inference that certain newsletter writers or online investment gurus have marvelous insight that no one else seems to have. Is it credible that these are the only people who can see these new trends or the only ones who can help ordinary people make money? Too many investors believe that a certain financial analyst or newsletter writer is the only one who truly knows what is happening. The truth is that most real experts do not do very well in their predictions,[2] so they shouldn't be the only ones to help you to profit.

The prudent investor will learn to listen to, follow, and strive to understand the major economic trends affecting the economy and the various markets, such as the stock, bond, commodity, and real estate markets. Both beginning and sophisticated investors would do well to read several financial newspapers and magazines and listen to the financial television and radio programs that are on regularly without letting one person's opinions move them to action.

---

2. Between 1929 and 1976, nine groups of experts picked the stocks or industries that they believed would do the best in the upcoming year. Not only did they fail to pick the best, but 76 percent of their choices underperformed the market. Source: David Dreman, "Contrarian Investment Strategy," as referenced in James K. Glassman, "A Contrarian View: Stocks' Risk Is Low," *The Washington Post,* May 10, 1998, p. H1.

Chapter 6

HOME BUYING

Mortgage Basics

A large part of the American dream involves owning your own home. Whether it is a condominium, town house, or detached house and whether it is a primary residence or vacation home, home ownership is venerated. The interest you pay on your home or on a home equity loan is tax deductible, and many people expect the equity built up in a home to provide part of their retirement nest egg.

A majority of baby boomers have already purchased homes;[1] they are concerned about paying off their mortgages early, refinancing, and taking out home equity loans. However, other boomers are still renting and may be in the process of deciding whether to rent or buy. Some boomers or their

---

1. 71 percent of boomers owned their homes in 1998. Source: "By the Numbers: A Boomer's Life," *Newsweek,* April 3, 2000, www.news week.com.

parents may suddenly become empty nesters and need to decide whether to sell the home they currently own; moving from a $250,000 home to a $150,000 home means more available cash, lower monthly payments, and lower upkeep expenses.

When you decide to buy a home, unless you are flush with cash or unless someone is going to buy it for you, you will need to borrow money. This is where mortgages come in. This chapter reviews the basics of mortgages, looks at some of the variables involved in deciding whether to rent or buy, and addresses the aforementioned issues specific to paying off mortgages.

Mortgages are a specific type of loan from a bank, savings and loan, or other financial institution. The terms for such a loan include the interest rate and the length of the loan. There may or may not be points on this loan (a one-time additional payment), and some mortgages allow changes in the interest rate. There may also be additional stipulations such as the ability to pay off the loan early.

Mortgage payments always include principal and interest, almost always include real estate taxes (which the lending institution pays to the proper state agency), and may include private mortgage insurance (PMI). In the initial years of a loan, most of the monthly payment goes to pay off the interest, so the equity you have in your home does not rise very much at first. Because this interest is deductible from your taxes, the actual cost of the loan is reduced. Often, if your down payment is less than 20 percent of the cost of the home, the lender will require you to purchase PMI, which is paid on a monthly basis. PMI helps to insure the lender against the consequences of default; this premium is not deductible from your taxes. Alternatives to PMI exist and are worth looking into.

Buying a house with a mortgage allows you to use leverage, or borrowed money, in a fairly safe situation. If you buy a $100,000 house with 20 percent down and the value of the house rises to $120,000, your investment has doubled. You invested only $20,000, and the bank or mortgage company lent you the remaining $80,000. When the price rises to $120,000, the bank's portion remains $80,000, but your stake in the house increases to $40,000.

The traditional mortgage has been the 30-year fixed loan. Under such a loan, you, the borrower, agree to make monthly payments to the lender, over 360 months, based on a specified interest rate. Such loans were the norm through the 1960s and the early 1970s. A variation on such a loan is the fifteen-year fixed loan, in which the home is paid off in half the time; the advantage to such loans is that you own the home much quicker, and the major disadvantage is that your monthly payments are higher.

As interest rates rose in the 1970s, the ability of many people, particularly those with modest incomes, to purchase a home declined. As interest rates and home prices rose, the total amount of the loan (and the monthly payment) needed by prospective home buyers also rose; this squeezed many people out of the real estate market.

Consequently, a number of variations on the fixed loan were born, many revolving around adjustable-rate mortgages (ARMs). The interest rate changes are specified in the terms of the contract; these changes are based on a specified index and are constrained by how much they can rise or fall in a given year and in total. To help new home buyers qualify, the first year's rate is lower than the prevailing thirty-year fixed rate, but the maximum cap is higher. Consumers should understand all the ramifications of these ARM variations; some of the pros and cons of fixed and variable rates are discussed in the next section.

A number of Web sites can give you good mortgage information; some of these promote their services as well. These sites include www.bankrate.com, www.e-loan.com, www.ilife.com, www.lendingtree.com, www.quicken.com, and www.youdecide.com.

Fixed-Rate vs. Variable-Rate Mortgages

Which mortgage should you choose? Given the plethora of mortgage choices, how should a home buyer go about choosing a mortgage?

As usual, this depends on a number of factors. There is no simple or right answer. Home buyers' goals and objectives differ depending, in part, on their risk level, age, and goals. Current and projected interest rate levels also play a part in these decisions. A few alternative situations are discussed in this section.

Risk-averse people probably would be more comfortable with a fixed-rate loan than with an ARM. Because a typical ARM might rise or fall as much as 2 percentage points with each adjustment (usually with a cap of 6 percentage points), risk-averse people might be uncomfortable with such volatility and opt for a fixed-rate loan.

Many first-time home buyers have low incomes and little savings. Such people might want to get into a starter home, a small condo or town house, so as to stop paying rent and start building equity. Once their income, savings, and equity increase, later on in life, or if other circumstances in their life change, they might aspire to trade up and sell this starter home to get a larger home. For such people, it might be wise to get an ARM. Because the first year's interest rate typically is lower than a fixed mortgage rate, they could probably qualify later for a larger loan, thus affording a more expensive home. In addition, because they do not plan to be in this house for a long period of time, the advantages of a stable interest rate from a fixed loan may not be that important.

Other buyers know that they probably will not be in their home for more than ten years. Although they might want the stable interest rate that comes from a fixed-rate loan, they also might want to consider a loan for which the interest rate is fixed for the first several years and then shifts one or more times. In such a case, the initial interest rate would be lower than on a thirty-year fixed rate. In most cases, even if the interest rate shifts upward, the total amount paid over an eight- or ten-year time frame might still be less than with a fixed-rate loan.

For someone who plans to stay in the home for a long time, there may be certain advantages to a fixed-rate loan. The buyer knows how much he or she must pay each month; this makes planning for the future easier. As the buyer's annual income increases, the percentage of his or her monthly pay going to these payments decreases.

The question then becomes which mortgage length to choose. Proponents of the fifteen-year fixed mortgage (as well as proponents of paying off one's mortgage early) argue that homeowners will save thousands of dollars in interest by adopting the strategy. The mathematics and the pros and cons of shorter and longer mortgages are discussed in the next section.

Paying Off Your Mortgage Early

A number of financial institutions and articles in the popular press encourage people to pay off their mortgages as quickly as possible so as to be able to save on their total interest payments. And it's true that the sooner you pay off your loan, the less cumulative interest you will pay. This sounds good, but is it a good idea?

If you currently have a thirty-year loan, paying additional principal each month will allow you to own your home sooner. Similarly, if you originally chose a fifteen-year loan, you would own your home sooner. And in both cases, you will pay out less money than you would if you simply made the regular monthly payments for a thirty-year fixed loan.

Given a thirty-year fixed loan for $100,000 at 7.5 percent and given the regular monthly payment (principal and interest) of $699, you will pay a total of $151,700 in interest over the life of the loan. If you added an additional $75 to your principal each month, you would pay off the loan about eight years earlier and would pay $104,600 in total interest. And if you had originally decided on a fifteen-year loan, you'd have monthly payments of $927, with cumulative interest payments of about $66,900. So with these accelerated payment programs, you can own your home either eight or fifteen years sooner and pay out $47,100 or $84,800 less in total interest charges, respectively. Sounds great, but should you do it?

For some people, the economics don't matter. They need security, and the need to own their home free and clear is paramount. Others don't like the idea of being that much in debt for that long a period of time. In such cases, accelerated payments are preferable.

However, it is important to remember that the principal you have in the home is not easily obtainable. Given some emergency or other need to get cash, real estate is not a liquid asset in the way that stocks, bonds, and cash are. You ordinarily cannot sell a portion of a home, and it is not very easy to sell a portion of the land on which your house sits to raise cash. You can refinance or get a home equity loan to obtain the needed cash, but, once again, you would be subject to monthly payments and interest payments. In addition, you will not have access to the money tied up in the home to take advantage of investment opportunities that come along.

Another consideration has to do with the income tax deduction for interest paid on real estate. If you pay a combined 33 percent in federal and state income tax, a 7.5 percent mortgage is, in reality, closer to a 5 percent loan. Most people are not readily able to borrow money at this low rate. Another advantage for stretching out your mortgage loans is that because inflation erodes the value of a dollar, you are paying off the loan with cheaper dollars each year.[2]

Finally, it is important to consider what you would do with the extra money that you do not pay out for these accelerated mortgage plans. If you opted for a thirty-year loan, compared to the twenty-two-year case, you would have an additional $76 per month, and for the fifteen-year mortgage, you would have an additional $228 per month. What would happen if you invested that money in common stocks?

Let's look at the following scenario. Three baby boomers, A, B, and C, each decide to buy a home when they are 40. All three have $1,000 each month to pay their mortgage or invest. Home buyer A follows the thirty-year plan and thus is able to invest an additional $300 per month for the thirty years. B follows the twenty-two-year plan and invests an additional $224 ($300 minus $76) per month for twenty-two years and then, from age 62 on, $1,000 per month. C follows the fifteen-year plan and invests $72 ($300 minus $228) per month for fifteen years, and then from age 57 on, $1,000 per month.

---

2. At 3 percent inflation, dollars in the fifteenth and thirtieth years will have lost 36 percent and 59 percent of their value, respectively.

They all invest in common stocks; let's see who has the most money when all the homes are paid off.

Amazingly enough, A winds up with the most money by the time all the mortgages are paid off. He or she has invested $108,000 in stocks, which have grown to $795,300. B has invested more money, $155,400, but has only $718,900. Meanwhile, C has invested the most money, $193,000, but has only $616,200. So even though A paid out $47,100 more in interest, he or she has had the greatest appreciation in net worth.

This result may not make intuitive sense, but it works because of the power of compound interest. The extra money A invested early on outweighs the increased investments by B and C later on. After fifteen years, the value of A's investments is $137,500, whereas C's is $33,000. Even though C can invest $1,000 a year for fifteen years while A is investing $300, the value of C's investment cannot catch up. However, if A or B spent this extra money rather than investing it, this analysis would give very different results. Table 6-1 shows the money contributed and its growth at the end of the year for selected ages.

Table 6-1   Growth of Investments

	A		B		C	
Year	Invest	Worth	Invest	Worth	Invest	Worth
1	$3,600	$ 3,996	$ 2,688	$ 2,997	$ 864	$ 959
2	3,600	8,432	2,688	6,324	864	2,024
3	3,600	13,355	2,688	10,016	864	3,205
15	3,600	137,484	2,688	103,113	864	32,996
16	3,600	156,603	2,688	117,452	12,000	49,946
22	3,600	324,532	2,688	243,399	12,000	198,818
23	3,600	364,227	12,000	283,493	12,000	234,008
30	3,600	795,287	12,000	718,891	12,000	616,152

From a financial point of view, it does not make sense to pay off your mortgage early. In such a situation, less of your money is tied up in the home, you are able to maximize the length of a low-interest loan, more of your payments are being made with increasingly cheaper dollars, and if you invest the difference, you'll be wealthier. However, as stated earlier, if you have nonfinancial reasons to pay off your mortgage early, including wanting to have your mortgage paid off before you retire, then all the reasoning in this section may not amount to a hill of beans.

Refinancing Your Mortgage

As mortgage rates have fluctuated, millions of homeowners have been able to refinance their mortgages. Why did rates drop in the 1990s, and what should you consider if you want to refinance your existing mortgage?

For much of the 1990s, interest rates declined because the annual rate of inflation declined and expectations about future inflation were low. Looked at one way, interest rates reflect these expectations: If you believe that inflation will average 3 percent in the foreseeable future, you certainly want to be paid more than 3 percent to lend your money for any period of time. If your expectations about future inflation fall, say to $1\frac{1}{2}$ percent, you would be willing to lend out your money at a lower rate. Thus, as inflation and expectations of inflation fall, interest rates fall.

In the 1990s, inflation, as measured by the consumer price index and the gross domestic product price deflator, fell from its high rates of the early 1980s. This decline in interest rates led to declines in all mortgage rates; in general, mortgage rates have been lower than they have been since the late 1960s.

Low mortgage rates mean that home buyers can borrow more, so they can afford a more expensive home. These low rates have allowed many renters to consider buying property. In addition, low rates allow many current homeowners to refinance their mortgages. Refinancing basically means that a mortgage payer trades in an existing mortgage for a new one; in a time of low mortgage rates, this new mortgage comes with a lower interest rate and lower monthly costs.

How much money could a homeowner save? Well, this involves comparing the terms of the existing mortgage with the terms of a new mortgage. It's impossible to say how much any one person could save, but let's look at an example after checking the steps to see whether it makes sense for you to refinance:

1. Compare your current monthly payment of principal and interest with that of your potential refinance.
2. Calculate the closing and other costs involved in refinancing.
3. Determine how long you intend to live in that home.

Let's look at the Joneses. They are at the beginning of their fourth year of a thirty-year, $100,000 loan at 9 percent, which means a monthly payment of principal and interest of about $805. Assuming that they could refinance their loan at 6³/₄ percent, which would equal a monthly payment of about $649, they would realize an apparent monthly saving of $156. Why would it be apparent savings? Because the amount of interest paid monthly, which is tax deductible, would be reduced. In their fourth year of their current mortgage, the average amount of interest paid each month is about $730;

assuming that they are in the 33 percent tax bracket, they can deduct one-third (a simplifying assumption to keep the math easy), or $243, from their taxes. Therefore, their real, after-tax monthly payment in their fourth year is $805 minus $243, or $562.

The total first-year interest on their refinancing package is $6,703, or about $559 per month. Again, because they are in the 33 percent tax bracket, they can deduct $186 from their taxes. Therefore, the real, after-tax monthly payment, in their first year, is $649 minus $186, or $463. These costs are summed up in Table 6-2.

Their net savings from refinancing would be $562 minus $464, or $99 per month. If closing costs are $4,000, or 4 percent of the loan, it would take about 40 months (almost 3⅓ years) for the net monthly savings to equal the closing costs. So if the Joneses were to stay at this home for at least 3⅓ to 4 years, refinancing would make sense.

A variation on the three steps just described would be to compare your current monthly payment with that of a refinancing package that adds the closing costs to the total principal. Many lending institutions today let you roll the closing costs into the loan amount, in effect allowing you to pay off the closing costs over the life of the loan. Of course, this increases the loan and monthly payment amounts, but you have no current out-of-pocket expenditures. This might not be a

Table 6-2 Real Monthly Cost of Loans

	Current Loan	New Loan
Principal and interest	$805	$649
Principal	75	90
Interest	730	559
Interest deduction	243	186
Real monthly cost	562	463

good alternative if adding the closing costs to the loan amount would force you to pay PMI.

Let's apply this variation to the example just cited. The monthly payment on a $104,000 loan (i.e., $100,000 loan plus $4,000 in closing costs), at 6¾ percent, is about $675. Monthly interest payments average about $562; still assuming that they can deduct one-third, they would be able to deduct $187 from their taxes, leaving an after-tax monthly payment of $488. Because this is less than their current after-tax monthly payment of $562, it would make sense for them to refinance this loan by rolling the closing costs into the total loan.

Home Equity Loans

You need money, so you look at your options. You could get a cash advance from your credit cards, you could get a debt consolidation loan, or you could tap into the equity in your home by taking out a home equity loan. The interest rates on these options average 18 percent, 12 to 15 percent, and 7 to 8 percent, respectively. In many cases, the interest on the home equity loan is tax deductible. This is why many people choose this option to obtain more cash.

Let's first look at what a home equity loan is. When you buy your home, you put a certain amount of money down, say 10 percent or 20 percent. This pays the equity in the house, so you now own 10 percent or 20 percent of the house. As you make your monthly payments, a portion of that payment goes to pay off the loan and a portion goes to increase the equity in your home.

Unlike money that you have in your savings account, checking account, or securities, the equity in your home is not liquid, not readily accessible. You can always sell 50 or 100 shares of XYZ stock or mutual fund to raise cash, but you can't sell a portion of your living room for the same purpose. The equity is locked up in your home.

So the way to tap into the equity in your home is to take a loan out against it, hence the home equity loan. As with all other loans, you will have to pay interest on this loan; it is one of the few loans that can be deducted from your taxes. So if your loan is 7.5 percent, and you are in the 33 percent combined federal and local tax bracket, the real cost to you is 5 percent (again, a simplifying assumption to keep the math easy). It is difficult to borrow money at this low a rate, so the home equity loan seems to be a much better option than credit cards or a debt consolidation loan.

However, there are drawbacks to home equity loans. What you are really doing is taking out a second mortgage on your home. Think about the consequences of this. Now you have two payments involving your home, not just one. If you default on either or simply don't pay either over a certain period of time, you could lose your home. This is why you should not take out such a loan lightly.

Some banks will lend you up to 125 percent of the equity in your home, pointing out how much cheaper this money is (in terms of interest rates) than any other option. Be very careful. The larger the loan, the more difficult it is to pay off. Some people have considered taking out home equity loans to invest in the stock market, but this is not a good idea; you have to make payments every month whether the market goes up or down, and the short-term direction of the market cannot be predicted.

In certain cases, a home equity loan may not be deductible. If you borrow more than 100 percent of the equity in the house, the amount over 100 percent is not deductible. In addition, if your adjusted gross income is above a certain level and you are subject to the Alternative Minimum Tax, the amount you can deduct could diminish.

The bottom line is that home equity loans are one of the cheapest ways to borrow money, but not always the best way.

Chapter 7

COLLEGE TUITION

Parents face many challenges in terms of saving money for their children's future education; one of the largest expenses parents face is college expenses.[1] Fortunately, there are some good resources available on the Web to help families plan expenses and look for loans and scholarships.[2] These sites include www.collegeboard.org, cbweb1.collegeboard.org, www.fastweb.com, www.finaid.org, www.ne-epc.com, and www.petersons.com.

With college costs rising, it is imperative that parents start

---

1. In 1998–1999 the cost of tuition, fees, and room and board at a four-year public college (rounded to the nearest $100) was $7,800 for in-state and $13,000 for out-of-state schools, and the cost for a four-year private college was $20,300. Students spend an average of $2,400 per year on books, supplies, transportation, and personal expenses. Source: *Average Student Expenses, 1998–99*, The College Board, October 1998.

2. About $64 million in financial aid was made available to students for the 1998–1999 school year, with loans making up about 58 percent of this amount. Source: The College Board, as referenced in *Scudder Perspectives*, Spring 2000, p. 3.

investing early for their children's college education. Although scholarships and loans are available, the former is never a sure thing, and the latter saddles you or your children with interest payments.

But what should you invest in? Generally, the longer the time horizon, the more risk a parent can take in investing for college. If there is less than five years before college, it is probably prudent to limit investments to short-term bonds, money market funds, and savings accounts. On the other hand, if a parent is investing for an infant, an investment vehicle such as stocks probably is a smarter and more profitable option. This is because, as discussed at the end of Chapter 9, based on historical data, stocks have outperformed bonds and Treasury bills a majority of the time and probably are a good option for accumulating funds for college.

Often unaware of how quickly wealth can accumulate by using stocks, many parents purchase U.S. Savings Bonds for their children's education because these bonds have tax advantages. Their appreciation is free of state tax and, in certain situations, free of federal tax if the money is used for the child's education. Given a typical annual return of 6 percent, $1,000 invested in savings bonds would grow to $2,900 over eighteen years. Meanwhile, at an annual rate of 11 percent, $1,000 worth of stocks would grow to $6,500 over eighteen years. The tax advantages of U.S. savings bonds do not offset this difference in returns.

Parents can decrease the annual tax they pay on investments by putting these investments in the child's name. This is done by setting up an account through the Uniform Gifts to Minors Act (UGMA). Until the minor reaches age 14, all income, dividends, and capital gains from a UGMA account are taxed partly at the minor's low rate and partly at the custodian's (presumably much higher) rate.[3] These tax savings can become significant as the money in the UGMA grows over time.

A major drawback with such accounts is that when the child reaches the age of majority, he or she controls the money and can choose not to use it for college. The donor or custodian has no legal say in this money's use. Because of this lack of control, some financial advisors counsel against setting up an UGMA account for a minor.

Money registered under the child's name (in an UGMA) may put him or her at a disadvantage in applying for financial aid. Many colleges determine a family's need before granting financial aid. Need is based on a standard formula that often requires 35 percent of the student's assets be used each year for higher education while only requiring about 6 percent of parents' assets. Therefore, much more money (from the student's assets) might have to be used for college expenses before financial aid would be granted than if the same money were in a parent or guardian's name.

Therefore, although UGMAs are a good way to set up a financial reserve to help your child later in life, they may not be the best way to accumulate money for college. Other options for saving and investing for college are discussed later in this chapter.

Once they're in college, it is important that your children don't fritter away your money or theirs. As was discussed in Chapter 4, as teenagers go off to college, they are subjected to a lot of pressure to spend money and take on debt in the form of credit cards. Without established guidelines, your children

---

3. The first $700 earned by the minor is tax-free, and the next $700 is taxed at the minor's rate (usually 15 percent). Income over $1,400 is taxed at the parents' rate if their rate is higher than the child's rate; tax form 8615 should be used in these situations.

could find themselves in debt. Teaching your children about budgeting and debt management could be an excellent way to prevent disaster.

Recent Tax Legislation

The 1997 tax law, the Taxpayer Relief Act, was great for higher education. It provided several different ways to help people afford to pay for a college education.

Before this act, almost all withdrawals from an individual retirement account (IRA) before age 59½ were subject to a 10 percent early withdrawal penalty. This act exempts withdrawals used to pay specific higher education expenses, including tuition, fees, books, supplies, equipment, and room and board. It is important to remember that these withdrawals, except for any portion attributable to the original nondeductible contributions, are still taxed as ordinary income.

One new option that originally received a lot of press attention is the so-called educational IRA. This name is a misnomer because this is actually an educational savings account rather than a retirement account. However, because the account works like a traditional nondeductible IRA, this name helps people to understand the mechanics easily. Anyone earning less than a certain amount can make a nondeductible contribution to an educational IRA for any child who is under age 18.

The most one can contribute in any one year is $500. Although this contribution is not tax deductible, the money grows tax deferred, as in an IRA. Suppose you invested $500 each year in an investment that averages 11 percent a year starting when your child is 1 year old; by the time this child is 18, the account would be worth about $28,000. This alone would not pay for an entire college education, but it certainly helps.

Withdrawals are tax free if used for specific types of college educational expenses such as room, board, and tuition. Income taxes and a 10 percent penalty are due on the investment's growth that is not used for these educational expenses. If money remains in an education IRA when the beneficiary reaches 30, both taxes and penalties are due unless the balance is rolled over to an educational IRA for another family member.

Many students pay for their college education with student loans. The deductibility of the interest on these loans was eliminated in 1986. Now, because of the act, interest on student loans is deductible for the first sixty months in which interest is payable. The maximum deduction was $1,000 in 1998, growing by $500 a year until it reaches $2,500 for 2001 and beyond. This deduction is allowed whether or not the taxpayer itemizes deductions.

The act includes two new tax credits for higher educational expenses; only one of these can be used per taxpayer in a calendar year. Both credits are subject to specific income caps. Tuition and fees are eligible for these credits, but room, board, and books are not. These new credits are as follows:

■ The Hope Scholarship credit: Taxpayers can claim a credit of up to $1,500 per student, for qualifying expenses, for each of the first two years of higher education.

■ The Lifetime Learning credit: Taxpayers can claim a credit of up to $1,000 per year for all students (rising to $2,000 per year for 2003 and later) for qualified expenses; this is not limited to the first two years, so it could be used for graduate or professional school.

Accordingly, if you have one student in college, a prudent strategy might be to use the Hope Scholarship for the first two years and the Lifetime Learning credit for all subsequent years. However, if you have more than one student in college at a time, you need to determine which credit would be best for each individual year.

Prepaid College Tuition

To help parents pay their children's tuition, a growing number of states have introduced prepaid college tuition plans. Although the details differ in each state, the broad outlines of the program allow parents living in a state that sponsors this plan to pay a certain amount of money now, thus locking in current tuition costs at any one of that particular state's public colleges and universities. The question that many parents are asking is whether such programs are good ideas and whether they are the best way to pay for college for their children.

The Taxpayer Relief Act authorized the creation of these plans as well as another plan, alternatively called the tuition trust and the Part 529 plan (after the section of the federal tax code that allows them), which is covered in depth in the next section. All of them allow parents, friends, and guardians to put away money now to help pay for college costs later. Unlike with educational IRAs, there is no adjusted gross income (AGI) limit to contributing to these plans, and they all allow much more than the $500 annual maximum that this IRA allows. As mentioned earlier, in the prepaid state college tuition plans, the plan purchaser pays money now to lock in college tuition costs, whereas in the tuition trust, the plan purchaser invests money in a state-sponsored plan for that money to grow to be used for educational expenses.

States participating in the prepaid tuition plans offer several payment options, which might include lump sum payments, a sixty-month (five-year) payment plan, and an extended program of equal monthly payments until the child reaches college age. These states typically levy a finance charge if the payer elects either of the latter two programs. Thus, the sum of the payments from the sixty-month plan would be roughly 20 percent higher than the lump sum payment, and the sum of the payments for the extended program would be even higher.

Although it would be nice to know when your children are young that their college tuition has been taken care of, there are several problems with these types of plans. Although the specifics of each program differ, there are flaws common to many of these programs:

- The prepaid tuition is just that: It includes only tuition and certain mandatory fees. Items such as room and board as well as books and supplies can make up as much as half of each year's college expenses, and this program does not pay for these items. Therefore, parents still need to save money for these items.

- To get the full benefit of the program, your child would have to go to one of your state's public schools. The program's promised payments usually can be applied toward tuition and mandatory fees at other schools, although these payments usually don't cover the full cost of tuition, so you would need additional tuition money. The state program would pay a private school or out-of-state college a certain amount of money.

Depending on the program, it might be the equivalent of the payments made on the contract plus an annual rate of return on those payments; in general, this rate of return might be 4 or 5 percent. Given the alternatives in the stock or bond markets, this rate is not good. If your child decides not to go to college, depending on the program, you will get back the amount you put in plus some interest; the return on your money will be quite low.

■ You will owe federal taxes. This can be a shock. Because your money has been appreciating for several years, this appreciation is treated as a capital gain. Many states offering this plan give residents state income tax deductions on the money in the plan and an exemption for all earnings and interest if the benefits are used in their state.

What is the best way to save for and pay for your children's college education? The prepayment plan sounds good as a way to escape the uncertainty of rising tuition costs and to ensure that your children's education is paid for. But it may not be the best way for you.

Part 529 Plans

Part 529 plans are sponsored by states and run by specific money management firms and mutual fund families. Under most plans, you can contribute up to $10,000 per year per beneficiary, which is the gift tax exclusion limit. Some plans allow you to contribute as much as $50,000 in one year, effectively using up five years' worth of exclusions at once; this gives the money longer to compound. Most plans allow total lifetime contributions per beneficiary of at least $100,000. If you have money in an educational IRA, you can use this money to invest in a Part 529 plan. However, you cannot contribute to both an educational IRA and a Part 529 plan in the same year.

Earnings grow in these accounts tax deferred until the money is withdrawn for tuition, fees, room, board, and other college-related expenses. When withdrawn, these earnings are taxed at the child's income tax rate. If the child suddenly opts out of school, the accounts can be transferred to a sibling or another college-bound relative.

Unlike the state prepaid tuition savings plans, with most of these Part 529 plans you don't have to live in the state that sponsors the plan to open and maintain an account. In addition, you don't have to use the money at a state school in the state that offers the plan. More than fifteen states offer such plans, most of which are open to out-of-state residents, and more states intend to offer such plans. Unlike many other tax breaks, these state tuition plans are available to everyone, regardless of income or AGI. Contributions aren't tax deductible at the federal level.

There is growing competition among the states for your dollars. Most states let couples deduct part or all of the amount of the contribution each year from their state taxes as incentive for state residents to invest in their plan. Some states match part of the contributions, given certain income limitations.

There is an estate-planning advantage to these plans. You keep control of the money even though it is not counted as being in your estate. This is unlike an UGMA, in which the money is out of your estate but you give up control of the money, or a mutual fund or brokerage account, which you still control and which remains in your estate.

The drawback to these plans is that you have no control over how the money is invested. And unlike state-sponsored prepaid tuition plans, they do not guarantee that your savings will cover future costs or grow at all. If the plan's investments do poorly, you have no recourse but to accept the losses; you cannot switch your funds from one state's plan to another. Therefore, it is important to research the different plans and to consider investing in more than one plan or keeping some of your college investment money under your own control.

Two good Web sites about these plans (as well as prepaid tuition plans) are www.savingforcollege.com and www.college savings.org; both Web sites provides information and links to each state's programs.

Almost all plans are managed in a life cycle mode, shifting assets from aggressive to conservative (and from stocks to bonds to cash) the closer the child gets to college age. However, not all life cycle plans contain the same percentage of stocks at the same time in a child's life,[4] nor do they all have the same number of gradations.[5] A few plans allow the beneficiary to keep the money wholly in stocks until college age. Several states offer more than one type of option, so that, for instance, investors can choose between individual funds and a life cycle approach. Initial setup fees and annual fees typically range from $0 to $50, and plan management fees range from 0.29 percent to 1.55 percent.

Because this industry is still in its infancy, the specifics of each state's plan and the number of states offering plans are changing. Therefore, it is vital that parents, guardians, and others who want to help out college-bound students do additional research.

---

4. For an infant, this percentage can range from as low as 55 percent in the New York plan to a high of 88 percent in the New Hampshire, Massachusetts, and Delaware plans.

5. As of June 2000, Iowa's plan, for instance, has four gradations, investing the same for all children ages 0 to 5 (the other three gradations are 6 to 10, 11 to 15, and 16 and above). Meanwhile, California's and New York's have nine gradations, thus allowing more precise life cycle mode investing.

Paying College Tuition:
Costing the Alternatives

Given all of these choices, what are the best ways to fund a child's college education?

Neither UGMAs nor educational IRAs would qualify, the former because there is no assurance that the money will be used for college and the latter because of the small amount of money that can fund it each year. Probably the best alternatives are the prepaid college plan, the Part 529 trusts, and investing funds by yourself. But which of these are best?

The best way to answer this question is to look at the costs of a prepaid college tuition plan available to you and compare them to alternatives. This means comparing the costs of the three common payment options, a lump sum payment, a sixty-month payment plan, and an extended payment plan to any alternatives.

Payments to the prepaid plans earn interest. You should calculate this interest to see what you would get if your child decided not to go to college or to go to a nonpublic or out-of-state college. A range from 4 to 5 percent would be a prudent way to calculate the returns from the prepaid plan. To make the math simple, you might want to assume that the effects of the state tax credits and federal tax deferral are roughly offset by the taxes that are ultimately owed at the federal level—a simplifying assumption at best.

The alternative to these plans is to invest in securities individually or as part of a tuition trust plan. This type of investment should get an annual average after-tax return of 6.5 to 8.5 percent; higher returns certainly are possible given good stock or mutual fund selection or if a particular tuition trust performs well. (After-tax returns are being used here, given the assumption to ignore federal taxes for prepaid plans.)

In all cases, these alternatives will produce more money. Most people can do much better investing on their own or in the tuition trust plan. The only exceptions might be if a prepaid plan is the only way the parent or guardian can save for college (i.e., lack of discipline) or, if the student is in eighth or ninth grade, a plan based on investing in securities might not be prudent.

Remember that you are saving for tuition as well as room, board, books, and supplies. Assume that you have $20,000 to invest for your child, and your child is 3, so you have a fifteen-year time horizon. At an annual growth rate of 7.5 percent, $20,000 over fifteen years becomes $59,200. The alternative is the prepaid plan, where you would be locking in only about half the costs and would be reimbursed for this at about 4.5 percent if your child does not attend a state school. At 4.5 percent per year, $20,000 over fifteen years grows to only $38,700, or about two-thirds as much.

Chapter 8

FAMILY

Life Insurance

As baby boomers age, life insurance plays an increasing role in ensuring the viability of their family and its plans. Life insurance should be considered an integral part of your financial plan, along with investments, retirement savings, and estate planning. Financial planning is more than asset allocation; asset protection is equally important.

Upon the premature death of one of the spouses, particularly the main breadwinner, life insurance can help the family maintain its current lifestyle and its longer-term plans. The heirs often are faced with large expenses, which can include income taxes, estate taxes, and debts. If the deceased's assets are tied up in nonliquid real estate or businesses, the surviving heirs may have to sell some of these assets, often at huge losses, to pay these unanticipated expenses. Life insurance can help pay these bills.

There are two basic types of life insurance: term and whole life. Term insurance is designed to provide protection for a specific period of time. Unless these policies are bought late in life, the premiums are lower than those for whole life, resulting in more protection for the same amount of cash. Term policies exist in lengths ranging from one year to thirty years. Because insurance risk rises as you age, premium rates rise with increasing term lengths; premiums become progressively more expensive after age 50.

There are three basic types of term policies:

■ Decreasing term policies, which have the lowest premiums, provide a death benefit that declines after a set period of time. This could be thought of as a good beginning policy.

■ Level term insurance has the same premiums and death benefits for the entire length of the policy.

■ Renewable term insurance pays the same death benefits while the premium systematically increases after specific periods of time. These policies can be renewed after each term period without additional evidence of medical insurability.

Whole life insurance combines a term policy with an investment component, which can be in stocks, bonds, or money market instruments. Over time, these policies accumulate an increasing cash value, which the policyholder can borrow against. Policies can be paid off in one payment, in a series of installment payments over a fixed period of time, or over an entire lifetime.

Whole life insurance is much more expensive than term for two basic reasons. Because permanent insurance insures you for the rest of your life, companies must charge more because there is no question that they will have to pay eventually. In addition, the premium encompasses both the insurance and the cash value. Most financial experts do not consider the latter portion to be a good investment. The high fees and commissions of these policies reduce the investment return. It is often difficult to calculate how much of the payment goes toward the investment. Therefore, permanent life policies can be difficult to compare.

Permanent life insurance policies are available in several varieties. The first three have a specified death benefit:

- Whole life has specified premiums.

- Adjustable life has adjustable premiums, which are recalculated every several years.

- Universal life allows flexibility in terms of pay schedules, subject to certain minimums and maximums.

- Variable life allows more flexibility because the policy's investments can help pay part of the premiums. Therefore, depending on the performance of the policy's choices, the death benefits and the cash values can fluctuate.

Should you buy term or permanent life? Term insurance coverage is designed to provide a large amount of coverage for a specific period of time at a low price and is also suitable for those who can't afford permanent life. Younger buyers, whose net worth is not high and who have cash flow problems, usually are better off with term. Companies on the Web such as www.quotesmith.com, www.selectquote.com, and www.reliaquote.com provide free insurance quotes. Permanent life is suited for people who want to build up a policy over a lifetime and accrue a cash value to help supplement future expenses. Although permanent life can help with estate tax problems, the added expense may not always be worth it.

Many financial experts believe that most people will do better buying term and investing the difference between term and permanent insurance premiums in investments such as stock mutual funds. Given anywhere near an annual increase of 11 percent, the value of these funds will exceed the cash value of the permanent life policy.

People often have trouble figuring out how much insurance they need. The first step is to calculate your family's short- and long-term financial obligations. Short-term obligations include food, clothing, rent or mortgage payments, utility bills, and doctor visits. Long-term obligations include projected or actual college expenses, the replacement of a car or major appliance, possible moving expenses, and possible job search. With only one spouse living, day care or nanny costs may suddenly become a reality. All of these expenses should be contrasted against existing assets; these include cash, all investments, the life insurance proceeds provided by your employer, and your spouse's income. Insurance proceeds should make up the difference between your assets and your expected expenses. Web sites that help with these calculations include www.smartmoney.com, www.life-line.org, and www.quicken. com.

There is no definitive rule about how much insurance protection you should purchase. One idea is to assume that you will put the insurance proceeds into a safe investment, such as a bond, paying around 6 percent, and draw on the interest for needed expenses. Thus, if you need $30,000 a year from insurance, you would purchase $500,000 worth of insurance ($500,000 $\times$ 6% = $30,000).

Before choosing an insurance company, you should also investigate each company you consider; this includes looking at its financial soundness, creditworthiness, reputation, and service. Personal references on the quality of each company's service can be useful, and there are rating services that can check the creditworthiness and claim-paying abilities of insurance companies. Several independent companies gauge the fiscal strength of insurance companies, including their claim-paying ability; the most financially sound insurers are rated AAA or the equivalent, and it is generally best to go with an insurer rated A or better. Web sites to consider include www. fitchibca.com, www.insure.com, www.moodys.com, www. ratings.standardpoor.com, and www.weissinc.com.

Medicare and Medicaid

As baby boomers' parents age, an increasing number of them will need help. Baby boomers may need to help their parents financially, may need to assist them with health-related issues, or may need to work with them on estate planning and wealth transfer issues. The purpose of much of this book is to help boomers increase their own wealth, so the topic of helping parents financially is not discussed in this chapter. However, health-related problems and wealth transfer strategies are discussed; the former is covered in this and the next two sections, and the latter is reviewed in the following two sections.

As people move into retirement, health-related costs become a large part of their annual budget.[1] A lingering disease,

1. An American Association of Retired Persons (AARP) study projected that Medicare beneficiaries age 65 and older would spend an average of $2,430, or 19 percent of income, on out-of-pocket costs for health care in 1999; this figure does not include the costs of home care and long-term nursing home services. The same study projected that about 25 percent of these beneficiaries will have out-of-pocket health costs exceeding $3,000 in 1999. Source: David Gross and Normandy Brangan, "In Brief: Out-of-Pocket Health Spending by Medicare Beneficiaries Age 65 and Older: 1999 Projections," AARP, December 1999, www.aarp.org.

chronic health problems, broken bones, and the need for long-term health care can rapidly eat into all but the biggest nest eggs. Proper medical planning and proper knowledge can help to alleviate some of the costs, reduce anxiety, and extend the length of time that the nest egg can support retirement.

The federal government provides medical care for older adults in a program called Medicare. For people without financial resources, both young and old, Medicaid can help pay for certain services. This section focuses on defining these programs and describing what they do and do not cover.

Medicare is a health insurance program set up by the federal government for people age 65 and older and for younger adults with certain disabilities. There are no means-related tests to qualify for this program. People qualify if they are at least 65 and eligible for either Social Security or Railroad Retirement benefits, are at least 65 and are married to someone who qualifies for these benefits, have been receiving Social Security disability benefits for at least two years, or have end-stage kidney failure. U.S. citizens at least 65 who don't fit these qualifications are eligible for Medicare but usually must pay Part A premiums; permanent legal residents who have lived in the United States for at least five years are also eligible for Medicare under these conditions.

Like most insurance plans, Medicare is divided into two parts. Part A covers basic hospital services and can be used for inpatient hospital care, skilled nursing facility care, home health care, and hospice care, and Part B is the equivalent to the major medical portion of private health insurance plans. Part A is free for most participants, whereas Part B, in most cases, charges a premium. Depending on the facilities and procedures used, there are specific deductibles and copayments for Part A services.

The length of time and type of services that Medicare will

cover vary. For instance, in 1999 Medicare paid defined costs for the first 150 days for inpatient hospital care. The program will pay all but a $768 deductible for the first 60 days, all but $192 a day for the next 30 days, and all but $384 a day for the next 60 days; after 150 days, the patient must cover all costs. (This amount of time can start again if the patient is out of the hospital for at least 60 days.) However, Medicare pays for at most 100 consecutive days of nursing facility care. In addition, Medicare pays for some services but not for others; for example, in a hospital, inpatient physical therapy is covered, but private nursing is not. People who qualify for Medicare should do research to determine what is covered and for how long.

Supplemental Medicare insurance, which fills in the gaps in certain Medicare coverage, is known as Medigap insurance. Boomers and their parents should seriously consider taking out this additional insurance because it covers some costs not paid by Medicare. One example is the aforementioned $192 per day hospital charges not covered in days sixty-one through ninety of hospital stays. Ten different plans exist and are known as Plans A through J; each plan covers different benefits, and their prices vary. Private insurance companies sell these policies; despite any differences in premiums that these companies charge, all plans with the same letter cover the same exact benefits.

Medicaid was set up to help poor people pay for basic health services. Each state sets its own standards for income eligibility within federal guidelines. For instance, people receiving Supplemental Social Security Income benefits automatically qualify for this program in some states but not in others. Much of the money spent on Medicaid is to help older adults in long-term care facilities such as nursing homes. However, to qualify for it, recipients generally must deplete their own resources.

In certain cases, Medicaid pays for some services not covered by Medicare. Thus, this program is a valuable resource to help the poor and those who do not qualify for Medicare. Medicaid pays some of the premiums, deductibles, and co-payments in the Medicare program for people at or below the poverty level.

Long-Term Care

A common fear among boomers and their parents is that at some point in the near future, their parents will need long-term care. People have a 40 percent chance of needing nursing home care after reaching 65 and a 10 percent chance of being there for at least five years.[2] The average nursing home stay lasts about 2½ years.[3] The type of care needed and the cost varies. Long-term care options are covered in this section, and the financing for these options is covered in the next. Web sites to look at include www.aarp.org, www.angelfire.com, www.alfa.org, www.benefitslink.com, www.ccal.org, www.elderweb.com, www.hcfa.gov/medicaid/ltc1.htm, www.ncal.org, and www.nursinghomereports.com.

Long-term care means helping people who have disabilities, chronic illnesses, or cognitive impairments (such as Alzheimer's disease) such that they need help with day-to-day or week-to-week activities or chores. The help needed in these circumstances can range from someone coming in a few days a week to go shopping or read to them to helping the person

---

2. "Long Term Care Insurance," AARP, www.aarp.org.
3. Howard Gleckman, "Someone to Watch Over You," *Business Week,* July 19, 1999, p. 130.

to bathe and dress. Conditions that can be treated in a short hospital stay or on an outpatient basis do not involve long-term care.

A growing facet of long-term care involves assisted-living and nursing homes. With assisted living, specific services, such as meals and health monitoring, are provided, and at a nursing home the person is cared for much more intensively. Therefore, assisted-living residences can be thought of as somewhere between living at home and living in a nursing home.

The term *assisted living* often is used to describe different tiers of living arrangements, and there are different types of assisted living. Independent living is made up of a community of residents in their own apartments with few or no personal services. Congregate care offers rental apartments, a communal dining room, and limited personal services. Freestanding assisted living facilities also include rental apartments and a dining room serving all meals but also have on-site nurses and provide assistance with specific personal needs; they qualify as intermediate nursing facilities (INFs) if they provide at least eight hours of nursing supervision a day. A continuing care community allows residents to stay in the same locale even as their conditions change because it includes independent living, skilled nursing, and a nursing home at the same site. Meanwhile, at nursing homes, also called skilled nursing facilities (SNFs), all services are provided for residents on a twenty-four-hour basis; at a minimum, SNFs provide medical, nursing, dietary, and pharmacy services and planned activities.

Before choosing any of these facilities, examine the terms and conditions of the contract. It should contain descriptions of the residents' rights and the staff's responsibilities; you should know exactly what is and is not included as part of the package. A partial checklist should include the facility's location, size, visiting hours, financing options, room selection, grievance procedures, and morale among the current residents. Each facility will have pluses and minuses, and some may have conditions that you are not happy with. For instance, are there clauses limiting the home's liability if a resident is injured or personal property is stolen? How secure would you feel if residents had to give all their income directly to the home? Is the staff-to-resident ratio too low? It might be worthwhile for the prospective resident to spend a night at the facility to see how comfortable he or she feels.

In addition, you should find out what happens to the resident's slot in the facility if he or she needs temporary hospitalization. What are the guidelines for moving a resident to a different part of the facility? How are prescription drugs provided and monitored? If there is a chance that Medicaid will be providing any of the money to pay, check with an elder law attorney to ensure that that facility is covered.

By law, a facility can discharge a patient only for specific reasons, such as when discharge is necessary for the resident's welfare, when the resident no longer needs the services provided by the home, and when the health and safety of other people are endangered, or if the facility ceases to operate or the resident fails to pay. Because these reasons can be applied subjectively, you should find out what kind of notice would be given and whether there is an appeal process. Checking into recent incidents can be very helpful.

Finally, in choosing an assisted living or nursing home, you should always check references and investigate the owner's financial viability. The facility should have adequate capital and not be highly leveraged, preferably being debt free. If it is a new facility, you should find out how quickly they expect to fill it and what contingency plans they have, in terms of fees and expenses, if these plans do not come to fruition. If it is an existing facility, investigate staff turnover and training. Keep in mind that this is a major decision, something that can affect the quality of life of your loved ones.

Paying for Long-Term Care

Long-term care is costly. Older Americans are projected to spend $52 billion of their own retirement savings for nursing home care a decade from now.[4] Some patients have spent more than $500,000 on long-term care expenses.[5] Depending on the services needed, costs range from $10,000 to $20,000 a year for home care, $12,000 to $42,000 for assisted-living facilities,[6] and $36,000 to $50,000 for nursing homes.[7]

Medicare does not cover long-term care. It pays for part of the first 100 days of SNF care but does not cover INF care. In addition, in a limited number of situations and over a short period of time, it can pay for a nursing home or for home health care for people who need the specific type of care known as skilled care after a hospitalization. Although this coverage can certainly help pay some bills, and Medigap may pay for some specific at-home care benefits in the short term, neither of these should be counted on to pay for long-term care expenses.

Medicaid can help to pay for nursing home care and, in certain situations, long-term care services at home. Currently, Medicaid pays for 52 percent of all nursing home care nationwide,[8] and about 70 percent of all people in nursing homes

4. Source: American Council of Life Insurance, as referenced in "The Cost of Long-Term Care," www.smartmoney.com.

5. Gary Hickerson, MSSW, "Financing of Long Term Care," www.angelfire.com.

6. "The Cost of Long-Term Care," www.smartmoney.com.

7. Hickerson, "Financing of Long Term Care."

8. Source: "Who Pays," www.nursinghomereports.com.

get some or all of their money from Medicaid.[9] However, Medicaid is only for the poor, so to qualify for Medicaid, potential recipients must pay for these services until their resources are nearly exhausted. The threshold limit for the assets you are allowed to keep varies by state, but in all cases it is around $2,000;[10] in addition, there are specific asset and monthly income limits for your spouse.[11]

There are several ways to circumvent this threshold. One involves giving away your money, often to children, with the idea that this money will still be available to you through gifts; this strategy also ensures that your heirs, not the nursing home or other creditors, get your money. The money must be given away at least thirty-six months before you apply for Medicaid for this strategy to work; money given away less than three years before still counts as your money and can prevent you from qualifying. Drawbacks to this strategy include a sudden estrangement between the parent and children, which can leave the parent destitute, or a divorce between one of your children and his or her spouse, which can eliminate access to some of the money.

You can retain access to money by using an irrevocable trust. Because this trust transfers control of the money, the money can no longer be considered yours in terms of Medicaid computations. The trustee cannot be a spouse, so before implementing such a trust, you should be very sure that the

---

9. Source: "Medicaid: Paying for Nursing Home Care," AARP, www. aarp.org.

10. Some assets are not counted, such as your home and burial fund. Source: "Medicaid: Paying for Nursing Home Care."

11. Depending on the state, your spouse can keep approximately $1,400 to $2,000 a month in income and approximately $16,400 to $82,0000 in assets, in addition to your home. Source: "Medicaid: Paying for Nursing Home Care."

appointed trustee is reliable. You can also retain access to the money by placing it in a variable annuity; the money in the annuity and the dividend checks are not counted in terms of Medicaid computations. Boomers and their parents should seek the services of an elder law expert to ensure that these strategies still allow access to Medicaid.

Until you have spent down your assets or transferred control of your money as discussed in the previous paragraph, you must pay for most of your long-term health care costs, generally out of your own assets. But unless you have amassed a lot of money, your personal wealth may run out, hence the need for long-term care insurance. This type of insurance was introduced in the 1980s as nursing home insurance but was soon expanded to cover more areas. Depending on the type of insurance purchased, it can pay for some or almost all long-term care needs; however, only 2 percent of nursing home costs are currently paid for by this type of insurance.[12] This type of insurance is deductible from federal income taxes and, in certain states, from state income taxes.

The time to buy such insurance is when you are still relatively young and in good health. Most financial planners recommend buying this insurance in your late 50s or early 60s.[13] Insurance companies will not sell such insurance if you've already developed conditions such as Alzheimer's disease. The longer you wait to buy such insurance, the higher the premiums; in any event, it is expensive and it must be purchased

12. This low percentage is not indicative of the number of residents that have private insurance "but rather reflects how infrequently the typical health insurance policy actually pays any costs involving skilled nursing services or long-term care. (These policies) are expensive and often riddled with exclusions that keep people from collecting." Source: "Who Pays," www.nursinghomereports.com.

13. Hickerson, "Financing of Long Term Care."

before age 80. Many policies cover preexisting conditions but don't pay benefits for any particular preexisting condition for a number of months, until after the policy has been triggered.

Because Medicaid is available as a safety net, these policies are not for everybody. People who have limited assets, cannot afford the premiums, are dependent on Social Security for their living expenses, or cannot pay for basic necessities probably should not buy such insurance. On the other hand, people who have significant assets and want to protect a portion of them and do not want to become dependent on help from others should consider purchasing such insurance. Depending on the policy's conditions, such as benefit period, monthly benefits, and level and type of home care, these annual premiums can be as little as $175 when the policy is purchased at age 45 to as much as $8,000 when purchased at age 70. Policies with inflation protection may cost 25 to 40 percent more than those without such protection.[14]

Different policies are triggered under different conditions. These triggers include the inability to do a certain number of daily activities, a doctor's certification of medical necessity, and prior hospitalization. In addition, insurance companies often use different triggers for home health care and nursing home care. Most policies have an elimination or waiting period before which the policy's benefits are paid; during this time period, the policy does not pay for long-term care.

The time spent reading the fine print on these policies carefully, then weighing the benefits and costs, is time well spent. Finding out exactly what is covered; whether the benefits are indexed to inflation; what the maximum daily, monthly, and lifetime limits are; and under what conditions

---

14. Source: UNUM Corp., as quoted in Howard Gleckman's "Table: The Cost of Long-Term Care Insurance," as used in "Someone to Watch Over You," *Business Week*, July 19, 1999, p. 130.

the policy can be activated are key determinants in deciding which policy to purchase. The insurance-related Web sites listed in the first section of this chapter can be used to check on the long-term viability and stability of these insurance companies.

As boomers do this planning with their parents, they should discuss wills (covered in the next section), durable powers of attorney, and health care proxies. A durable power of attorney, unlike a regular power of attorney, has staying power in the event of a disability. You don't need a lawyer to complete these forms, and you can buy them at stationery stores for a few dollars. Otherwise, in the event of an emergency, a child (or another designated person) must hire a lawyer and file to become his or her parent's guardian, an expensive and time-consuming process. A health care proxy instructs the hospital or other caregiver, in the event of terminal illness or injury, not to put the person on life support if there is not a reasonable chance of recovery.

Basics of Wealth Transfer

Over the next forty years, $8 trillion will be passed on to the next generation.[15] With proper planning, much of this wealth can be passed on tax free. With poor planning, the estate tax burden on the baby boom generation will be huge.

Below a certain threshold, no federal estate taxes are owed on inheritances. This threshold, known as the unified credit, is $675,000 per benefactor in 2000 and 2001 (in effect, $1.35 million per couple) and is scheduled to rise, in small

---

15. Source: Federal Reserve Board, "1989 Survey of Consumer Finances," as referenced in Peter Lynch, "Fidelity's Guide to Investing Responsibly," www.fidelity.com.

increments, until it reaches $1 million in 2006. Net worth, in the case of an estate, includes real estate, proceeds from a life insurance policy, securities (stocks, bonds, mutual funds), and retirement plans such as a 401(k).

Stocks have greatly appreciated in value during the long bull market that started in 1982. Houses that were bought in the 1950s and 1960s, before inflation and before the runup in real estate prices in the 1970s and 1980s, are now worth a lot of money. Thus, many people's (or couples') net worth is above this threshold and they are not aware of it. Above this threshold, estate taxes start at 37 percent and rise to 55 percent. These taxes apply regardless of whether the assets are transferred by a will or a living trust.

If your net worth is modest, a will may be the best way to distribute assets. A will is a legal document that gives instructions about how you want your property distributed after your death. A will must have a few specific things. It must name an executor and, if you have minor children, it must name a guardian. Spelling out, as specifically as possible, how the property is to be distributed can help to prevent the possibility of legal challenges. If you don't have a will, the laws of the state in which you live will determine how your assets are distributed. Currently, about three-quarters of Americans do not have a will.[16]

If your assets are large enough, it may not be a good idea to distribute all your assets through a will. A major disadvantage to using wills is probate. Probate is the legal process that transfers property from a deceased person's estate to his or her beneficiaries. This procedure involves a lawyer and an accountant appearing before a judge, and after certain questions are

---

16. Jeff Wuorio, "The Sandwich Generation: Taking Care of Aging Parents," www.quicken.com.

answered (such as whether the will is valid, whether the deceased had any debts, and whether anyone is contesting the will), the process continues and, eventually, the assets are distributed. Probate takes a number of months and can be costly. Wills are public documents, accessible to anyone and thus open to challenges. If you have property in more than one state, multiple probate proceedings may be needed.

Some people use living trusts as a way to get around probate; using a living trust and avoiding probate can save 3 to 10 percent of the estate's value from lawyer fees and appraisals.[17] This involves setting up a trust (with the help of a lawyer) and then retitling all the assets to the trust. All assets in the trust pass to the beneficiaries without going through probate and without public scrutiny. Working with a lawyer to set up a living trust is usually less costly than writing a will.[18] Unfortunately, many people set up the trust but then do not retitle the assets to the trust's name, which accomplishes nothing.

Although there are numerous strategies for reducing the size of the estate tax bite, some people try to do this by retitling assets in both the parents' and the children's names, which actually makes things worse. The idea behind this thinking is that retitling assets will allow the assets to pass directly to the children, reduce inheritance taxes, and circumvent probate. This can be a very costly mistake.

When assets are transferred using a will or a living trust, the beneficiary gets a stepped-up basis for each asset. For example, if XYZ stock was originally purchased at $10 a share and it is now worth $100 a share, it has an unrealized capital gain of $90 a share; if that stock were sold now, capital gains

---

17. Mike Janko of the National Association of Financial and Estate Planning, as referenced in Robert J. Samuelson, "Darling, It'll All Be Yours—Soon," *Newsweek*, April 3, 2000, www.newsweek.com.

18. "Wills and Living Trusts," AARP, www.aarp.org.

taxes of $90 a share would be owed. If the price is $100 a share when the original owner dies, the new basis, for the beneficiary, becomes $100 a share, wiping out this $90-a-share capital gain. However, if the ownership of this stock is retitled to include both the parents and the children, the basis would remain $10 a share. If the children sell at $120 a share, they will owe capital gains tax of $110 a share rather than $20 a share if that stock had not been retitled. Thus, retitling assets greatly hurts, rather than helps, beneficiaries.

Another excellent reason to avoid retitling assets is that they are now subject to legal proceedings against either owner. So if there is a monetary judgment against the child, the parent's money could be used to pay off such a judgment, potentially rendering the parent penniless.

Wealth Transfer Strategies

One of the simplest ways to transfer assets is to give them away. Each person can give up to $10,000 a year to another person. If you are planning to leave the money to certain beneficiaries anyway, this strategy allows you to give the money away earlier and thus reduce the amount of the estate that would be subject to estate taxes. If you give more than $10,000 in any one year to a particular person, you must fill out specific Internal Revenue Service (IRS) forms, and the amount over $10,000 is subtracted from the estate tax threshold; in other words, estate taxes would kick in at a lower threshold level. One way around this limit is for a husband and wife to give up to $10,000 each, for an effective gift of up to $20,000, but they need to document how much came from each spouse.

Another solution is to donate securities such as stock to

any nonprofit organization that is designated as a 501(a) organization or has a 501(c)(3) tax exemption granted by the IRS. Major benefits accrue to both the donor and this nonprofit organization, as shown in the following example.

Suppose you have a choice of donating to an organization 100 shares of stock that were originally bought at $10 per share and are now worth $30 per share or selling the shares and donating the money. In the former situation, you would be able to donate and write off your taxes, as a charitable donation, the full $3,000 that the shares are now worth. In the latter situation, you would owe tax on the $2,000 of capital gains appreciation. If you are in the 28 percent tax bracket and these were short-term capital gains, you would owe $560 worth of tax; you would be left with only $2,440 to donate. Thus, not only would you have to pay taxes and be able to donate less money, but you would be able to write off less as a charitable donation. Again, if you are in the 28 percent bracket, a $3,000 donation could reduce your taxes by $840, whereas a $2,440 donation could reduce your taxes by about $685.

The nonprofit organization benefits as well. It does not have to pay tax on any increase in the value of the stock, whether through appreciation or through dividends. So if the stock increases in value over time or pays dividends, your gift actually is worth more to the organization.

A number of nonprofit organizations have another mutually beneficial program to help you decide to donate. They will set up an annuity for you in exchange for cash or a security. Such annuities are designed to pay you a fixed monthly income for the rest of your life. So if you were to donate $10,000 worth of stock, the nonprofit organization might pay you $700 a month for life. This monthly payment would be based on the amount donated and the appropriate actuarial table, showing your life expectancy. Such a program is a fine way to support a favorite charity, obtain a constant income stream, and reduce the size of your estate and estate taxes.

A third way to reduce estate taxes is through the use of a bypass trust; this strategy works only for married couples. Most couples' wills are what are known as sweetheart wills; they leave everything to each other. However, such wills can cost them a lot of money. Many people use such wills because they have heard that you are never taxed on the money you leave to your spouse. And this is true. But by doing so you are giving up one of your threshold exemptions. An example will help explain.

Let's suppose that you and your spouse have a net worth of $1.15 million (which is under the $1.35 million cap in 2000), and you do no estate planning. If you died tomorrow and if you and your spouse had sweetheart wills, you would leave your share to your spouse, who pays no taxes. But when your spouse dies, he or she will have only one exemption available. For instance, if this happened in 2000 or 2001, $475,000 of the original $1.1 million estate would be taxable to your heirs, leaving them with taxes of approximately $185,000. (It actually could be higher if the $1.1 million appreciated at all.) So by leaving all your money to your spouse, you've given up your own exemption, currently at $675,000.

Under a bypass trust, however, instead of leaving everything you own as a couple to your spouse, you specify assets worth $675,000 to be put into this trust. The rest ($475,000) can be left tax free to your spouse. He or she can tap into the trust for reasonable living expenses, and when your spouse dies, the money from the trust goes tax free to whoever is specified as your ultimate beneficiaries. The surviving spouse's estate will not be liable for any estate taxes because it's below the exemption level. Therefore, if you use this strategy (at a cost of about $2,000 in legal fees), your heirs will save approximately $185,000 in taxes. Because the threshold will increase through 2006, it is important to modify the trust document periodically to ensure that the maximum amount is sheltered.

Another type of trust that can help reduce estate taxes is an insurance trust; this type of trust can reduce the size of your estate. As mentioned in the previous section, if you own your insurance policy, the proceeds from this policy are included in computing your net worth as it relates to the unified credit. A $500,000 policy would almost certainly move you above that credit threshold. If you set up an irrevocable trust and transferred ownership of that policy to the trust, your heirs would still get the money but would not owe inheritance tax on those proceeds.

In all cases, you should consult with a qualified elder law attorney to ensure that any such strategies are both appropriate and applicable to you and to ensure that these strategies are executed properly.

Additional Family Matters

So far this chapter has covered situations that most people will face during their lives. Additional family-related matters can come up that are unique to limited segments of the population. This section covers a few of these; it is not intended to be exhaustive.

Many boomers are in second or third marriages, so ensuring that the children from previous marriages get their fair inheritances can be an important consideration.[19] Trusts can be

---

19. Currently, the divorce rate is more than 50 percent, and the average length of a marriage is a little more than seven years. A good quick guide to the dos and don'ts of dividing up assets can be found in the June 2000 issue of *Smart Money*.

valuable in such situations. One of these is called the Qualified Terminable Interest Property (QTIP) trust; it is a variation on the bypass trust discussed in the previous section. Under a QTIP trust, your children are named as the final beneficiaries, but they won't get the money or have to pay taxes on it until your spouse dies. The money goes into your spouse's estate, and the spouse gets the income generated by the trust. After he or she dies, the children get the assets.

One of the major controversies in a divorce has to do with dividing up retirement benefits. The most effective strategy is to settle on this division as part of the divorce settlement. However, not using the correct forms during and immediately after the divorce settlement can result in taxes and penalties. By using a qualified domestic relations order (QDRO), you can transfer money from a 401(k), individual retirement account (IRA), or other qualified retirement account to your soon-to-be-ex-spouse's IRA without penalty. By using this form, you can transfer money without it being treated as a taxable distribution.

Many parents or guardians want to give away money to reduce their estate taxes and to help out minors or young adults. The major catch to gifts such as the $10,000-a-year gift and the UGMA is that it belongs to the recipient, either as soon as he or she receives it or when he or she reaches the age of majority. That creates a problem for a donor who wants to transfer money out of his or her estate to a minor or young adult; the benefactor may want the recipient to go to college, but he or she would rather purchase a beach house. In addition, if the minor or young adult is notorious for being irresponsible, he or she may spend the money very quickly, using it in a careless manner. However, the parent or guardian may still want or need to give money to him or her for a specific purpose.

One solution is to set up a Crummey trust. You put the gift, such as the once-a-year $10,000 gift, into a trust written to give the recipient temporary access to it, but only for a limited time period. The recipient probably will not take the money, knowing that such an action could limit future gifts from you. After this specified time period, the recipient can withdraw the money based on the provisions of the trust. These provisions can ensure, for example, that the money be spent only for college, for medical expenses, or to set up a business. A provision of such trusts is that if there is any money remaining when the recipient reaches a specific age, such as 35 or 40, he or she gets the balance of the trust.

Parents of children with mental or physical disabilities face additional challenges because such disabilities can spell increasing medical bills. There are certain things that parents should do in such situations. Social Security covers people with certain disabilities under Supplemental Security Income (SSI) benefits. About 100,000 claims for SSI benefits are adjudicated each year for child disability claims.[20] A person is eligible for SSI benefits if his or her income and financial resources are below a certain level and if he or she is disabled. A child is considered to be disabled "if he suffers from any . . . impairment of comparable severity" to one that would render an adult "unable to engage in any substantial gainful activity."[21] If your child has such a disability, you should file as soon as possible after your child has become disabled; the benefits begin after a five-month waiting period. Your child will continue to receive a disability benefit as long as the condition

20. Social Security Administration, Office of Disability, "Preliminary Staff Report: Childhood Disability Study," September 20, 1989, p. B-1.

21. There are specific definitions of disability that would enable a child to qualify for these payments; these definitions are spelled out in 42 U.S.C. § 1382c(a)(3).

remains; however, his or her condition will be reviewed periodically.

Given certain physical or mental disabilities, such a child might need lifelong care. There are specific minor trusts that parents can set up to ensure that the child will have sufficient funds to obtain proper care even after the parents are gone. These trusts can be set up so that a competent and trustworthy person is legally assigned to care for the child and manage his or her portfolio in a reliable manner. This usually means structuring the trust such that it holds conservative investments, such as dividend-paying stocks and bonds; this money must last for the rest of the child's life, and an aggressive investment strategy could result in serious losses. Because a primary goal of such trusts is to provide current income for the child, the composition and weighting of the stocks and bonds should be selected carefully to provide an adequate income stream. The bond strategies discussed in Chapter 13, bond ladders, Treasury Inflation Protected Securities (TIPS), and convertible bonds, as well as the way to obtain an increasing stream of stock dividends, as explained in Chapter 16, all have a place in this portfolio.

A growing trend has been increasing numbers of same-sex partnerships. Although some companies extend medical and other benefits to a same-sex partner as if the employee were in a traditional marriage, this is by no means universal. Few states or municipalities recognize same-sex marriages or give them the same legal protections as traditional marriages. Therefore, it is incumbent on the partners to seek competent legal advice in setting up wills, trusts, and other estate-planning documents. A well-drafted legal document can stand up to any court challenges from family members or former partners.

However, such legal documents cannot be the sum of all financial planning. Given the lack of legal protection for same-sex partners and the extreme difficulties in getting spousal survival benefits, it is even more important for these partners to have a sound financial plan constructed for them and to follow through with such a plan. Such a plan should certainly encompass the basic steps discussed in Chapter 1, but given the lack of spousal survival benefits for same-sex partners, there should be more emphasis on accumulating retirement assets. Because there will be no spousal Social Security benefits and because there almost certainly will not be company pension benefits, both partners should maximize all of the options discussed in Chapter 3. This means, at a minimum, contributing the maximum each year to 401(k)s and IRAs. It also means making it a priority to fund self-employment retirement accounts, such as Simplified Employee Pension IRAs, if applicable, and making it more of a priority to set up and fund variable annuities. Although nonretirement assets can be left to a same-sex partner, having this partner be the beneficiary of these retirement accounts may better ensure that he or she will receive this money.

Chapter 9

BEGINNING INVESTING

Invest in Yourself—Now

One of the big keys to financial success is investing in yourself, realizing that you are important enough to invest money in. This means making a conscious decision to allocate money from each paycheck to start and maintain an investment program dedicated to you and to pay money into this program before you pay for anything else.

A common complaint among baby boomers goes something like this: "After paying the mortgage, bills, transportation costs, food expenses, and other bills, I just don't have any money left over to invest. I'd love to invest—maybe after the kids are done with college, or after I finish paying off this car, or after my daughter's wedding." Expenses always come up; if you wait until they all go away, you'll wait a long time and will not invest anything.

Before getting a raise, most people have great ideas

about what they will do with the extra money. Once the raise kicks in, however, people often fritter this extra amount away. Instead, consider earmarking the extra money for investment.

Consider this: If your pay were reduced by 5 or 10 percent, you'd find ways to get by. So invest that 5 or 10 percent in an investment program and pretend that your salary was reduced. People find that they can adapt to most new budgets pretty soon; a lower spending level translates to higher levels of savings and investment and less money frittered away. The earlier you can start saving and investing and the more seriously and rigorously you take your saving and investing program, the faster your wealth will grow.

There are many easy ways to invest. If your company has a 401(k) or 403(b) retirement program, the money comes directly out of your paycheck. If you, like a growing number of baby boomers, have developed a side business, you should set up and contribute to a Simplified Employee Pension Individual Retirement Account (SEP-IRA) or Keogh from your net profit. If you are investing in a mutual fund or a stock that has an automatic investment program, the money can be taken directly from your checking account or, in some cases, your paycheck. Or you can set up a program to send a check to your mutual funds every month. All these plans are easy to set up and take little effort on your part.

It is important to start investing in yourself now, and not put it off. One of the most important ways to accumulate money is to use time wisely; procrastination is your enemy. As was shown in Chapter 3, delaying even a couple of years can result in a lot less money. The important thing is to start and start now.

Common Investing Misconceptions

Two common reasons why people do not invest are that they can't seem to save enough money to start investing and they believe that they need a lot of money to start investing.

It is amazing how much money people fritter away without thinking about it. A newspaper here, a candy bar there, a soft drink with some friends, and you spend several dollars a day without thinking. One sign of the growing influence of baby boomers in the economy is the proliferation of gourmet coffee bars; how much do you spend on such treats each day? Several dollars a day does not sound like much, but over a year it adds up.

As shown in Chapter 4, you can save at least $1,000 a year simply by making your own lunch every day. Think of this money as seed money for your investment program. If you have twenty years to go before retirement, bring your lunch to work and invest this $1,000 in the stock market each year. Given the annual average return of 11 percent, you will have added more than $70,000 to your net worth by the time you retire.

Another idea for "finding" money to invest involves paying for everything you buy during the day with dollar bills, not with any change in your pocket or purse. At the end of the day, put this change in a jar at home. At the end of every month, put the accumulated change in the bank as seed money for your investment program or use it to write a check to your mutual fund. Depending on your spending habits, you could save $25 to $50 a month.

It does not take much money to start investing. Some mutual funds have minimums of $1,000, and others reduce this minimum to $500, $250, or even $0 if you sign up for an automatic monthly investment plan; these minimums often are lower for IRAs. Under such a plan, you agree to allow the mutual fund to take a fixed amount, usually at least $50, from your checking account or paycheck on a designated day each month. Most people who participate in such plans do not miss the money. By doing this, you are putting yourself first and making sure that you, your future, and your retirement are paid first.

Mutual funds are discussed further in Chapter 14. There are many good reasons for investors, particularly beginning investors, to invest in mutual funds rather than individual stocks or bonds. These advantages include professional managers (who can keep abreast of the market on a constant basis), instant diversification (which helps reduce risk), and the ability to make initial or subsequent investments with relatively small sums of money. The average investor normally does not have the time or expertise to investigate the market and stay informed about market trends and changes. There are currently more than 10,000 mutual funds; they can be the ideal way to start an investment program.

Declare Your Financial Independence

There are many ways to get money. They include inheritances, gifts, lotteries, and investments. Gifts and lotteries are the most serendipitous; rarely can they be planned for. An inheritance has a little more certainty to it; given a well-to-do parent or grandparent, one can expect to get some portion of this wealth. Indeed, as noted in Chapter 8, the baby boom generation stands to inherit trillions of dollars, and some may be basing their retirement planning on a large inheritance. There can be two major problems with this expectation. One is that wills and trusts can be modified at any time, shutting out the would-be beneficiaries. Given the possibility of significant wealth distribution, legal problems can hold up this distribution for months or years. Planning your future based on inheritances can be very disappointing.

So it's mostly up to you. Unfortunately, the strategies you need to become financially independent and secure a comfortable retirement are not stressed in this society. While people dream of winning the lottery or inheriting large sums of money, popular culture often equates wealth and financial independence with ruthless, self-centered people. The message that many movies, television shows, and books send is that you need to run over your friends and family to get wealthy. How to become financially independent without doing so is not well publicized.

Fortunately, such information is readily available. For those who are clueless about finances and investing, the initial guiding principle should be to collect enough information so that it all begins to make sense. It doesn't take a lot of energy or effort to start asking questions at your bank or credit union, read books and articles, attend seminars, listen to radio programs, or send away for general reading materials from some of the well-known mutual fund companies. The business pages of many newspapers are filled with notices for classes and seminars, many of which are free. Libraries are packed with books and magazines on finance and investing for all levels of interest and sophistication; many of these books and magazines, as well as many of these classes and seminars, are geared toward the interests and needs of baby boomers. The Internet is crawling with Web sites devoted to financial advice and information. Many radio and television stations specialize in providing business and financial news and information for people of all levels of interest and sophistication. Mutual fund companies have free information on how mutual funds work, and brokerage houses have good material on stocks and bonds. You can get all this material without needing to expend a lot of effort.

Once you begin to get the information, set aside time to absorb it. This will probably be a struggle at first, as almost any new thing is. Weigh the initial discomforts of absorbing this material against the knowledge that you are taking control of a major aspect of your life, one that can pay major dividends and help to secure the rest of your family's life financially. Keep in mind that if you were to plan a vacation or a party or to build an addition on your home, you would take enough planning time to leave little to chance. Why should you do any less with your financial future?

The important thing for any investor to do is to break the sound barrier. Breaking the sound barrier for the beginning investor means beginning to understand terms such as *bull market, bear market, price-to-earnings ratio,* and *cash flow* and beginning to understand how to make money in stocks and bonds. Continuing to break through the sound barrier for the more sophisticated investor can mean learning the difference between short-term and long-term trends and learning which financial commentators and advisors are credible.

There are many fine strategies for building wealth; some are discussed in the last chapter of this book. Whichever strategy you choose, it is important to trust it, give it time, and stick with it. Although it is important to review and possibly fine-tune your strategy over time, it is equally important not to make large modifications too often. Stick with your strategy and don't let your emotions cloud your investment logic.

Risks of Not Investing

Given the historical volatility in the stock market, typical responses to investing in stocks include comments such as "I'm scared," "I could lose my money," "I can't stand volatility," and "I want to be safe and secure, so I'll put my money into a savings account or certificate of deposit." A number of baby boomers remember lessons from their parents or grandparents, some of whom lost money or were financially ruined in the Great Depression. Yet are these prudent responses?

Certainly, if you want to avoid change or focus on stability, these are prudent responses. However, if you want to increase your net wealth and are acting from ignorance or misinformation, then these responses probably are not in your best interest.

Why? What is wrong with putting your money into a savings account or a CD? For your safe money, nothing is wrong with this approach. Safe money is money that you might need quickly for emergencies. Prudence dictates that you keep three to six months' worth of living expenses as safe money; boomers with many obligations might find it prudent to have even more safe money. But in the long term, you are risking your future by avoiding risk.

What many people fail to realize is that there are two types of risks here. One is the risk of losing money in a down market. The other is the risk of losing money by not investing; this is known as opportunity cost, the cost of not doing something else. By not availing yourself of these different investment options, you are losing an opportunity to increase your wealth.

You will never get rich investing in CDs and savings accounts. The average return for a CD is fixed for the term of the deposit, but the yield you can get on another day is different. These yields move up and down in relation to the bond market; the interest rates on bonds depend on the inflation rate. The double-digit rates on CDs that were common in the early 1980s were that high only because inflation was high. Inflation has since waned, so interest rates and yields on bonds and CDs have fallen. The historical difference between the yield on the long (thirty-year) bond and inflation averages about 2 percent.[1] Thus, when inflation is running at 3 to 4 percent, long-term bond yields are at about 5 to 6 percent. The yield on CDs generally is a little lower than it is on bonds; the issuer of the CD needs to make a profit, too. Because interest paid on savings accounts is lower than what is paid on CDs, the real, after-tax and after-inflation return can actually be negative.

If CDs or money market mutual funds are paying 5 percent interest, after subtracting out taxes (roughly one-third) and inflation (roughly 2 to 3 percent), the real return on these investments is, at best, 1 to 2 percent. Even at 2 percent, it will take thirty-six years for your money to double; this is not a good plan for long-term wealth.

On the other hand, stocks have averaged 11 percent per year. You can defer paying taxes on stocks by not selling them and can reduce these taxes by holding stocks for at least twelve months to take advantage of the (lower) long-term capital gains rates. The real return on this investment averages about 7 percent.[2] At a real return of 7 percent, your investment in stocks doubles approximately every ten years, or much faster than these safer investments. Using these real return assumptions, $1,000 invested in stocks would be worth as much as $11,400

---

1. William Bernstein, "The Gospel According to Ibbotson," *Efficient Frontier,* February 1999, as found at www.brill.com.
    2. Source: James A. Glassman, "As Investors Reappraise Risk, Stock Prices Will Go Higher," *In the Vanguard,* Spring 2000, p. 3.

in thirty-six years,[3] whereas $1,000 in these less risky invest-ments would be worth $2,000 at most. Therefore, the oppor-tunity cost of not investing in stocks is the loss of this real return, this added appreciation for your assets.

But isn't the stock market volatile? What about Black Monday, in October 1987, when the stock market dropped 22 percent in one day? Doesn't such volatility argue against investing in stocks?

Certainly, in any month, quarter, or year, the stock mar-ket can (and often does) go down. Therefore, it is not prudent to put money into stocks that you might need three months or a year or two from now. If you have children who will be going to college in a year or two, you should not put the tuition money into the stock market. Too often, novice investors, hop-ing to drastically increase their modest stake, put most or all of their money into a stock or a mutual fund on a hot tip, only to see it drop 10 percent. The saying "once bitten, twice shy" applies here, for such people rarely invest again.

It is true that investing in stocks is risky and that people lose money. It is also true that people make money, lots of money. Boomers looking to increase their wealth should keep the following points in mind:

■ The stock market has dropped 10 percent or more fourteen times since 1968, but over the same thirty-one-year period it has risen more than 15-fold.[4] Despite the crash in

3. Because you do not pay taxes on stocks until you sell them, you can control the effects of taxes on the long-term appreciation of stocks.

4. Jeremy Siegel, *Stocks for the Long Run,* (New York: McGraw-Hill, 1998), and Bloomberg and Fidelity Investments, August 1999, as reported in Peter Lynch, "Fidelity's Guide to Investing Responsibly," www.fidelity.com.

1987, an investor who stayed fully invested did better than one who went to cash just before the crash and stayed in cash or one who went to cash but slowly put new money back into the market.[5] Therefore, you can (and should) use volatility to your advantage to buy on the dips.

■ Looking at five-, ten-, twenty-, and thirty-year time horizons, based on historical data, the return on stocks beat those of bonds and bills about 70 percent, 80 percent, 90 percent, and almost 100 percent of the time, respectively.[6]

■ The volatility of a stock, as measured by its standard deviation, decreases the longer you hold on to it.[7] In addition, stocks, if held for twenty years or more, are no more volatile than government bonds or Treasury bills.[8]

■ There's been no twenty-year period in which investors lost money in the stock market and only two periods of ten years, 1929–1938 and 1930–1939, in which stocks lost ground. With one exception, the 1929 to 1932 Depression bear mar-

5. A study by T. Rowe Price showed that if all three types of investors started with $10,000 and then added $100 per month, the one who stayed in stocks would have had $76,000, the one who moved all to cash would have had $30,000, and the one who switched into cash but put new money into stocks would have had $65,000. Source: James K. Glassman, "Panic Selling Almost Always a Bad Move," *The Washington Post*, September 3, 1998, p. E01.

6. Siegel, *Stocks for the Long Run*, p. 28.

7. Standard deviation, as a measure of volatility, is discussed in Chapter 10. Based on historical data, in any given year, stocks have a standard deviation of 20 percentage points, which means that two-thirds of the time, their returns will vary in a range between −9 percent and 31 percent. However, over fifteen years the standard deviation drops to about 2 percent, so that about two-thirds of the time, the average annual return varies between 9 and 13 percent. Source: Glassman, "As Investors Reappraise Risk, Stock Prices Will Go Higher," p. 3.

8. James K. Glassman, "Is This Time Different," *The Washington Post*, February 23, 1997, p. H1.

ket, market dips have never lasted more than two years. So, although prolonged crashes can happen, they are unusual.[9]

Historically, the bias of the stock market has been to the upside, reflecting the growth in the U.S. economy. Thus, given a time frame of at least five years, it appears to be prudent for boomers to invest in stocks and risky not to do so.

9. Roger Ibbotson, "I Am a Bull," *Forbes,* June 16, 1997, www.forbes. com.

Chapter 10

DEVELOPING AN INVESTMENT PHILOSOPHY

Know before You Buy

Developing an investment philosophy will help to keep you in the market or out of the market when your emotions, echoing sentiments reflected in the media, are telling you to do the opposite. The majority of people underperform the market; from 1984 to 1998, the average stock mutual fund made an annual return of 10.7 percent, whereas the average investor made only a 7.3 percent annual return.[1] Over this time span, a 3.4 percentage point difference is quite significant; money invested in the market in 1984 appreciated 459 percent, whereas the average investor's appreciation was 288 percent, or only about 63 percent as much. Clearly, the average inves-

---

1. Charles W. Kadlec, "Strategy Beats Tactics," *Mutual Funds Magazine*, May 2000, p. 116.

tor has not developed a successful investing philosophy; because the time is growing short for baby boomers to accumulate money for retirement and other needs, they must develop an investing philosophy. This chapter discusses some of the beliefs and convictions boomers will need to develop to become successful.

Too often, boomers make an investment based on a whim, a tip, out of fear, or out of hope—all the wrong reasons. They do it because they are scared that this investment is the one-in-a-million opportunity that will make them rich, and if they don't jump on it, then all such opportunities will have passed them by forever. Or they do it because they feel lucky, their neighbor or colleague at work invested in it, or they read about it somewhere. In other words, they are investing without knowing anything about the risks and the rewards.

The average boomer probably spends a fair amount of time researching the best buys in refrigerators, cars, stereos, or clothing. Often they know the make and model of the best brands. More important, they know why they are buying the specific make and model. The idea of buying a refrigerator or a stereo based mainly on a hot tip seems ludicrous. The idea of taking a vacation without doing some basic research or going to a travel agent for advice and recommendations is not something they will consider. Some won't even try a new restaurant without reading or hearing the recommendations of a restaurant critic. Yet when it comes to investing, many of these precautions seem to go out the window.

Why? This is a good question. It stems in part from the idea that investing is no different from gambling, that there is no real reason why investments rise or fall, whether it be technology stocks or pork bellies. Why do any research, and why not follow a hot tip? Your luck may change if you wait too long.

Too often, people invest in a stock, bond, or mutual fund if they see the same security mentioned in several places, whether it be in newspaper articles, radio shows, or magazines. The thinking seems to be, "If so many people are making the same recommendation, it must be good." Unfortunately, it doesn't work that way. Often, writers and analysts simply parrot what they heard or read elsewhere. In addition, how sure are you that that particular source is an authority; following this "authority's" guidance may be the equivalent of following medical advice from a lawyer or plumber.

In addition, many boomers do not think through what they are investing in. A recent report showed that more than 30 percent of 401(k) plan money was invested in money market funds or their equivalent.[2] Although this may be appropriate for investors in or nearing retirement, this percentage may not be appropriate for boomers looking to increase their wealth. Often, boomers who know that they will need a certain amount of cash in the short term, such as to help their parents or children, invest this money in stocks, trying to increase their net worth without realizing the risk they are taking; there is a good chance that they will wind up with much less money.

Many boomers purchase a mutual fund because it is hot, having performed well over the last three months or so. Often this fund is purchased near its high. If that fund plummets during the next three months, it is sold in a panic and the money is shifted into the next hot area. It is easy to lose money buying high and selling low. After doing this several times, the tendency is to swear off investing in the belief that there is no way the average person can succeed.

---

2. Paul A. Merriman, "17 Steps to Improve Your 401(k) Returns," October 1999, as found at www.brill.com.

You work hard for your money. Why throw it away, possibly on a bad investment, without knowing what you are doing? Before investing a cent, you should consider the following questions:

- How much do I have in savings for an emergency?

- How soon will I need this money?

- Why am I putting money into this particular investment?

- Does this particular investment complement my other investments?

- What are the possible risks to this investment?

- How much can I afford to lose before I bail out?

- If investing in a company, what does this company do, and what are its prospects over the short and long term?

- If investing in a mutual fund, what has been the manager's track record, especially in bear and bull markets?

When you know these things, you won't be as upset if you lose 10 percent of your investment during a sudden market slide. The wrong thing to do then is to sell in a panic. Yet people tend to sell without answers to these questions. It may be that the best thing to do during this 10 percent drop is to buy more of this particular investment, as if it were on sale. Without knowing your reasons for investing, you may miss out on this sale.

If you consider the reasons you are investing and take the time to do the necessary research, you will feel more comfortable and do better with your investments.

Asset Allocation

Did your stocks or funds do as well as everyone else's last year? Are you getting ready to switch your money into the most recent winners? Well, don't do it; doing so may be hazardous to your financial health.

Open up any financial magazine or newspaper or listen to programs on radio or TV and you will be pummeled with advertisements claiming that some fund or fund family or some brokerage firm's recommendations were number one over some recent time period. Americans love instant gratification and love going with a winner. The thinking is that if XYZ Fund was up 50 percent last year, then it probably will be up 50 percent this year. Everyone else is getting rich, so why not me?

There are many problems with chasing the winner; in fact, this is why many boomers get burned investing. As discussed in Chapter 14, given the thousands of mutual funds and other investment vehicles, the manager of a fund or the management of a company has to do something extraordinary to do that much better than everyone else. Sometimes, superior records are indeed accomplished by excellent management; the best way to find this out is to look for a superior long-term track record. However, such exceptional records often are accomplished by taking greater than average risks, making unusual gambles. An investment that is up 50 percent one year can fall 40 percent the next.

A major reason many of these gambles can work out or not work out is market rotation. As discussed in Chapter 14, no one sector of the market stays hot. Fund managers who concentrate their portfolios with strong sector bets need to be right a lot of the time to make up for the volatility inherent in such decisions. Using baseball terminology, the hitters who always go for the home run often strike out.

A less volatile approach to investing is to pursue a strategy of asset allocation; the overall makeup of your portfolio will affect your returns much more than one or two superstars.[3] Therefore, the way to wealth is to concentrate on how well your entire portfolio is doing rather than on one or two stocks or funds that did extraordinarily well. Investors wanting long-term financial success should have a broadly diversified portfolio consisting of multiple asset classes.[4]

A mathematical example will help show the importance of diversifying your assets. Suppose that investor A decides to rely on one investment, which gives a steady return of 10 percent a year. Over twelve years, $1,000 becomes a little more than $3,100. Investor B decides to diversify, finds four investments, and puts $250 into each. These four average annual returns of zero percent, 8 percent, 12 percent, and 20 percent. How much does B have after twelve years?

On the surface, one might say that B would have the same amount of money as does A, for the arithmetic average of zero, 8, 12, and 20 percent is 10 percent. However, this would not be correct because the compound results from the 12 percent and 20 percent investments more than make up for the poky results from the zero percent and 8 percent investments. After twelve years, B would have almost $4,100, nearly $1,000 more. B concentrated on finding a number of investments, which included some winners.

---

3. "Many academic studies have revealed that asset allocation is the most important factor in predicting a portfolio's investment return. Asset allocation also determines the overall volatility or 'risk' of a portfolio. Most investors, and especially retirees, seek to maximize return and minimize risk." Source: John P. Greaney, "Asset Allocation for the Ages," September 1, 1998, http://www.geocities.com.

4. Source: David Bugen, "Why Diversify," February 26, 1999, www.morningstar.com.

Beating the Pros?

How can you, working your everyday job, possibly having a family, wanting to do things such as watch TV, go to the movies, and take vacations, hope to do better than investment professionals? These people have been professionally trained, have the benefit of highly paid research staffs, have developed expertise in understanding trends in their industry, and are paid to spend their entire day analyzing their particular markets. It seems as if the odds are stacked against the average investor, but this may not be correct.

Whether the "average" investor can do better than investment professionals is irrelevant because you and the professional have different goals. You are not competing against an investment professional any more than you are competing against someone who drives a different car or someone who takes a different sort of vacation. For instance, if you are happy in a moderately priced hotel in the Rockies, are you doing worse than someone who prefers a deluxe hotel in the Caribbean? If you don't like cruises and prefer the nearby beach, are you doing worse? Bringing this analogy back to investing, if your goal is to earn 10 percent from your mutual funds or to have $3,000 a month in retirement income, it really doesn't matter if an investment professional is making twice as much with his or her investment strategy. The important thing is to define your goals and work toward them, not to compare yourself with someone else.

Things are not stacked in favor of the professionals because you are not being judged as these professionals are judged. This is their livelihood, and if they don't produce, they might be out of a job. You don't have dozens of clients or thousands of shareholders peering over your shoulder, demanding superior performance. You don't have to justify any gutsy or questionable investment decisions to your supervisors and your clients. You don't have to sell certain holdings near the end of each quarter, as many mutual fund managers do, so that when a list of holdings is published in a quarterly report, it looks as if they are not taking undue risks.

In addition, you are free to investigate and invest in small or unusual opportunities. There are thousands of investment possibilities; you are not limited to the ones that someone has researched; you can do your own research and discover hot opportunities long before the investment professionals learn of them. In the industry or environment in which you work, you have knowledge about your specialty and can pick up on trends or new ideas long before the pros do. In your everyday shopping, at the supermarket or mall, you can identify new products or stores that generate new demand and then investigate whether these products or companies might be worth investing in. You can grab on to ideas that you hear on the radio or see on television and see whether they make sense to you. These investment strategies are ones that Peter Lynch, the famous manager of the Fidelity Magellan Fund from 1977 to 1990, constantly stresses.[5] You have the freedom to pursue areas that many professionals do not have because no one is looking over your shoulder.

It is important to understand that investing is not a zero-sum game in which one person has to lose for another person to win. Both you and the investment professional can win in the marketplace.

Pulling the Trigger

The stock market has been in a bull market since August 1982, and has appreciated dramatically since 1995, so it

___

5. Peter Lynch, *One Up on Wall Street* (New York: Penguin, 1989), pp. 14, 18.

would be reasonable to expect that many boomers would be much wealthier. Unfortunately, many are not. There are a number of reasons why people lose or do not make much money in a rising market. One is the desire to time the market. As shown in Chapter 11, people who try to time the market lose out on much of the market's increase.

Another major reason some boomers haven't made money is that they haven't invested; they are afraid to make a decision and to commit themselves, or, in market speak, they are afraid to pull the trigger. Many of them know that they should be investing but are still scared.

Why do people hold back? Let's look at several reasons:

■ Ignorance. People are afraid of what they don't understand. Often, when they don't know about something, they are too afraid to investigate and learn about it.

■ Fear. This may be the biggest reason. They are afraid of various things, such as the market going down and staying down. Or they remember horror stories from the Great Depression. They may be afraid of picking the wrong investment, or they have a friend or neighbor who lost money in the market. But basically, they are scared of failing and losing everything.

■ Perfectionism. This is also known as paralysis by analysis, which occurs because people feel that they haven't done enough research and haven't found the best investment. If only they can do a little bit more research, they are sure that they can find the perfect investment, the idea that is guaranteed to make them the most money risk free.

How can you overcome ignorance, fear, and paralysis by analysis?

- Realize that everyone is ignorant of some things and that such ignorance is nothing to be ashamed of. The important thing is to accept that you are ignorant and to do something about it. There are many ways to learn about investing, some of which are discussed in Chapter 9.

- There are many ways to overcome fear. The important thing to remember is that all investors make mistakes; no one is perfect. If you can look at your mistakes as a learning experience, you can put them behind you and move on. No one is right all the time; however, if you do not invest, you will not be right any of the time and you will not make any money.

- It is good to spend time researching and investigating your different investment options. However, eventually you must move forward and make a decision. Too much analysis may be as bad as too little; you should look for a happy medium.

No one can make the perfect investment choice each time, but as the market rises, your choices probably will make money too. For instance, rather than spending an inordinate amount of time looking for the perfect mutual fund, you should simply find a good one and move on. When it is time for the market to move up, most funds move up to some degree. As shown earlier in this chapter, much of the increase in a portfolio comes from asset allocation and investment in the different sectors rather than one perfect investment.

Meaningless Facts Related to Market Performance

Many boomers base their investing philosophy and program on information they gather from the media. They do little independent investigation and are swayed by sensation-driven headlines and a doomsday mentality. One day, they hear a good reason to invest, so they do it. A week later, they read a report "proving" that a major recession is in the offing and the market is about to fall, so they adjust accordingly. This is a sure recipe for failure.

Much of the media-driven hype sounds good and actually may have some basis in fact. Yet much of it does not stand up to serious scrutiny. Let's examine some of these "facts" in this and the next two sections:

- From 1991 through 1998, it was widely held that the market hadn't had a 10 percent correction since 1990, so a major correction was imminent. It is true that market corrections are a fact of life and are necessary for the long-run stability of a market, and seven years is a long time to go without one. But there are a couple of major problems with this reasoning. First, where did this magic 10 percent number come from? It is simply a handy, round number. The market, as measured by the Standard & Poor's (S&P) 500 and the Dow Jones Industrial Average (DJIA), had a 9.8 percent correction in 1997 and was down more than 10 percent in interday trading in 1994 and 1996.[6] If the "magic" correction number is 9 percent or even 9.5 percent instead of 10 percent, then the original statement loses its validity.

In addition, the S&P 500 and the DJIA are not the entire stock market; as discussed in Chapter 11, they are large-capitalization stock indexes. There are thousands of domestic stocks, many have little correlation with the stocks in these indexes, and these have had their own ups and downs.

In sum, the overall stock market has had normal corrections.

---

6. Peter Lynch, "Investing in Volatile Markets," www.fidelity.com.

■ Another belief is this: Not only can stocks can be risky, but investors may suffer through long periods of flat or stagnant returns; after all, the market was at the same level in 1983 as it was in 1966. It is true that stocks can have flat periods, and it is true that the market, as measured by the DJIA, peaked just below 1,000 in January 1966 and, but for a few short intervals, did not break through this barrier for seventeen years.

Once again, we are faced with the problem of confusing one index for the entire market. Many mutual funds made money during this seventeen-year period by ignoring the over-valued stocks and finding other good companies. Had you invested in the market in late 1974, after the two-year bear market, with the DJIA below 600, you would have enjoyed good profits over the next few years. Proper diversification would have helped make you money even though the DJIA was flat.

■ Another belief is that the current stock market is way overvalued. The "evidence" is that the price-to-dividend ratio is at historic highs. Once again, the sentiment is partially true: This ratio is at historic highs. But why is it so high?

Technical analysts are constantly looking for numerical trends and ratios that have worked in predicting market turns in the past to help them to forecast the future. At times, such trends and ratios are helpful predictors of the future. Yet it is important to look at the assumptions underlying these trends and ratios to see whether they still hold.

Many companies pay out a certain percentage of their profits in the form of dividends. As profits increase, dividends increase. Historically, the ratio of stock price to dividend has been one way to discern whether the stock price had gotten ahead of the dividend; if this ratio became too high, the stock was overvalued.

Increasingly in the 1990s, however, companies have been deciding not to increase their dividends to keep up with an increasing stock price and to use this money to buy back stock or make more profitable investments, including putting more money into research and development. Therefore, the companies are still profitable but are using the money for different purposes.[7] Thus, in many cases, companies' not funding increases in their dividend is no longer a sign that the company is in trouble or that the stock price is too high; rather, the fundamental underlying assumptions have changed, and the company is using the money differently.

It has often been said that the low dividend rate of the S&P 500 shows how overvalued the market is. However, for much of the 1990s the profits of S&P stocks grew nearly three times as fast as their dividends.[8] In addition, the weighting of technology stocks in this index rose from 10 percent in September 1994 to 24 percent in September 1999.[9] Given that technology stocks pay few or no dividends, this percentage increase almost guaranteed that the S&P 500's dividend rate would fall.

Meaningless Facts Related to Market Declines

Another belief about stock market investing that does not stand up under close scrutiny is that because the stock market has been rising so rapidly, what goes up must come down. Like most prognostications, this statement has some basis in

---

7. James K. Glassman, "Is This Time Different," *Washington Post,* February 23, 1997, p. H1.
8. Ibid.
9. Source: BARRA as referenced by Lewis Braham, "The Shifting S&P," October 19, 1999, www.smartmoney.com.

fact. As described in Chapter 11, almost all markets experience fluctuations and rarely shoot up or down without a change in direction. However, to suppose that because the market has gone up it must come down is to misunderstand what drives the market. This supposition comes from beliefs such as the following:

- The market is a crapshoot, and there is no particular reason why stocks move up or move down.

- There is little historical basis for the current stock market to continue to rise; over the previous several decades, the market has not acted this way.

There are factual problems with both beliefs:

- Many boomers, swayed by advertisements and articles showing them how to make a quick killing, do not understand how the stock market works. Without such knowledge, no long-term strategy will make any sense. In the short run, emotions can sway the market, but over the long term, fundamental components such as companies' sales and earnings, interest rates, and the supply and demand for stocks tend to move the market.

- As noted in the previous section, many prognosticators use numerical trends and ratios that have worked in the past to help forecast the future. However, it is important to see whether the assumptions underlying these trends still hold. In the late 1990s and moving into the new millennium, the U.S. economy has been growing steadily, with low inflation, relatively stable interest rates, and low unemployment. It is vital to realize that this current economic environment is very different from anything seen since at least the mid-1960s.

Inflation began to kick in and accelerate in the late 1960s. This was followed by the drastic oil price increases of the 1970s as the economy suffered from what was then known as stagflation: stagnant growth coupled with high inflation. Inflation reached double digits by the end of the 1970s and started to decline only in the 1980s. As inflation declined, unemployment crept up, and it was believed that unemployment had to stay high to keep inflation low.[10] In the 1980s and into the early 1990s, American industry, castigated as being bloated and inefficient, engaged in costly reengineering projects that involved major layoffs, which led, at the time, to lower productivity.

Given such different conditions, how can one look at the economic and market conditions existing in the late 1990s, compare them to what has happened in recent decades, and then make forecasts based on what was the market norm in the 1970s, 1980s, and early 1990s? Yet this is what many analysts did when they looked at the spectacular market rise in 1995 and said, in late 1995 and early 1996, that the stock market could not do well in 1996 simply because there had not been two good years in a row in a long time, or that 1997 would have to be a poor year simply because the U.S. stock market has just had two good years in a row, and there haven't been three good years in a row in more than a generation. There is no evidence to support the idea that a period of low returns must follow a period of high returns.[11]

---

10. As taught in many undergraduate economics classes, the Phillips curve relates levels of unemployment to inflation. In the 1960s, it was believed that if unemployment fell below 4.5 percent, inflation would pick up. Based on the experience of the late 1960s into the 1980s, this theory was modified so that the point at which low unemployment ignited inflation moved well above 5 percent.

11. Roger Ibbotson, "I Am a Bull," *Forbes,* June 16, 1997, www. forbes.com.

The direction of the stock market is determined much more by current fundamentals than by a misguided view of what "should" be happening.

Meaningless Facts Related to Taking Risks

Another statement that sounds plausible but may not stand up to hard scrutiny deals with risk and reward aphorisms such as "To make money, you have to take a lot of risk." As with many popular statements, there is some truth to these remarks, but only within limits. Leaving your money in a passbook savings account or investing in a certificate of deposit is basically a risk-free investment but guaranteed to pay small returns; as discussed in Chapter 9, by using vehicles such as these, you will not increase your wealth substantially in the long run.

In looking at investments, boomers should weigh the risks against the rewards of each investment. If two investments yield the same result but one is twice as risky as another, it seems to makes little sense to choose the riskier path. Or if investment A potentially yields only 10 percent more than investment B but is 50 percent riskier, you must weigh whether the additional reward is worth the extra risk.

One way to measure risk is to examine the amount of volatility. This is done through a statistical measure called standard deviation, which measures the amount of variation from an average. (Another way to think of this is the amount of "wiggle" in the price, as seen on a graph.) A higher standard deviation means more volatility, the potential for lower lows, and the possibility of longer periods of time in which the investor can lose money on the investment. All of this becomes important if the investor needs to sell in a hurry, is likely to sell an investment if he or she is scared out of the market, or can't take such volatility. Thus, an investor should learn how much volatility is likely with each investment and should strive to get more reward for a greater amount of risk.

One measure of reward to risk is the Sharpe ratio. The return on an almost riskless investment, such as a Treasury bond, is subtracted from the return for a specific investment. This result is divided by the investment's standard deviation. Therefore, this ratio measures the reward divided by the risk. For example, if the investment returns 20 percent, a riskless investment yields 6 percent, and the standard deviation is 7 percent, then the Sharpe ratio would be 2.0 ([20 − 6]/7). The higher the investment return or the lower the standard deviation, the higher the ratio and the higher the overall reward. If another investment has returned 22 percent but has had a standard deviation of 16 percent, its Sharpe ratio would be 1.0. The higher Sharpe ratio for the former investment is telling the investor that there is not enough additional reward in the second investment (an additional 2 percentage point return) to take this additional risk (an additional 10 percentage points in volatility).

Tools such as the Sharpe ratio allow the investor to examine two investments and weigh their reward to risk ratio. As discussed in Chapter 9, over the long run, bonds have outperformed cash, and stocks have outperformed both of these. It is true that in any given month or year stock prices can fall precipitously. However, over the last seventy years research has shown that in successive rolling ten-year periods (e.g., 1926–1935, 1927–1936, etc.), stocks have almost always yielded a positive return.[12] Historically, the rewards from stocks have been worth the risk.

---

12. Over ten-year periods, average annual returns have ranged from − 0.8 percent to 19.9 percent. Over fifteen-year holding periods, average annual returns ranged from 0.6 percent to 18.1 percent, and over twenty-

Why You Should Ignore Hot Tips

"Knowledge is power" and "Time is money" are two popular sayings. Maybe "Ignore hot tips" should be another one. This section discusses how these three sayings are related and why the first two imply the third.

Let's first define these three sayings. "Knowledge is power" means that when you know something and others do not, you can use this knowledge to your advantage. You might have specific information about a particular company or industry, sometimes your own. Often, because of your job, you have knowledge in your area of expertise that the average investor, industry analyst, or stockbroker knows little about. As mentioned earlier in this chapter, Peter Lynch has held that individual investors can do well by investing in companies or areas with which they are familiar. By investing in what you are knowledgeable about, you gain an advantage over other investors.

The saying "Time is money" can also be used in investing. One major application is linked to "Knowledge is power." If you know of an imminent development that others do not know about, for instance, you can use this time-sensitive information to buy or sell, thus increasing your profits or minimizing your losses. Time-sensitive information is very powerful. (Another application of "Time is money" deals with the power of compound interest; the longer your hold your investments, the more profitable they become.)

So we see that using time-sensitive specific information can lead to great profits. The value of using such information

---

year holding periods, average annual returns ranged from 3.1 percent to 17.7 percent. Source: "Plain Talk: Realistic Expectations for Stock Market Returns," The Vanguard Group, www.vanguard.com, 1999.

is that few people know about it and it must be used fairly quickly. If many people knew of it, its advantage would be lost. So there are great advantages to speed and secrecy.

But there is a big difference between this specialized knowledge and hot tips. Hot tips proliferate everywhere. People hear them on buses and subways, on the radio, walking down the corridor, or in a phone call from a friend or a stranger. People pay attention to them out of both fear and greed: the fear of losing out on something big and the greed of wanting easy money. If you are getting this tip, you probably are not the only one getting it, which diminishes its value. You need to ask yourself how valuable this information can actually be and how many layers of people has it passed through. For instance, if you are told that a certain company has had some sort of a major breakthrough that few people are aware of, how likely is it that you are among the first to know?

Think of a stream starting in the mountains. At and near its source, the water is pure and the stream is narrow and fast. The further it gets from its source, the greater the chance for the water to be polluted or run into obstacles. The closer it moves to its destination, the broader the river and the less it resembles the original stream near its source. This is analogous to information. Close to its source, the information is pure, accurate, and timely. The further it gets from its source, the more distorted it gets and the less powerful it is. Usually by the time it gets to you, this information is more like the water in the broad, sluggish (often polluted) river than the mountain stream. At this point, the information is rarely powerful or time sensitive. The people who can use it to profit already have. By the time you use it, the information often is worthless or might cost you money.

Get Rich Slowly

Something in the human psyche seems to revel in the roller coaster ride involved in getting rich quickly. The sudden pop upward of the investment vehicle, whether it be stocks, options, futures, or lottery tickets, can be exhilarating. The rags-to-riches story is part of the American culture, and people dream of tripling their net worth in a very short period of time. A slow, methodical approach to building wealth does not fire the imagination and is not the subject of novels or movies.

Yet, although it is boring, a get-rich-slow approach has a more certain outcome. Many more people get wealthy using a slow, systematic approach than an abrupt approach. This is because there are proven systems and historical bases for this more boring formula; there doesn't seem to be a surefire way to get rich quickly.

The basis for a lot of investing and wealth creation comes down to probabilities, expected values of success, and a comparison of risk and reward. Certainly the payoff from a lottery can be high; guaranteed payments of $200,000 a year for twenty years is a typical payout. However, the odds of winning such a payout are very small. The expected value of success, which is obtained by multiplying the payout by the chances of winning, is usually less than the price of admission. For example, if the after-tax payout is $4 million, the chance of winning is 1 in 16 million, and the lottery ticket costs $1, the expected value of success of $0.25 ($4 million/16 million) is less than the cost of playing, $1. The risk of not winning more than outweighs the potential reward. Under these conditions, it appears to be foolish to play the lottery and expect to come out ahead.

Expecting the lottery to make you rich quickly is an extreme example. However, the principle is the same for boomers who believe that they need to take large risks to get wealthy or that there is a direct correlation between risk and reward. What else would explain the vast numbers of people who play the commodities market? Unlike the stock market, in this market, for every winner there is a guaranteed loser. Even professionals lose money, so the odds are not good for the nonprofessional. Yet nonprofessionals continue to play this market because of the stories of the occasional investor who strikes it rich, turning $2,000 into $20,000. Many boomers, particularly those with a modest net worth who are hoping to retire soon, look for the miracle approach in which they don't have to sweat and plan and think and analyze day after day. This is not too different from all the quick ways of losing weight; people want the results quickly without having to pay the price.

Historically, an approach that has worked well is investing in common stocks. Compared to the rapid and huge payouts from these riskier approaches, an 11 percent average return sounds boring. Yet over time, thanks to compound interest, 11 percent can turn small sums of money into fortunes. Using this average, investing $1,000 a month in common stocks gets you to $1 million in twenty-one years. (If this monthly investment amount seems high, don't forget that it can include your 401(k) and IRA contributions.) Saving and investing the often-advised 10 percent of take-home pay can make you rich in a slow and measured way.

Yet this slow and measured way frustrates some investors. In an attempt to speed up this process, some baby boomers believe that by being more aggressive, investing solely in small companies or penny stocks, they can get rich quicker and move the time for retirement that much closer. Again, there are stories of such stocks quintupling nearly overnight, making investors wealthy. However, looking at the risk-to-reward ratio, in most cases people do not become rich, and many wind up losing money.

The negative effects of one or more bad years on a portfolio cannot be overemphasized. This can be shown with an example of two investors, A and B. A is fairly cautious and invests $1,000 in a mutual fund that returns the long-term market norm, 11 percent a year. Five years of investing turns this into $1,685. B wants to take more chances and finds an aggressive fund that averages 18 percent for the first four years. However, in the fifth year this fund drops 18 percent. B winds up with less money in the fund, $1,590. B has taken more risk and experienced more volatility; even though B's fund outperformed A's fund four of the five years, A ended up with more money.

The problem with a get-rich-slow approach is that it takes work, discipline, and time. It will not turn $2,000 into $200,000 overnight. Yet on a risk to reward basis, it has the highest potential reward.

Using Time Wisely

Every baby boomer who decides to invest has a hidden ally: time. In the long run, markets reward investors appropriately. Over time, compound interest can work miracles for you.

In the United States, since the end of World War II, there have been numerous market declines of at least 10 percent, as measured by the DJIA. In addition, there have been countless disasters, as defined by the news media. These disasters have included three major wars and countless other military skirmishes, a presidential assassination, a presidential resignation, the worst recession since the Great Depression, and two dramatic increases in oil prices. Yet the DJIA is more than fifty times higher than it was at the end of World War II.

Too often, boomers who invest don't want to give their investments time to grow. By withdrawing their capital early, they are robbing themselves of their greatest rewards; the big growth in capital comes at the end, not at the beginning of the process. An example will more clearly illustrate this principle.

Assume that in a pond, there is a water lily species that reproduces itself once a day. After thirty days, the pond is covered with water lilies. This means that on day 29, the pond is only half covered and on day 28, the pond is only one quarter covered. Therefore, three quarters of the growth came in the final two days. If the full (thirty-day) process were lacking only two days (such as starting two days late or ending two days early), three-quarters of the growth would not take place.

Common stocks will not increase at such a fast pace. But investors who sell their investments earlier than necessary are robbing themselves of the greatest part of their reward. Similarly, those who put off investing for a few years because they just can't get around to finding the time, doing the research, recognizing the importance of planning for the future, or deciding that investing is more important than buying something today or tomorrow are robbing themselves of the greatest part of their reward.

Let's apply this principle directly to baby boomers. Suppose a 45-year-old man suddenly realizes the need to start investing. He puts $10,000 a year into an investment that returns 11 percent through age 65; at age 65, he will have about $800,000. By waiting three years to start this same program (or withdrawing the money three years early), at age 65, he will have roughly $240,000 less.

Let's apply this principle another way. The man now realizes that he should have started earlier, but because he is earning a lot more money and can invest more money each month, he is certain that he can make up for lost time. How easily can he do this?

Assuming the 11 percent annual return on his investment and assuming that the same amount is invested each year, a 45-year-old would have to invest about fifteen times as much as a 20-year-old, nine times more than a 25-year-old, and five times more than a 30-year-old to wind up with the same amount at age 65. Let's look at this another way. In an investment that returns 11 percent, $1,000 invested each year would give a 20-year-old nearly $1.2 million at age 65; starting this same program at age 45 will result in only $80,000 by age 65. So, to make up ground, this 45-year-old would have to invest roughly $15,000 a year for the next twenty years.

Substantial wealth creation comes to those who plan, take action early, and are patient.

Chapter 11

MARKETS

What Drives the Market?

Boomers new to investing usually have no idea how the stock, bond, and money markets work. Without such knowledge, novice investors are flying blind.

What do the stock market and the local farmers' market have in common? To the uninitiated, they seem to have little in common. The former is a model of high technology, complete with computers and fast-breaking news events. The latter often is held in a parking lot and usually is a model of low-key, friendly service. But the dynamics that propel both are the same.

Both are driven, as are almost all markets, by supply and demand. In both, as the demand for a good, whether it is stocks, bonds, or fresh tomatoes, increases, the sellers of this good can increase the price. And in both, when the supply of the good increases, the buyers can decrease the price that they are willing to pay.

In a market where perfect (or nearly perfect) competition takes place, both buyers and sellers operate with perfect (or nearly perfect) knowledge of the prices and quantities of the goods they are interested in and all substitutes. At any given time, the price charged and quantity purchased are at or near an equilibrium point. At equilibrium, the amount of the good that people want to purchase and the amount that people are willing to supply are equal. If the price were any higher, fewer people would want to buy; therefore, there would be excess supply. If the price were any lower, fewer people would be willing to supply the good; therefore, there would be excess demand. As the demand for a good increases, sellers can raise the price until once again an equilibrium point is reached.

The more freely competitive the market, the more this relationship holds. At a farmers' market, the buyers can choose from many different sellers, so it is rare that there is much variation in the price of the same type of good.

These supply and demand fundamentals fuel all securities markets, be they stock, bond, commodities, or options. So let's look at the dynamics in the stock market. In the short run, the supply of stock is pretty much fixed, so the main driver of the market is demand. In the short run, the increase or decrease in the demand for stocks is driven largely by emotion. People react to the latest news on inflation, interest rates, commodity prices, foreign events, politics, the latest economic numbers, or the chief executive officer of a major firm resigning. In other words, there is little rhyme or reason to the short-term direction of the market, and this direction is almost impossible to predict. This is one reason why market timing does not work; no one can tell when there will be a sudden surge of optimism or pessimism, based on one of the aforementioned factors, that will change the price of stocks, at times dramatically.

In the long run, both supply and demand are factors. The

supply of stock can increase as firms bring new stock onto the market or decrease as firms buy back their own stock or enter mergers. The demand for stock varies based largely on people's long-term expectations of the domestic and, to a lesser extent, foreign economies, as well as the profit potential of specific companies. It can also include trends in interest rates and inflation. The long-term demand is driven less by emotions than is the short-run demand.

What Drives the Stock Market?

Given that supply and demand drive the stock and bond markets, what are the current and projected dynamics in the U.S. markets?

Over the last several years, the U.S. stock market has been rising. Throughout the 1990s, the market, as measured by the Dow Jones Industrial Average (DJIA), Standard & Poor's (S&P) 500, and the National Association of Security Dealers Automated Quotation (NASDAQ), has risen dramatically. Major questions being asked include how much longer it will continue to rise, how high it can rise, and when the next major correction or bear market will be. No one has a definitive answer; however, looking at some of the major trends can help people understand what has been happening. This discussion is not meant to be definitive or predictive.

The available supply of stock has declined. With every merger and acquisition, stock is retired; given the large number of recent mergers and acquisitions, the total quantity of stock has been reduced. As corporate profits have been rising, many companies have been repurchasing their own stock, again reducing the total amount of stock available. New companies have been coming out with initial stock offerings, increasing the amount of stock available, and some companies have been recruiting or keeping highly trained employees, including many baby boomers, with stock options, but the total quantity of stock represented by these stock offerings and options has been far outstripped by the first two factors.

A decrease in the supply of stock, with all else remaining equal, leads to an increase in prices. This can be understood by going back to the farmers' market analogy. If the quantity of tomatoes falls yet the demand remains the same, suppliers can raise the price because some consumers will be willing to pay more. A new higher equilibrium price evolves at which supply equals demand.

Demand for stock has been rising. A major factor behind the stock market rise has been the river of money baby boomers have been pouring into the market in an attempt to save for their children's college education and their own retirement. The current perception, right or wrong, is that the stock market is the only place to make the double-digit returns necessary to make money grow quickly enough. An increasing demand for stock, all else remaining equal, also leads to an increase in prices. Again, going back to the farmers' market example, if enough consumers are willing to pay more for tomatoes than they were the week before, sellers would be foolish not to raise the price.

Another factor has been the restructuring of corporate America. Throughout much of the 1980s, American corporations were bloated with extra layers of mismanagement and were not competing profitably in the global economy. The large numbers of layoffs, restructurings, and mergers that have been in the national news are evidence of American corporations becoming and remaining competitive. As a result, many American companies, in different segments of the economy, have become more profitable. Because consumers increasingly want to own shares of successful companies, rising profits (also known as earnings) translate into a rising demand for stocks. As the demand for specific stocks rises, all else remaining equal, the price of these stocks also rises.

Many countries whose economies were once very regulated have adopted less regulatory and freer capitalist systems. As a result, economies that were once moribund have started to flourish, demand for consumer goods has been rising, and many of these countries have established stock exchanges. The increase in consumer demand and these burgeoning stock markets have led to increased trade and expanded capital flows, leading, in large part, to a greater demand for American-style goods and services. Greater demand for specific American goods and services has made the stocks of companies that can serve this growing worldwide demand much more attractive. The rising demand for these stocks has pushed up their prices.

The advent of the Internet is also driving up stock prices. This has nothing to do with the "dot com" mania that drove up certain Internet shares in 1999 and early 2000. Rather, the Internet allows faster and better information, data transfer, and communication. These components allow more efficient and cheaper acquisition and procurement programs, better logistics, and faster service, leading to improved overall business efficiency, lower costs, and higher profits.

Companies are now able to shop for raw materials and components from around the world, rather than just in their local area. The larger number of suppliers and the speed with which pricing information can spread through the marketplace will cut costs and keep prices low. Given the proliferation of procurement sources and faster communications, many components can be ordered much more cheaply and received sooner, allowing product orders to be filled that much faster.

The faster turnover of product orders and lower capital requirements translate into growing profits; growing profits, over time, lead to rising stock prices.

What Drives the Bond Market?

Although supply and demand also characterize the bond market, different forces are at work than in the stock market. The price of bonds depends on both current interest rates and the perception of future interest rates. If consumers believe that increased inflation is or will become a factor or if they believe that interest rates will rise, they will demand higher yields (interest rates) to compensate them. If inflation is perceived not to be a factor or if interest rates seem to be falling, consumers will accept lower-yield bonds.

The issuers (suppliers) of bonds also set bond yield rates in anticipation of inflation and future interest rates. The higher the perceived rate of interest or inflation, the higher bond yields must be. If the perception is that interest rates or inflation will be lower, lower-yielding bonds will be supplied.

Throughout much of the 1980s and into the early 1990s, as inflation and the perception of inflation subsided, interest rates declined and the price of bonds rose. As discussed further in Chapter 13, interest rates and bond prices are inversely related; as investors believed that inflation would decline, the demand to lock in high-yielding bonds increased, pushing up their price and further lowering their yield. This increase in prices resulted in a high total return for bonds.

Since then, however, there has been more confusion about the future rate of inflation. Thus, depending on short- and long-term news and rumors, supply and demand have been dancing around these changing perceptions, driving interest rates up and then down. For instance, in 1994 there was a sudden spike up in interest rates, as the Federal Reserve Bank (Fed) increased short-term interest rates to try to ward off inflation; these rate increases were reversed in 1995. The volatility in the Asian markets in the second half of 1997 led the Fed to lower rates to help stave off financial collapse. However, because the Asian economies have largely recovered and the U.S. economy continued to expand, the Fed reversed course starting in mid-1999 and has increased rates.

As the federal budget has been stabilized, going from deficit to surplus, the supply of Treasury notes, bills, and bonds has fallen. The U.S. Treasury Department has started buying back bonds to help reduce the national debt, thus decreasing the supply of such bonds. This decrease in supply increased the price of such bonds, lowering yields, leading to a strange anomaly in mid-2000 in which the short-term rates, set by the Fed, were rising, while long-term rates, set by the decrease in supply, were falling.

Thus, the bond market, like the stock market, has many factors that can influence the price of securities. These two markets do not operate in a vacuum; the action of one influences the other. Investors are constantly weighing the relative safety of the bond market against the potential growth in the stock market. When the yield on bonds becomes high enough, stock investors will begin to consider the guaranteed returns on a bond as outweighing the possible gain in stocks. Conversely, when bond yields drop, bond investors begin to gravitate toward stocks, seeing the gains in that market as outweighing the guaranteed returns in bonds. Inflation fears, which lead to higher bond yields but lower bond prices, hurt the stock market.[1] Therefore, there is a constant dynamic between these two markets. One of the catalysts of the bull market in stocks in the 1980s and into the 1990s was the decline in bond yields, sending bond investors searching for higher overall returns in stocks.

Stock Market Indexes

Often, the first question investors ask during or after a stock market trading day is how the market is doing or how the market did. The answer, more often than not, reflects how one or more of the stock market indexes did.

These indexes were designed to give a quick snapshot of market activity. There are thousands of publicly traded companies, so it is difficult to compress the stock market action of all these companies into one succinct answer. Probably the three most widely known indexes are the DJIA, the S&P 500, and the NASDAQ. It is important to realize that these three indexes are not the entire stock market; thousands of domestic stocks are not represented by any of these indexes. However, because so many indexes are followed so closely, given sudden index changes, the gut instinct often is to buy or sell in a panic and forget about taking the long-term perspective that is necessary, in most cases, for long-term wealth creation. Because there are many stocks not reflected in the popular indexes, this gut reaction could cause you to sell good stocks, which may be rising even as the indexes are falling.

There are problems with following the indexes closely. If

---

1. Higher interest rates, meaning that future dollars will be worth less, decrease the value of a stock's future earnings, thereby decreasing the stock price and the desirability of stocks. The opposite occurs when interest rates decline.

you had noted the level in the DJIA on January 1, 1987, gone to sleep, and woken up one year later, you would have seen that this index was higher than it had been a year before and would feel that all was right with the world. By watching it day by day, you would have lived through a very rapid increase into August, followed by incredible declines in October. You would have seen this index finish the year higher, but you would not be happy with the state of affairs. Same results, different perspectives.

Each index was designed to help show how a different part of the market is doing. The DJIA, made up of large blue chip companies, is an arithmetic average based on adding up the prices of the thirty stocks in the DJIA and then dividing by a certain divisor. When the index started, the divisor was thirty; however, Dow Jones, Inc., adjusts the divisor to reflect stock splits. In addition, because the companies that make up the DJIA change periodically, the divisor must be modified to reflect the prices of these new companies. The current divisor is around 0.2. Thus, a $1 change in the share price of any of the Dow stocks moves the average by about 5 points. Years ago, a 100-point Dow move was a major event that reflected a large percentage gain or loss. Now, a move of 75 cents in every Dow stock in the same direction yields about a 100-point change, and this change represents less than a 1 percent change in the DJIA as long as this index remains over 10,000. Two major problems with using the DJIA as a barometer are that the selection of the thirty companies is somewhat arbitrary and that these thirty companies do not represent all aspects of the stock market. As a result, changes in the Dow do not always correspond to changes in the rest of the market. On the other hand, it is the most widely known stock market index, so it will continue to be watched.

The S&P 500 is an index of 500 companies, including the

largest publicly traded companies, and the NASDAQ is an index of the nonfinancial companies that are traded on that stock exchange. Both are capitalization-weighted indexes. This means that the larger the company's capitalization, the more influence it has on the index.[2] Therefore, the effect of Microsoft, for instance, on either index is much larger than that of a much smaller company. Because the capitalization of the two largest stocks in the S&P 500 equals that of the smallest 250, the price movement of these large companies often masks the price movement of the rest of the stocks in that index; the same anomaly is present in the NASDAQ. In 1998 and 1999, the S&P 500 rose by more than 20 percent, yet the average stock in both indexes did not do well; most of the increase came from price movement in only a few stocks.[3]

Three broader measures of the stock market include the Wilshire 5000, the Russell 3000, and the Value Line index. The Wilshire 5000 covers the entire stock market and includes 7,300 publicly traded companies. It is also a capitalization-weighted index; there is a very close correlation between its 500 largest companies and the companies in the S&P 500. The capitalization of these 500 largest companies makes up around 75 percent of the Wilshire 5000. The Russell 3000 is made up of the 3,000 largest companies, measured by their stock capitalization; the market capitalization of this index makes up about 95 percent of the market capitalization of the Wilshire

---

2. A company's capitalization is calculated by multiplying the number of shares outstanding by its market price.

3. In 1998, five large-cap stocks—Intel, Cisco, Microsoft, Lucent, and Dell—were responsible for 25 percent of that year's rise in the S&P 500. Source: Pat Dorsey, "Bigger Was Better, and Price Was No Obstacle," December 30, 1998, www.morningstar.com. In 1999, eight stocks accounted for half of the index's rise. Source: Terrance Odean and Brad Barber's article in the May 2000 issue of *Bloomberg Personal Finance,* as referenced in "Tweedy Browne American Value Annual Report," March 31, 2000, p. 12.

5000. The Value Line index is a non–capitalization-weighted index made up of the 1,700 stocks that Value Line Inc. follows. These stocks are among the largest in the stock market, and changes in this index represent a good cross-section of the market's action.

There are several measures of small-cap stocks; these are generally defined as stocks with a market capitalization of less than $1 billion. Probably the best-known index is the Russell 2000. This index actually is a subset of the Russell 3000; the Russell 2000 measures the price action of the 2,000 smallest of these stocks and so reflects the valuation of many small-cap stocks. Because there are a lot of small-cap stocks in the NASDAQ, some argue that that is a good measurement of small-cap stocks. However, a majority of the price action in the NASDAQ is based on the large-cap stocks in the index.

The use of indexes gets murkier outside of the United States. One broad international index of countries with developed economies is the Europe, Australasia, and the Far East (EAFE) index. This index, which is a country capitalization-weighted index, attempts to weigh the amount of capitalization of each country against all the international stock markets in this index. So if the market capitalization of a certain country were 4 percent of these stock markets, the EAFE would have 4 percent of the larger stocks from that country.

Combining most international stock markets into one index may not make the most sense; Japan's stock market lagged in the 1990s, whereas most of Europe's markets did well in the mid- to late 1990s. Therefore, the EAFE was dragged down by the poor performance in Japan. Another difficulty is the efficacy and wisdom of combining very different country markets into one index: How much do these countries have in common? A third problem with international indexes is that these countries' economies often are at different phases of the economic cycle.

In addition, there is a fair amount of subjectivity in selecting which stocks to use to represent each country in any particular index. Many financial institutions have tried to put together countrywide or regionwide indexes, but there has been no consensus on the effectiveness of these indexes.

The S&P 500, Wilshire 5000, and Value Line indexes represent different aspects of the U.S. market. But finding good benchmarks for the rest of the world has not been as easy.

Time in the Market

When it comes to amassing wealth, time in the market, rather than timing the market, is critical.

All investors and many noninvestors dream of discovering a way to divine market tops and bottoms, to be able to know when to sell (market top) and when to buy (market bottom). Stories abound of people who bought a particular stock (or other investment) right at the market bottom or sold it the day that prices peaked. Many newsletters and strategies cater to such desires, and many of these target boomers looking to make up for lost ground. However, to date no one has discovered such a strategy; the *Forbes* 400 (list of richest Americans) includes long-term investors, not market timers. No mutual fund has been successful in using a market timing strategy over a long period of time. It is almost impossible to discover such a strategy because, in the short term, the market moves on emotion. Indeed, many large directional swings and major market moves occur in a single day (or a single hour), caused by some late-breaking news. When you try to time the market, you have to be correct twice: when to get out and then when to get back in.

The long-term trend of the stock market has been up. As the economy has grown and as firms have become more profitable, the stock market has risen. This has certainly been true in the United States, in many other developed countries, and in many developing countries. Certainly, there will be market contractions and corrections and major stock price fluctuations in the short or even medium term. But in the long term, the direction of the stock market, reflecting the direction of the economy, has been positive.

As long as the direction has been up, and given a belief that the economy will continue to grow, it is important to invest now and not wait. The following four examples emphasize the greater importance of time in the market rather than short- and medium-term swings in the market.

- An analysis of the S&P 500 from 1926 to 1992 showed that out of the 816 months in this time period, the returns in the 60 best months (7 percent of the time) averaged 11 percent per month. In the other 756 months, the average return was 0.01 percent per month. Clearly, the market does not inch along at an average of 0.01 percent per month; this is merely the average of the ups and downs occurring in all but the best 60 months.[4]

- An investor who put $1,000 in the S&P 500 index in 1960 would have seen it grow to $19,450 by 1990. But if the investor had pulled this money from the market for the best ten months of that period, the return would have fallen to just

---

4. Alan R. Feld, "Market Timing Is Harder Than It Looks," *The CPA Journal Online,* February 1995, www.cpajournal.com.

$6,580. Thus, 66 percent of the gains were accumulated in just 3 percent of this time period.[5]

■ From January 1, 1984, to March 31, 1996, the S&P 500 returned 491 percent, but an investor in mutual funds averaged about 20 percent of the S&P's return, as shown in a report by Dalbar, Inc. "The difference is attributable to poor market-timing attempts by investors and the fact that investor cash does not remain invested [in stocks] for the entire period." The report's findings were summed up this way: "Investment return is far more dependent on investor behavior than on fund performance."[6]

■ Another study looked at three hypothetical people who invested in the S&P 500 each year starting in 1965 for thirty years. The first invested in this index at the start of each year; this strategy's average annual return was 11 percent. The second invested at the market peak each year; the average annual return was 10.6 percent. The third was able to invest at the exact market bottom each year; this strategy's average annual return was 11.7 percent. Thus, the difference of investing on the best day of the year and the worst day of the year, over this time frame, was 1.1 percentage points.[7]

The moral: In the long run, what works is to invest and stay invested. Time in the market is much more important than timing the market. Accordingly, baby boomers wanting to invest for retirement should not wait for the "perfect moment" to invest but should jump right in.

---

5. Charles Ellis, "Winning the Loser's Game," as referenced by James K. Glassman, "Panic Selling Almost Always a Bad Move," *The Washington Post,* September 3, 1998, p. E01.

6. James K. Glassman, "To Buy and to Hold, for Richer, Not Poorer," *The Washington Post,* September 15, 1996, p. H1.

7. Peter Lynch, "Investing in Volatile Markets," www.fidelity.com.

Bull and Bear Markets

Many Americans always seem to fear the worst. Many investors (as well as some noninvestors) are always looking for, talking about, and trying to predict the next recession, depression, correction, or bear market. Certainly it pays to be cautious at times, especially when it comes to your own financial well-being. However, given the duration of bull markets and bear markets (and economic recoveries and recessions), are people being too pessimistic?

Bull markets are markets in which the value of the commodity involved, such as stocks, bonds, gold, or pork bellies, rises for a sustained period of time, and a bear market is just the opposite. These names get their designation from the fact that when bulls charge or attack, their heads are in an upright position, whereas when bears charge or attack, their heads face down. The average bull market and economic recovery usually are measured in years, whereas the average bear market and recession usually are measured in months.[8] After bear markets end, stocks return to their prior peaks rather rapidly and then climb higher; on average, this return to the prior peak takes eight months.[9] In the worst bear market since the Great Depression, which lasted from December 1972 to September 1974, the S&P 500 lost 43 percent of its value. It took less than two years, until June 1976, to regain its pre–bear market level.[10]

Based on history, in any given year, the average investor

8. Since the mid-1950s, the average duration of a bear market has been twelve months, ranging in length from three months to nearly two years. Source: The Vanguard Group, "Plain Talk: Realistic Expectations for Stock Market Returns," www.vanguard.com, 1999.

9. Feld, "Market Timing Is Harder Than It Looks."

10. Glassman, "Panic Selling Almost Always a Bad Move."

has a better than 2 to 1 chance of making money.[11] Yet many people are determined to wait for the next major correction or bear market before they invest. Much of what people see on the newsstands and in other media are predictions as to when the next bear market will begin—as if anyone knows.

A long-term approach to investing will be more calming on the nerves because it is generally much more profitable. Markets correct; this is a fact of life. A correction normally is defined as a 10 percent drop in the stock market; during the 20th century, there have been fifty-three declines of 10 percent or more, or one every two years. A bear market usually is defined as having a decline of at least 20 percent; since 1956, there have been nine downturns of at least 20 percent, averaging one every five years.[12] Yet the long-term trend has been up. Therefore, boomers will be better off finding a strategy that they are comfortable with and sticking with it rather than jumping in and out of the market and paying the resultant taxes.

Why do market corrections occur? The price of any commodity rises when more people are buyers than are sellers, and vice versa. If the market has been rising for a while, everyone (or almost everyone) tends to be optimistic and wants to be a buyer. However, when everyone wants to buy, no one wants to sell, so there is no one to buy from. This necessarily defines a (temporary) market top. Suddenly, the market psychology shifts and people start selling. Therefore, markets generally rise only when there is a fair amount of pessimism and skepticism. So you can almost see this pessimism and skepticism as a sign that it is time to buy, not to sell or to wait. Markets tend to climb a wall of worry.

---

11. In the seventy-three years from 1926 to 1998, stocks finished the year with a gain in fifty-three of these years. Source: The Vanguard Group, "Plain Talk: Realistic Expectations for Stock Market Returns."

12. "How to Prepare Your Portfolio to Bear a Bear Market," In the Vanguard, Spring 2000, p. 9.

One way to measure the effects of bull and bear markets on a portfolio is to look at the five best and worst years using two different strategies over the thirty years from 1969 to 1998. For strategy A, assume a portfolio of 100 percent in stocks, whereas strategy B allocates one-third each to stocks, bonds, and cash.[13] For strategy A, only two of the worst five years for this time period had negative double-digit returns: 1973 and 1974. The losses in the other three worst years were less than 10 percent. Meanwhile, each of the five best years averaged increases around 20 percent. Because the stock market has risen more often than it has fallen, this strategy would have made money.

For strategy B, only two of the worst five years had negative returns. This means that by following such a strategy over this thirty-year period of time, you would have had only two down years. The latter strategy, because of the high amounts of cash and bonds, would be less volatile and would have appreciated less than strategy A.

This is not to advocate either of these two strategies. It is to show that it is important for each boomer to find a strategy that fits his or her temperament and goals and stick with it. Certainly it is important to stay informed about long-term trends and certainly it is okay to modify a plan as conditions warrant, but switching strategies often will not improve one's overall results.

What's Different Now?

Embedded deep in the American psyche are the ravages of the Great Depression. People alive today lived through it, or their

---

13. This approach uses the S&P 500 as a proxy for stocks, U.S. Treasury bonds as a proxy for bonds, and U.S. Treasury bills as a proxy for cash.

parents or grandparents lived through it. This awful period of time, stretching from 1929 well into the 1930s, was a time of poverty, ruined lives, and despair. Many people still live in fear of another Great Depression and base their economic lives on this fear. As a result, many baby boomers refuse to invest in stocks.

Ironically, the term *depression* was coined during the Hoover years to try to convince the American public that things weren't so bad. America had actually lived through six such depressions before the Great Depression, but they were called panics, as in the Panic of 1837 or the Panic of 1907, and the thinking was that the word *depression* was more benign than *panic*. These panics came about, to a large extent, because of the still developing banking and stock market systems; the lack of uniformity, in terms of acceptance of money and regulations, was a chief culprit. The effects of each of these panics were as devastating as those of the Great Depression.

Part of the mythology stemming from the Great Depression was that the stock market crash in October 1929 helped to cause this major economic downturn. During this month, stocks tumbled, helping to end a nearly decade-long bull market. At the depths of the crash, the DJIA had fallen 90 percent. Stocks did not regain their October 1929 levels for years, leading many to wonder, in the October 1987 crash, whether investors in the American stock market were in for another Great Depression. Indeed, during every major stock market decline and every bear market, the major fear is whether the market will continue to crash and whether we are in for another Great Depression.

The truth is that less than 1 percent of the American public owned stocks in 1929.[14] Therefore, 99 percent of Ameri-

---

14. Lynch, "Investing in Volatile Markets."

cans were not affected directly by the stock market crash. There were very few mutual funds in 1929, and certainly no 401(k) plans or individual retirement accounts. The mindset about investing and making money was very different.

Since the end of World War II, the American economy has had numerous recessions and bear markets, yet we have never come close to the severity suffered in the 1930s. This stands in stark contrast to the depths of the Great Depression, when one out of every four Americans was out of work. Similarly, no bear market in stocks has been nearly as severe as the one from 1930 to 1932, when the average stock lost more than two-thirds of its value. Why not? What's different now? The answers are complex but include the following:

- From an economic point of view, two actions that helped to prolong the Great Depression were the Fed drastically cutting the money supply and Congress passing a major tariff. Because there was less money in circulation, less commerce could take place, thus severely retarding job creation. By slapping large tariffs on imported goods, Congress severely inhibited trade, again severely retarding job growth. Lessons have been learned from history; for instance, after the October 1987 stock market crash, the first thing the Fed did was to increase the money supply.

- There were few social safety nets in the 1930s. There was no unemployment insurance and no other countercyclical federal government programs to help cushion the effects of higher unemployment. In addition, there was no Social Security at the start of the Great Depression; the guaranteed payments that older adults get certainly play a large role in preventing poverty.

- The rules by which one invests have changed. In the 1920s, an investor could go 90 percent on margin. This means that an investor could borrow up to 90 percent of the value of the security purchased and put only 10 percent down. Such a strategy works well when the market is rising, but when the market is falling, one must constantly come up with money to maintain the margin level. A rapidly falling market could cause many people to sell some of their securities to prop up others; these actions exacerbated the downward pressures. Today, margin levels are at 50 percent.

  ▪ The investment community is more heavily regulated and insured by the federal government. The guarantees on banks (and savings and loans) of up to $100,000 help to prevent runs on banks; these runs on banks helped to create wide-scale panics. There are similar regulations and guarantees on stock brokerage accounts and other investment vehicles. In addition, there are tighter regulations on mutual funds and on stock and bond brokers; a major byproduct of these regulations is to instill confidence in the investment system.

  None of this means that another Great Depression can never occur; no one can truthfully predict that. But the chances are greatly diminished, as evidenced by the economic record since the end of World War II. Accordingly, it is important to realize that things have changed, and it is equally important, for boomers making investment decisions that could affect the quality of the rest of their lives, not to be scared by the past.

Chapter 12

STOCKS

Stocks Aren't Lottery Tickets

A common misperception about investing in the market can be found in the attitude of boomers who say they are going to "play the market." That phrase speaks volumes about their attitude and understanding of the stock market; they think that buying stocks is little different from buying lottery tickets, playing craps, or betting on horse racing. Within this mindset, there is little or no rhyme or reason why money is made in the stock market because luck, more than any other single factor, seems to predominate. The idea of holding on to stocks for a long period of time seems to make as little sense as holding on to a lottery ticket for a long period of time. Therefore, when the market rises, there is a desire to cash in quickly, for who knows when the market will turn around. And when the market declines for a day, week, or month, there is panic and a tendency to want to sell immediately. Little money is made, and a lot of money can be lost.

Let's review exactly what stocks are. Stock represents ownership of a company or corporation. When a company needs to raise money, it can generally do so one of three ways: borrowing money from a lending institution; issuing bonds, which are promissory notes to repay the principal at a certain time and to make specified interest payments; or issuing stock, which represents ownership in the company.[1]

If the company decides to issue stock, it will make an initial public offering (IPO); revenue from this IPO will benefit the company directly. What most people do not realize is that only when one buys stock directly from a company in an initial or subsequent public offering does the money flow directly to that company. In almost all other instances of buying stocks (and other securities), one buys those shares in a secondary market from the previous owner.[2] The beneficiary of this purchase is the previous shareholder, not the company. That company does not get the investor's money; the investor is associated only by means of an annual report, a proxy vote, and a dividend.

When you purchase shares of stock, you become a partial owner of the means of production. As the economy grows and as firms become more profitable, the stock market rises. This has certainly been true in the United States and many other developed countries, and this has been happening in many developing countries.

Baby boomers who invest in stocks usually should look at them as long-term investments. In any given time period, such as a month, or a quarter, or a year, the economy or individual

---

1. Often the company's management holds on to a large block of the stock so that it retains a controlling or major interest in the company.

2. It is the existence of a secondary market that encourages investors to buy initial stock offerings; these investors know that they can eventually sell this stock. This secondary market also encourages companies to issue stock.

companies can go up or down, and stock prices can fluctuate accordingly. However, over time the economy has grown, and over time the profitability of many companies has grown, leading to rising stock prices.

It is these daily, weekly, and monthly fluctuations and volatility that cause many people to look at stocks as the equivalent of the lottery. This lottery notion also comes from not understanding what stocks really represent. True profits come about by identifying good companies that are increasing their profits (earnings) and their market share; they do not come from buying and selling frantically on a daily or weekly basis.

Purchasing Stocks

As discussed in Chapter 11, the price of a stock on any given day is determined by supply and demand. This demand is a function of the overall market; the sector in which that company operates; the short-, medium-, and long-term prospects for that company and that sector; the overall economy; what is happening in foreign markets; and people's perceptions of these factors. So if the company is a good one, its prospects are good, and it is increasing its earnings, all else remaining equal, the company's stock price should rise. Unfortunately, other factors often intervene.

In the short run, investors vote their preferences by buying or selling shares of specific companies. In the short run, emotions and market psychology hold sway, so the decisions that take place in the short run generally are based not on fundamentals but rather on fear or exuberance. When fear gets hold of an individual investor or a mutual fund manager, the fact that a company is a good buy is ignored and shares are sold, forcing the price down.

This is where the insightful investor can profit. Often, the way to riches is to go against the crowd and buy shares in companies that have been ignored and whose stock price is depressed. It is not an easy thing to do, for fear is contagious. It helps to recognize that most investors are not successful and are not wealthy, so going against the crowd means doing the opposite of what the unsuccessful investors are doing.

Another way to think of this is to realize that as stock prices are going down, the savvy investor can purchase these stock shares at a discount if he or she has concluded that that company is worth owning. A couple of analogies might help in recognizing what is happening. Assume that you go into a department store and see a suit that you are interested in on sale. Do you buy it or wait until it has risen back to its original price (or maybe a little higher) before you buy it? Most people would buy it. Or suppose you go into your local supermarket and see cans of tuna fish marked down by 25 percent. Do you stock up or wait until the sale is over before buying any? Again, most people would buy.

Stocks seem to be the only commodity that people want less of when the price drops and more of when the price rises. The thinking seems to be, "If no one wants it (and the price is falling), then there must be something wrong with it, so I don't want it, and if everyone wants it (and the price is rising), I want it too." Fear and greed take over. This often occurs because many investors simply don't know why they are investing and don't understand the fundamentals of investing; boomers are no different from other investors in following the herd. You should invest in a company only if you know what the company does and what its prospects are; do not base buying decisions on a hot tip or a magazine article. A falling stock price may enable you to purchase an attractive company at a bargain price; acting on tips and trends will cause you to buy and sell at the wrong times and lose money.

It is a common fallacy to base investment decisions only on the price of the stock. Some shy away from a stock that costs $100 a share but gobble up a stock that is priced at $5, thinking that it is easier for a "cheap" stock to rise than for an "expensive" stock to rise: "If the $5 stock increases by only $1, I've made 20 percent, whereas if the $100 stock also increases by $1, I've only made 1 percent." However, it is just as easy (or difficult) for a $100 stock to increase by 20 percent as for a $5 stock; the $100 stock will tend to increase (or decrease) by larger increments than the $5 stock. In addition, the absolute price of a stock is somewhat arbitrary; it depends, to some extent, on the number of shares outstanding.[3]

There are many good places to find information on stocks. A premier source is from Value Line, Inc.; this publication is available by subscription, but you can find it at most public libraries. Value Line evaluates 1,700 stocks, and each stock page includes an incredible array of statistics. Unfortunately, most people look only at the timeliness and safety ratings and read the analyst's blurb in deciding which stocks to purchase; such investors are shortchanging themselves and not taking advantage of the other information available on each sheet. Investors should obtain recent annual reports on the

---

3. Assume that ABC Inc.'s stock is selling for $40 a share and it has 100,000 shares outstanding. The company decides to undertake a 2-for-1 stock split, so it now has 200,000 shares outstanding, and the price of the stock drops to $20. Its total market capitalization remains at $4 million; before the stock split, there were 100,000 shares at $40 per share, and after the stock split there are 200,000 shares at $20 per share. Nothing has changed.

companies they are interested in and the relevant financial reports filed with the Securities and Exchange Commission; most of this information is also available on the Web.

In addition, there are many good Internet sites with pertinent data for thousands of stocks in addition to good research material. These include www.companysleuth.com, www.excite.com, www.freeedgar.com, www.hoovers.com, www.infobeat.com, www.investorama.com, www.morningstar.com, investor.msn.com, www.quicken.com, www.smartmoney.com, www.stockdetective.com, www.thestreet.com, www.wallstreetcity.com, quote.yahoo.com, and www.zacks.com. Information on large company and small company IPOs can be found at www.ipocentral.com, www.ipohome.com, www.iposyndicate.com, www.mainstreetipo.com, and www.openipo.com. In doing research online, investors should be wary of information or hot tips that they pick up in these Web sites' chat rooms. Such information is questionable at best and harmful at worst; chat rooms are wonderful places for negative rumors and misinformation to be disseminated.

Buying a Company

What if you suddenly were given $5 billion and told that you had to buy a company with this money? How would you select a company, and what would you do after you purchased it?

For one, you would spend a lot of time researching all your potential candidates. It is very unlikely that you would buy this company based on a whim, a hot tip, or an article. Instead, you would take the time to look at what products or services it creates or provides and how unique these products and services are. You would learn as much as you could about your prospective purchase. How well known is the company and what it produces? How secure is its market share, and could it be expanded? Are its products or services subject to obsolescence, or is there a steady or growing demand for them? Are revenues and earnings growing, and is it paying down debt? What are its medium-term and long-term strategies for increasing earnings and market share? What plans does it have to overcome or acquire its competition? In short, you would ask these and other similar questions before spending a nickel of your money to purchase the company.

Once you had purchased the company, you would continue to gather data and track its progress. One thing that you would not do is panic and sell based on a rumor or a sudden dip in its stock price. You would pay much more attention to its annual earnings trends and financial fundamentals than to a magazine article slamming the company. And you probably wouldn't look at its day-to-day stock price movements in deciding whether this company's prospects were good.

So why is it any different when you buy shares of stock in a company? After all, with this purchase, you become a partial owner, albeit on a smaller scale. If you are investing your hard-earned cash in a company with the hope that it will increase its profitability and increase your net worth, why wouldn't you proceed as if you were buying the company? Why would you buy or sell on a rumor, someone's unsolicited opinion, or the way the recent stock price lines up on a chart? Why would you sell a company soon after you bought it, given how much time and work you put into researching it?

Yet this is what many boomers who are trying to get wealthy do. Instead of investing in businesses, they speculate on stock movements and look for quick profits, often not realizing that these profits can be eaten up by transaction costs and short-term capital gains taxes. They throw away the possibility of long-term gains by not understanding what they bought and why they bought it. They fail to look for companies that are increasing their earnings, revenues, and market share and instead buy when the mood hits or when fear that they will miss a golden opportunity takes over. Baby boomers who can train themselves to think that they are the actual owners of a business and hold on to its stock are much more likely to see good long-term returns than are those who move rapidly in and out of stocks.

The Price-to-Earnings Multiple

Probably one of the most important and talked-about measures of a stock is its price-to-earnings (P/E) multiple. This is usually called the P/E, the PE ratio, or the multiple. What does this mean, and why is it so important?

Earnings are another name for profitability. Few companies can survive for long if they are not profitable, if they do not make money after meeting their fixed and variable expenses. A major aim of companies is not only to be profitable but also to increase their earnings over time.

To obtain the P/E, you divide the price of the stock by its annual earnings per share. Earnings per share are obtained by dividing the total company earnings by the total number of shares. So if XYZ Corp. has earned $1 million in a certain year, has 250,000 shares of stock outstanding, and is selling for $20 a share, its earnings per share would be $4 ($1 million divided by 250,000 shares), and its multiple would be 5 ($20 a share divided by $4 earnings per share). If its stock price suddenly rose to $24 a share, its P/E would rise from 5 to 6.

Earnings are calculated over a twelve-month period. This period normally occurs during a calendar year, but it can represent a fiscal year; many companies' fiscal years run not from

January to December but for some other consecutive twelve-month period. The P/E is expressed in terms of current year earnings or projected or estimated earnings for the following year. For example, if XYZ Corp.'s projected next year's earnings are $1.5 million, its projected earnings per share would rise to $6 ($1.5 million divided by 250,000 shares), and its projected multiple would be 3.3 ($20 a share divided by $6 earnings per share).

One reason that the P/E is useful is that it gives you a measure by which to compare companies and to determine their relative worth. This can be done by comparing its multiple to the growth rate of the company's annual earnings. If the multiple far exceeds this growth rate, then the stock may be overvalued or richly valued; conversely, if the multiple is less than this growth rate, the stock may be a good value. Therefore, if a stock's multiple is 38 but its earnings are growing at only 10 percent per year, then this stock probably is overvalued. A comparable company with a multiple of 15 and earnings growing at 20 percent per year is almost surely a better value.

Assume that ABC Corp.'s stock is selling at $50 a share, and its earnings are $5 a share. Therefore, its P/E ratio is 10 ($50 divided by $5). Let's see what happens with different earnings growth rates:

- Assume that the earnings growth rate is 10 percent per year. That means that in a year, ABC Corp.'s earnings would be $5.50 a share. The stock price could grow at 10 percent, to $55, and maintain the same P/E ratio.

- Assume that the earnings growth rate is 5 percent per year. In a year, ABC Corp.'s earnings would be $5.25. If the stock price were to go to 55, its P/E would be greater than 10.

In fact, it would take about two years, at this growth rate, for earnings to support a P/E of 10.

- Assume that the earnings growth rate is 15 percent per year. In a year, ABC Corp.'s earnings would be $5.75. At a price of 55, the P/E would be less than 10.

What we see is when the earnings growth rate is well below the P/E, the stock price often does not grow as quickly as when the earnings growth rate is higher. Conversely, when the earnings growth rate exceeds the P/E, a faster increase in the stock price becomes likely.

In the third example, at a stock price of $57.50, the P/E would become 10. If this earnings growth rate were to remain at 15 percent, over time, the P/E often will tend to move up as investors, intrigued by rapidly growing earnings, will become more interested in the stock, bidding up the price sharply. Meanwhile, if the growth rate were 5 percent, as in the second example, the P/E would tend to decline, leading to either a slow increase or a contraction in the stock's price as investors start to shy away from this stock.

Over time, price tends to follow earnings. If you graph a company's earnings and its stock price over time, in general, you will see a fairly close correlation.[4] There will certainly be exceptions over periods of time that can be measured in days, weeks, months, and possibly years. However, this correlation tends to be true much more than it is not true. This fact gives investors an idea whether a stock is too expensive, too inexpensive, or fairly priced. But this is only one piece of the puzzle. As discussed in the next section, there may be many other reasons why the stock price is out of line with the earnings.

---

4. Peter Lynch, *One Up on Wall Street* (New York: Penguin, 1989), p. 159.

Using P/E for Investing

One approach to investing is to look for stocks selling below what they "should" be selling for, that is, if all the information about that stock were correctly understood. This approach is known as value investing; one of the prime measures used is the P/E ratio.

There is no such thing as a "correct" or "perfect" P/E ratio. Not only does the P/E multiple vary by stock, but it also varies by sector. What is an expensive multiple for one sector is inexpensive for another. Fast-growing small companies usually can command a higher P/E than established blue chip companies because they are growing at a faster rate and because investors believe that they have more potential.[5]

Some established companies that have major recognizable trademark names or that dominate their particular sales market, such as Coke and Microsoft, can command high P/Es. In most cases, however, choosing whether to invest by comparing their P/Es to their earnings growth rates appears to be one prudent way to find good companies to invest in. Another would be comparing that company's P/E with the P/E of the sector it's in or the P/E of the entire market. If the P/E of the market is 30 and the P/E of a specific sector is 25, but the P/E of a specific stock in that sector is 15, this stock may very well be undervalued and thus a good buy.

Sometimes, because of some external event, investors get scared in the short run and significantly bid down the price of a stock or a sector. On a long-term basis, however, such stocks

---

5. This is one reason why some people invest mainly in small company stocks. Unfortunately, it is also more likely that the earnings growth in small companies will falter than it is in established companies, usually leading to a plummeting stock price, so the strategy of investing mainly in small company stocks is much riskier.

may be cheap. Once investors get over the shock of this event, the price of these stocks often rebounds.

An example might be useful. When President Clinton announced his comprehensive health care plan in 1993, the stock prices of major pharmaceutical companies plummeted; this was largely caused by fears that such a plan would permanently cripple the ability of these companies to earn a profit. This is an example of the sort of fear that drives the stock market on a short-term basis. Some investors, doubting that any plan would emerge that would cripple these companies so much, saw these lower prices (and low P/Es) as a major buying opportunity. The companies seemed sound, their balance sheets looked good, and they were still earning money at the same rate; the only thing that had changed was the perception of the future and the perception of future earnings. Once it became clear that such a comprehensive health care plan would not be enacted, the prices of these stocks moved back up quickly; any investor who purchased shares of these companies at the artificially low prices made a nice profit.

It is vital to understand that a low P/E can also mean that a company should not be invested in. If a firm's quarterly and annual earnings have declined, this often is a bad sign, and many investors may sell. If investors begin to recognize that a company's management is not doing a good job and the fate of this company may not be good, investors may begin to sell even before the company's earnings begin to fall. In such situations, the lower P/E ratio may signal anticipated disaster. If a sector falls out of favor, such as the oil services sector through most of the 1980s and the early 1990s, this can be a signal to stay away from all companies in this area. On the other hand, when the pharmaceutical industry fell out of favor, it turned out to be a time to buy. The bottom line is that there are no easy ways to get rich quickly or find good companies to invest in; investors need to do their homework.

Investing Styles

The search for good stocks does not depend only on P/E. Different investors and different money managers use different investing styles and favor different types of stocks.

Value and growth are two types of management styles. A stock that is classified as a value stock is one that, for some reason, is temporarily out of favor, and its share price has been beaten down. Value investors look for companies that they can purchase at a good value. The previous section used the pharmaceutical industry in 1993 and 1994 as an example of value stocks. Investors who favor these stocks are looking for the stock price to return to a fair market value by using measurements such as P/E, price-to–book value ratio, and free cash flow. This type of analysis also looks at and sums the value of each of the company's components; if the value of these components exceeds the current stock price, this company's stock usually is selling at a good price. Value stocks become more popular when the market outlook is less certain and investors get more defensive. Value investing as a strategy is discussed in Chapter 16.

Meanwhile, growth stocks are those whose revenue and profits grow steadily each year. Often, these companies' earnings are growing faster than the stock market as a whole, and their P/E usually is higher than that of the market. In the most recent quarters, these stocks' earnings growth often has accelerated, and they have been increasing their earnings faster than most other stocks. As long as their earnings keep growing at or above the rate expected by analysts, their stock price usually continues to rise. However, given a bad quarter, if their earnings grow at a slower pace than is expected, the stock price can plummet.

The difference between a growth stock and a value stock is that when you buy a growth stock, it is like boarding a train that is already in motion in hope that it continues and maybe accelerates. When you buy a value stock, you are boarding a train that is at a standstill with the hope that it turns out to be an express.

In addition, some investors favor large-company stocks, whereas others prefer small-company stocks. In this case, a company's size is based on its capitalization; as defined in Chapter 11, capitalization is the product of the number of shares outstanding and the price per share. Established companies usually have a large capitalization; large-capitalization (or large-cap) companies have total capitalization greater than $7 billion. Smaller, developing companies, called small-cap companies, usually have a capitalization under $1 billion. Mid-cap companies are those with a capitalization that falls in between. These distinctions are important; a 1981 study of stocks on the New York Stock Exchange showed that small-cap companies have outperformed large-cap companies since 1926.[6] However, criticism of this study has surfaced; one criticism was that much of this outperformance can be traced to several individual years in which small caps did much better than large caps.[7]

At different times, the stock market favors value stocks over growth stocks and vice versa. In addition, at different time, the stock market favors large, well-established companies over small, up-and-coming companies and vice versa.

---

6. Rolf Banz, "The Relationship Between Return and Market Value of Common Stocks," *Journal of Financial Economics*, Vol. 9, pp. 3–18, 1981.

7. John Rekenthaler, "The Long Wait: Will Small Company Stocks Ever Outperform," October 30, 1998, www.morningstar.com.

Value stocks have less downside risk because they already have been beaten down in price; growth stocks have the potential for greater gains but also have the potential for greater losses. Similarly, large, established companies have demonstrated some durability, so they usually have less immediate downside risk; smaller companies have the potential for greater gains but also have the potential for greater losses. Therefore, a portfolio that combines large and small stocks and both growth and value stocks can be a good way to spread risk while participating in the stock market's increases.[8]

Discount and Online Brokers

Everyone loves to save money; everyone loves to buy something on sale and get a bargain. Does it make sense for boomers to do this by using a discount or online broker?

Until the early 1970s, investors could purchase securities only from what are now known as full-service brokers, and they paid essentially the same commission for transactions at all brokerage firms. Since then, discount brokerage houses, where commissions on securities transactions have been set much lower, have developed and grown in popularity.[9] At dis-

---

8. Looking at how six investment styles—value and growth indexes for large-, mid-, and small-cap stocks—have done from 1976 to 1999 shows great diversity. For instance, in eight of the years, the small-cap value index had the best record, but for four of the years it had the worst. Meanwhile, in six of the years, the large-cap growth index had the best record, and in nine of the years it had the worst. Source: Maggie Topkis, "There Is a Season, Turn, Turn, Turn," *Mutual Funds Magazine,* June 2000, pp. 50–51.

9. In 1980, 1.3 percent of retail brokerage commissions went to discounters; by 1997, this figure was 14.5 percent. Source: The Securities Industry Association, as referenced in James M. Clash and Maura Smith, "Discounters," *Forbes,* June 16, 1997, www.forbes.com.

count brokerage houses, investors generally are not assigned their own individual brokers, and there are fewer extra services (such as advice and research) than at full-service brokers. A more recent occurrence is the advent and proliferation of online (i.e., Internet) brokerages, some of which are online versions of discount brokerages. At these online brokerages, the commission on each trade is a small fraction of what it costs with a full-service broker and also lower than with a discount broker. Does it make sense for investors to use a discount or online broker?

On the surface, it appears to make sense. An investor can buy or sell shares of stocks, bonds, and mutual funds and get price quotes from online as well as full-service brokers. Why pay more money to buy or to sell the same product?

When you buy a stock, bond, or mutual fund from a broker, you are actually buying more than that investment. You are also paying for service and information. This is somewhat analogous to buying a car or a computer; the level of service varies among dealerships and distributors, and the amount of service each customer needs or wants varies as well. If you thoroughly understand cars or computers, or if you feel comfortable diagnosing and possibly fixing problems, your need for full service is less than that of someone who does not understand or is not comfortable with cars and computers. So it is with brokerage houses.

Some boomers enjoy and are good at researching and analyzing different stocks and other securities. They know what to look for and feel comfortable with buy and sell decisions. Others get what they feel is valuable information from financial newsletters, magazines, or radio and TV. For them, purchasing securities using a discount or an online broker generally is the right thing to do.

Unfortunately, the very ease of buying with a quick

phone call or from your own computer and the low cost of each transaction can be seductive, so seductive that there is a strong tendency to use this medium too much. Investors using discounters tend to trade too frequently, and their gains are less than what they anticipate and often do not offset trading costs.[10] Boomers whose main job does not involve purchasing or analyzing securities usually do not have the time or energy to keep abreast of the market. Therefore, the user of the discount or online service may hear only snippets of information about a particular security; the moment any bad news becomes available, it can be very easy, too easy, to sell. Prudent decisions about buying or selling securities work better when they are dispassionate, not emotional.

Many online brokerages are new and may not have all the problems worked out of their computer programs or have enough capacity. There have been cases of people opening accounts but being unable to trade because of computer foul-ups. Even larger problems have come up when a person is unable to withdraw money or can't get hold of a responsible employee to straighten problems out. During particularly busy times, an investor may not be able to connect to the online broker for a number of minutes and cannot buy or sell at his or her preferred price. People new to an online broker's Web site often misunderstand some of the instructions and buy or sell when they did not mean to. Therefore, cheaper doesn't always mean more profitable.

Sometimes, investors actually pay more at discount and online brokerages. When you buy a stock, there is a spread between the prices at which stocks are bought and sold. Spreads on the New York and American stock exchanges rarely

10. This was a conclusion of a 1996 study by Terrance Odean, as referenced in Clash and Smith, "Discounters."

exceed one-eighth of a point. However, on the NASDAQ, where many online investors do much of their trading, spreads can be three-quarters of a point or higher. Often, with a full-service broker, you can shave the spread; this rarely happens with discount or online brokers. This extra quarter or half percent can more than outweigh the higher commission from full-service brokers.[11]

For those who want to find a good online broker, financial magazines such as *Smart Money, Mutual Funds Magazine,* and *Worth* regularly publish their evaluations of the best online brokers, and these evaluations often are available on their Web sites (www.smartmoney.com, www.mfmag.com, and www.worth.com, respectively). Another option is www.gomez.com.

If you can develop a good relationship with a competent broker, it may be worth paying the extra money in commissions. If this broker can give timely advice and analysis on prospective purchases or existing positions, paying this extra money in commissions may in fact be a bargain. In addition, if this broker can serve as a dispassionate voice against buying or selling too often or in a panic mode, then the higher commission could be money well spent. It is important to contrast this extra money spent with the potential profit to be made or the potential loss to be avoided. As in other professions, there are good brokers and bad brokers, so it is important to get recommendations and shop around.

Stock Investment Programs

A major investing fallacy is that you can buy shares of stock only through a broker. As the last section showed, a stock (or

---

11. Clash and Smith, "Discounters."

bond) broker can be a good place to go, especially if you are ignorant about the market or if you want an experienced hand to guide you. What is less known is that you can purchase shares of stock directly from certain corporations. In addition, you can reinvest any dividends directly with that corporation to buy additional shares.

A number of publicly traded corporations allow investors to purchase initial shares directly; this program is known as a direct investment program. Each has its own set of rules, including the minimums and maximums of the initial and subsequent purchases, as well as how frequently subsequent purchases can be made. These purchases are made with little or no commission; if there is a commission, the investor is charged a few cents per share or a flat fee per transaction. Therefore, the investor does not have to pay the sales commission normally charged by a stockbroker and can purchase fewer shares than would normally be purchased from a broker.

Many corporations pay quarterly dividends. Investors who participate in these programs have the option of receiving these dividends in cash or reinvesting the proceeds with the corporation, purchasing additional shares. Such a program is called a dividend reinvestment program (DRIP). Participating in a DRIP allows the investor to buy these additional shares and make additional profits if the stock price increases. In reality, participating in a DRIP is a form of dollar cost averaging, in which the investor is purchasing shares on a consistent basis and is buying proportionally more shares if the stock price dips. Participants in DRIPs usually can buy additional shares on a weekly, monthly, or quarterly basis, thus increasing their participation in this form of dollar cost averaging.

Investors who purchase shares from a broker can also request that they be put on a DRIP. In some cases, the brokerage firm handles all the paperwork, and these additional shares show up on their monthly statements. In others the shares are, in effect, transferred to the corporation, and the investor deals directly with and gets statements from that corporation. In both cases, dividends are reinvested; typically, only in the latter case can an investor purchase additional shares directly from the corporation.

The major problem with these programs is the lack of flexibility in buying and selling shares that were purchased directly from the corporation. This lack of flexibility could cost you money in both buying and selling shares. Because usually you can buy or sell only once a week, month, or quarter, depending on the investment program, you might not be able to take advantage of specific information about the stock or sudden rises or drops in the share price. Such precipitous changes could cost you money if you want (or need) to buy or sell immediately and cannot. This difference could be a lot more than the commission you paid to a broker (which gives you the flexibility to buy or sell immediately). In addition, if you suddenly need the money and cannot get it by selling these shares immediately, you may be forced to liquidate another investment.

To sum up, the major advantages of buying stock directly from a corporation are the savings in commission and dollar cost averaging. The disadvantages are the increased paperwork and lack of flexibility. These programs make more sense if you intend to hold on to the stock on a long-term basis.

Selling Stocks

After buying a stock, holding on to it for a period, and potentially reinvesting its dividends, when is the proper time to sell, and what do you need to consider in deciding whether to sell?

It's all very good to find a good stock, do the research, and buy it, but all profits (or losses) are paper profits (or losses); until you sell it, your net worth has not changed.

Some sell decisions are driven by events totally unrelated to the market, the global economy, or news events. Events that occur in an investor's life, such as college tuition, a sudden emergency, a wedding, helping one's parents, or a vacation, can all lead one to need money and thus to sell stock. It may or may not be the best time to sell that stock (or bond or mutual fund), but if you need the money, that need is the primary controlling factor.

However, boomers, like most other investors, often sell out of fear. A precipitous drop in the market, a bad series of economic reports, some negative global news, a set of rumors, or a negative report in the media can lead many investors to suddenly decide to sell. These emotion-driven decisions often are based not on logic but on the fear of suddenly losing large sums of money.

Some investment advisors recommend that when you buy a stock, you should set a price target or a percentage rise to sell at. For example, if you buy a stock at $10, you might set a price target of $15; when you sell, you will have made a 50 percent profit. Given a short enough time span, a 50 percent profit is quite remarkable. At this point, you would take your profit and reinvest in another stock to try to parlay that money into more profit. According to this logic, you should be quite satisfied with your 50 percent profit, and if you can string enough of these profits together, you should do quite well. This is the sort of strategy traders often use. However, this strategy may be wrong if the stock still has potential to rise.

Before thinking about selling a stock, you should consider why you bought it in the first place. Again, you are buying part of a company. If you were comfortable with that company when you bought the stock for specific reasons, you should check it from time to time to make sure that these factors are still in effect. If they are, and the stock price has gone down, you might consider buying more shares instead of selling it. After all, if it made sense at a certain price, it should make more sense at a lower price. If the price has gone up but your reasons for the initial purchase still hold, you might still consider buying more shares.

However, if the picture has changed, then you might want to consider selling the stock. In making this decision, you should consider how much things have changed, whether that change makes the stock a little or a lot more undesirable, whether the stock is in a nontaxable or taxable account, and what else you would do with this money. Can you purchase another stock (or investment) that has a potential return better than that of the stock you are considering selling? Or would it make sense to sell and keep the money in a money market fund for a while? If the company's circumstances are about the same but you have found another situation that is much better, you might consider selling, but you should be very sure of your facts.

Unfortunately, some investors ignore most of these considerations; rather, they wait for the stock to return to the price at which they originally bought it. Such a strategy is based on emotions, principally on the desire not to lose money on the investment. Unfortunately, there is no guarantee that you'll get your original money back. If the stock you bought has gone down 50 percent, you'll need it to double to get you back to par. In a situation like this, you need to decide whether the stock has that type of growth potential or whether another investment has a better chance of giving you that return. Your stock may never return to its original price. In addition, when you sell at a loss in a taxable account, the government, in effect, becomes a partner in your loss; selling at a loss generates a capital loss and reduces your taxes, reducing the amount of money that you've actually lost.

Other investors face a different dilemma: Their investment has shot up so much that they don't know whether to sell. They are torn between fear (in case it plummets) and greed (in case it continues to go up). One solution is to sell part of it, so as to lock in the gain (even though you'd have to pay some taxes). This way, you have locked in some gain and still have the possibility of getting more gain. One way to do this is to sell your original basis, so you are "playing" with profits only. Suppose you had invested $10,000 and the stock is now worth $40,000. If you were to sell $10,000, you'd have recouped your original basis, and everything left on the table would be your profit. Another way would be to sell half your stake and let the other half ride; this way, you'd have your basis and $10,000 of profit, so no matter what happens to the rest of the money, you have ensured yourself a sizable profit.

In sum, investors do better when they make sell decisions based on an objective look at the reasons they bought the stock rather than a subjective reaction to factors beyond their control.

Chapter 13

BONDS

As boomers contemplate retirement, having a dependable source of income becomes important. Boomers' parents, most of whom are in or nearing retirement, depend on such a steady stream of income. When the primary focus is current income, bonds become important. A bond is like an IOU; it is a promise to repay a set amount of money at a certain time, with interest payments paid at regular intervals, usually each quarter. Corporations, state and municipal governments, and the federal government issue bonds to raise money.

Bonds are issued for a set period of time, ranging up to thirty years. These periods of time are known as maturities. Under most circumstances, the longer the time period (i.e., the longer the loan), the higher the interest rate paid. Think about it: If you are going to give up the use of your money for five years instead of two years, you want a higher reward for doing so.

Bond investors are concerned primarily with the safety

and the yield (interest rate) of the bond. You might find an incredibly good yield, but if the issuer of the bond defaults on the loan, not only do you not get your interest payments, but you may not get all of your principal back. Therefore, a bond issuer's ability to pay its debts—that is, make all interest and principal payments in full and on schedule—is a critical concern for investors.

There are rating services that determine how creditworthy the bond issuer is; the higher the creditworthiness, the more likely you are to get interest payments and your principal back. Two of the best-known rating services are Standard & Poor's (S&P) and Moody's. Both use a letter scale; the highest-quality bonds are assigned AAA by S&P and Aaa by Moody's. Investment-grade bonds are considered to be of medium quality, rated at BBB by S&P and Baa by Moody's; bonds with ratings at or below BB or Ba are considered junk bonds. The lower the rating, the higher the interest rate that the issuer must attach to the bond. This makes intuitive sense. You want to be compensated for taking additional risk; this compensation takes the form of a higher yield on the bond. Accordingly, junk bonds have the highest yields but also the highest risk.

The safest bonds one can invest in are those issued directly by the federal government; the chances of default are almost nil. These might be a good choice for older adults who are afraid to invest or are still haunted by the Great Depression. These bonds are backed by the full faith and credit of the U.S. government. The government issues bonds known as Treasury bills, notes, and bonds with varying maturities. Bills have maturities of one year or less, notes range from one to ten years, and bonds range from ten to thirty years.

The next safest bonds are those issued by federal agencies, such as the Government National Mortgage Association (Ginnie Mae), and congressionally chartered agencies, such as the Federal National Mortgage Association (Fannie Mae). The former are as safe as Treasuries, but the latter are not directly backed by the full faith and credit of the U.S. government. However, their chances of default are very low because it is very unlikely that Congress would allow a congressionally chartered agency to default on its loans. In addition, these bonds usually offer a better rate of return than do Treasuries.

When a state or municipality needs to raise money, one option is to issue a bond. These bonds are known as municipal bonds. In general, these bonds have a lower yield than federal government or corporate bonds for similar time periods, thus lowering the cost to such municipalities. These entities can issue bonds with a lower yield due because in almost all cases the interest from such bonds is exempt from federal taxes. In addition, the interest is exempt from state tax for taxpayers in the state that issues the bond. Therefore, it would make sense for a Virginia resident to consider purchasing a municipal bond issued by Virginia or by a Virginia municipality. For residents of Washington, D.C., and Puerto Rico, the interest is exempt from state tax regardless of where the bond was issued.

When should an investor purchase a municipal bond instead of a corporate or a government bond? This can be answered by looking at that investor's tax rate. Suppose that that investor has a choice between a $10,000 government bond yielding 5 percent and a $10,000 municipal bond yielding 4 percent. If the investor is in the 28 percent tax bracket, after taxes he or she would have $360 from the government bond ($10,000 × 5 percent × 72 percent) and $400 from the municipal bond ($10,000 × 4 percent). For this investor, the municipal bond would be the better choice. For an investor in the 15 percent tax bracket, after taxes the government bond would pay $425 ($10,000 × 5 percent × 85 percent), and the municipal bond would pay $400. For this investor, the government bond would be the better choice.

The aforementioned rating services also rate municipal bonds for all states. States and municipalities strive to maintain high credit rankings to minimize their costs of borrowing. Most investors probably should consider only AAA municipal rated bonds because the additional yield from lower-rated bonds is slight.[1] Both states and counties have defaulted on their bonds; two of the most famous in recent memory are Washington State and Orange County, California.

Private corporations also issue bonds. Like states and municipalities, corporations strive for the highest rating on their bonds so as to lower their cost of borrowing. The yields on corporate bonds usually are higher than those issued by the federal government; this is often because the credit quality of corporate bonds usually is not as high as that of government bonds. There are many corporations with minimal credit risk.

Buying and Selling Bonds

Bonds are sold at what is known as par, or face, value. At par, a $1,000 bond sells for $1,000. If you hold the bond until maturity, you will get your $1,000 back unless something happens to the issuer. However, if you sell the bond before maturity, you might not get back the face value. This is because bond prices vary inversely with interest rates. As interest rates fall, the price of a bond rises (and vice versa). An example will help to explain. Assume you have a $1,000 bond paying 8 percent. A month later, interest rates fall to 7 percent. Suppose you

---

1. Gerri Willis, "A Fixed-Income Plan for Bond Cynics," www.smart money.com.

suddenly need to sell this bond. You will be able to sell the bond at a premium, for more than $1,000, because it is more valuable than anything currently selling for $1,000 is. Accordingly, when interest rates are falling, the price of the bond rises. This inverse relationship between bond prices and bond yields is confusing to most new investors.

Usually, the longer the maturity (i.e., fifteen years versus two years), the greater the degree of price volatility. This is because there is less uncertainty in interest rates in the short run than in the long run. With the shorter time frame, you are much more assured of getting your money back than with the longer time frame. If you plan to hold the bond until maturity, you will probably be less concerned about these price fluctuations because you know that you will receive the face value of your bond at maturity.

Boomers who bought bonds in the early 1980s, when interest rates were well above 10 percent, profited in two ways as interest rates fell throughout the 1980s and early 1990s. They received higher interest payments than they could get with newer-issue bonds, and if they needed to sell their bonds, they received a substantial premium to the bond's face value. On the other hand, boomers who bought bonds in late 1993 and early 1994 lost in two ways because the Federal Reserve raised rates several times in 1994. They received lower interest payments, and if they needed to sell their bonds, they received a substantial discount to the bond's face value.

The bond's yield is the amount the bondholder will receive in interest payments. Because of the price volatility of bonds, you need to be aware of other types of yields. One is the current yield, which is the annual return on the dollar amount paid for a bond. If you were to purchase a $1,000 bond at face value, and the bond's yield is 6 percent, your current yield is 6 percent. However, if interest rates had gone down and you bought the bond for $1,100, your current yield is 5.45 percent (6 percent × [$1,000/$1,100]).

Another way of looking at yield is called the yield to maturity; this tells you the total return you will receive if you hold a bond until maturity. Yield to maturity includes all the interest you'll receive for the life of the bond plus or minus any capital gains. So, using the previous example, assume that the $1,100 bond you bought has a maturity of three years. Because you'll get $1,000 from the bond issuer when the bond comes due, you'll have a capital loss of $100. Because you can write off 20 percent of the capital loss on your taxes, the yield to maturity is 9.09 percent ([3 years × $60 interest − $80]/$1,100). Calculating yield to maturity allows you to compare bonds with different maturities and coupons to ensure that you are getting the best deal.

Web sites with good information about bond investing include www.bondagent.com, www.munidirect.com, and www.dljdirect.com. Boomers can purchase Treasury bills, bonds, and notes directly, and commission-free, at www.treasury direct.gov.

Bond Ladders

Bond ladders are an efficient way for income-oriented investors to lock in current yield without giving up their flexibility to lock in higher yields in the future.

The interest rate you can get on any individual bond varies over time. One question boomers ask when considering bonds for themselves or their parents is whether they should invest their money now or wait for the possibility that interest rates may rise so that they can get a better yield. An additional problem is that if interest rates rise and you have to sell your lower-yielding bond, you would have to sell it at a loss. On the other hand, if interest rates go down, you would have to settle for a lower yield. Therefore, if you buy now, you might miss out on higher yields, but if you don't buy now, you might have to settle in the future for a lower yield. This is where bond ladders are useful.

In constructing a bond ladder, you initially divide up the money to be invested to purchase bonds of different maturities. When the shorter-term bonds mature, you simply reinvest them for a longer period of time.

An example will help flesh this out. Assume that you have $10,000 to invest. Break this amount into five blocks of $2,000 each, and invest in bonds of increasing maturities. One possibility might be two, four, six, eight, and ten years. This way, you'll capture the higher yields with the longer-maturity bonds while leaving open the possibility of having your money available in the short term to take advantage of new possibilities. If interest rates rise, the money that comes due in two years can be used to purchase a higher-yielding ten-year bond. If interest rates fall, you know that you have already locked in the higher current rates. With this strategy, you always will have money available for new investments every two years and can purchase higher-yielding longer-term bonds.

This example is only one way to do this. Depending on your available cash and personal needs, you could use the money to construct a ladder of shorter maturities (i.e., one, two, three, four, and five years). Another alternative would be to divide the available money into more blocks of cash to purchase more bonds of a lesser value; this would yield more years in the ladder (i.e., one, two, three, four, five, six, and seven years). The bottom line is that by using this strategy, you'll get the best of both worlds: flexibility and high current yields.

Treasury Inflation Protected Securities

In an effort to protect bond buyers from inflation, in 1996 the U.S. Treasury introduced an inflation-indexed bond. These bonds are known as Treasury Inflation Protected Securities (TIPS). Because a sudden spurt of inflation can reduce the desirability of buying and owning bonds, the idea behind TIPS is to protect the investor from inflation. Boomers and their parents who remember the crippling inflation of the 1970s and early 1980s can well remember how this inflation reduced the value of their income; inflation particularly hurts those on a fixed income because their fixed amount of dollars is able to buy progressively less. Therefore, inflation protection should interest those in or nearing retirement. How do TIPS protect against inflation, and are they right for you?

As noted in Chapter 11, interest rates are set by both actual and perceived future inflation. Bond yields typically run about 2 percent above the rate of inflation. So if inflation is running at 3.5 percent, the thirty-year Treasury bond should yield around 5.5. The problem is that if you purchase such a bond and rates rise, your real (after-inflation) return will fall. This is where TIPS come in.

To show how they work, let's assume that TIPS bonds are issued for ten years with yields averaging around 3.5 percent. They are indexed to the Consumer Price Index (CPI). So on a $10,000 bond, with no inflation, the bondholder would obtain annual payments totaling $350. But given inflation, higher payments would be received.

TIPS bondholders are paid twice a year. If inflation ran at 2 percent for the first six months of the year, the $10,000 par value would be increased by $10,200 to reflect the 2 percent inflation. Consequently, the bondholder's payment would be $178.50 ([$10,200 × 3.5 percent]/2) rather than $175.00 if there were no inflation protection. If inflation picked up during the second half of the year, say to average 5 percent for the entire year, the second payment of the year would be $183.75 ([$10,500 × 3.5 percent]/2), again showing inflation protection.

A normal Treasury bond does not have this inflation protection. Bondholders receive the same payment regardless of what inflation is. Given a $10,000 bond paying 6 percent, the bondholder will be paid $300 twice a year. If inflation averages less than 2.5 percent over the life of the bond, this bondholder comes out ahead; if it averages more than 2.5 percent, the TIPS bondholder comes out ahead. This threshold of 2.5 percent is obtained by subtracting the TIPS yield of 3.5 percent from 6 percent.

The yields of both types of bonds are taxed as ordinary income. However, the bondholder receives the inflation adjustments on the bond when the bond matures, and the adjustments are taxed as capital gains. Both this added premium in dividend payments and the extra payment when the bond comes due make TIPS a good choice for conservative income-oriented investors. Therefore, baby boomers and their parents should seriously consider TIPS when constructing the income part of their portfolio.

Convertible Bonds

Convertible bonds are unique in that they have features of both stocks and bonds. They have the ability to participate in most of a market's rise, but their dividends can help buffer any market declines. Because these investments are good for the investor who is looking for growth, income, and some safety, they can help baby boomers who are just starting to invest, boomers who want more safety in their investments, and boomers' parents.

Convertibles are issued as interest-paying bonds that can be converted to stocks if the stock price rises to a certain level. Convertibles can rise almost as much as stocks but usually don't fall as much.[2]

One way in which a corporation can raise cash is to issue convertible bonds. By issuing convertible bonds, the company allows purchasers to know that they will get their money back when the bond matures and entices them with the possibility that if the company does well enough and the stock price rises, the lender can become a partial owner.

Why would a company issue convertible bonds? The main reason is to lower the cost of doing business. By holding forth the promise that a lender can become an owner, they can issue the bonds at a lower interest rate than they would have to for a regular bond, thus saving money. When a company issues a convertible bond, it typically sets the conversion price way above the current stock price. For example, assume that a stock is selling at $12 a share and pays a 1 percent dividend, whereas its corporate bond is yielding 6 percent per year; a convertible bond might be issued to sell at $16 per share, yielding 4.5 percent, and be convertible into stock at $24 per share. In the near term, because the conversion price is so far away from the current stock price, the convertible acts more like a bond, paying its dividend and falling and rising in price as interest rates rise and fall. As the stock price rises, the price of the convertible rises but at a slower rate. As the stock price nears $24, so does the convertible, hence the ability of a con-

2. As a group, these securities delivered 69 percent of the gain and only 50 percent of the loss of the overall stock market. Source: Ibbotson Associates, as referenced in Gerri Willis, "A Fixed-Income Plan for Bond Cynics," www.smartmoney.com.

vertible to participate in a stock market rally but at a modified pace. On the other hand, if the stock price declines, the option to convert becomes more and more worthless. Thus, as the stock price falls, the convertible falls, but it falls more slowly for its dividend, which is higher than the stock dividend. This higher dividend can still pay the investor a decent return.

Because convertibles can participate in the stock market's gain and also have loss protection, they can fit into the portfolio of a conservative investor, help provide some growth and income to a retired person, or make up a portion of a broadly diversified portfolio. From 1973 to 1999, the compound annual returns for convertibles were 12.6 percent, close to the 13.9 percent return of the S&P 500.[3] Investors can purchase convertible bonds from their broker or invest in a broadly diversified convertible securities mutual fund.

---

3. Ibbotson Associates, as referenced in Willis, "A Fixed-Income Plan for Bond Cynics."

Chapter 14

MUTUAL FUNDS

Mutual funds have grown in popularity; since 1980, the total number of mutual funds available to American investors has grown from fewer than 1,000 to more than 10,000. They are an ideal way for boomers to invest in the market, from the novice to the sophisticated investor. Currently, 83 million Americans own mutual funds.[1]

Mutual funds are investment companies that pool money from different people and hire a manager to decide where the money should be invested and to track these investments. The advantages of mutual funds include professional managers, who can devote the time to follow the market closely; diversification, which reduces risk;[2] and the ability to make initial or

1. Source: Investment Company Institute, as referenced by Russell Kinnel, "Fund Investors Stay Cool Under Fire—Again," www.morningstar. com, May 2, 2000.
2. Because mutual funds have a number of securities in their portfolio, their chances of falling drastically in value are much less than those of individual stocks. From 1994 to 1999, on average less than 1 percent of all

subsequent investments with small sums of money. The average boomer normally does not have the time or expertise to study the market and to stay informed about market trends. Mutual fund investors have ready access to their money and can receive it in a matter of days with just a phone call or a letter.

Boomers who are knowledgeable or wealthy enough to buy enough stocks to achieve proper diversification still should consider using mutual funds to invest in areas of the market with which they are less familiar. Examples of such areas include small-cap stocks and international stocks (which are discussed in Chapter 15). These are areas that most investors do not have the time or expertise to follow or understand. This is in contrast to well-established and well-researched areas of the market that large-cap stocks exemplify; there are few surprises among such stocks.[3]

Each mutual fund specifies a minimum amount necessary for an initial investment, which usually ranges from $1,000 to $3,000, and a minimum for subsequent investments, which

U.S. stock funds lost more than 20 percent in a year, whereas more than a quarter of all stocks lost more than 20 percent in a year. Source: Susan Dziubinski, "Using Stocks and Funds Together in a Portfolio," April 10, 2000, www.morningstar.com.

3. For instance, there are only a limited number of automobile manufacturers. There is plenty of information about these companies, so comparisons can be made easily. There are significant barriers to entry; it would not be easy for a new, startup automobile company to gain a foothold in the market. These factors are not true about most companies that small-cap stocks represent. There are thousands of such stocks, some of which may not exist several years from now. There is less information about most small and even medium-sized companies to help in making informed decisions about investing. The different industries and their products often are in flux; for example, compare the computer industry today with five or ten years ago. In most cases, the average boomer does not understand and probably could not follow all of the changes. Mutual funds certainly make sense for small- and even medium-cap stocks.

usually ranges from $25 to $250. Some mutual funds lower their initial minimum to $500 or less under an automatic monthly investment plan. Under such a plan, the mutual fund takes a fixed amount, usually at least $50, from a checking account or a paycheck each month. These programs are an ideal way for boomers to start a mutual fund investment program and are a good way for all boomers to ensure that money is flowing constantly to build up their wealth.

Investing a fixed amount per month also is a feature of dollar cost averaging. This popular investment strategy can help boomers begin to accumulate wealth over time and smooth out market fluctuations. Dollar cost averaging allows an investor to buy more shares when the price goes down, which is to the investor's advantage when the share price goes back up. The following numerical example shows how this system works for two investors, A and B. Assume that A and B both invest $1,500 into a fluctuating market. A invests all the money at once, as shown in Table 14-1:

Table 14-1   Investing All the Money at Once

Month	Amount Invested	Price per Share	Number of Shares Purchased	Total Number of Shares	Value of Investment
1	$1,500	$20	75	75	$1,500
2	0	15	0	75	1,125
3	0	10	0	75	750
4	0	15	0	75	1,125
5	0	20	0	75	1,500

B invests $300 a month for five months, as shown in Table 14-2 on the next page.

Investor A puts $1,500 in the fund all at once; at the end of five months, the net worth is the same as after the first month. Meanwhile, investor B's investments are spread out over five months. When the price goes down, B is able to pur-

Table 14-2   Investing the Money over Several Months

Month	Amount Invested	Price per Share	Number of Shares Purchased	Total Number of Shares	Value of Investment
1	$300	$20	15	15	$300
2	300	15	20	35	525
3	300	10	30	65	650
4	300	15	20	85	1,125
5	300	20	15	100	2,000

chase more shares for the same amount of money (thirty shares at $10 per share as opposed to fifteen shares at $20 per share). When the price comes back to $20, investor B is ahead by $500.

This is an extreme example; mutual funds normally do not fluctuate anywhere near this much in such a short period of time. However, it shows how an investor can use this strategy to advantage. So in making an investment, is it better to plunk all your money down at once or flow the money in over several months?

There is no answer guaranteed to help boomers in all situations. For low-volatility funds or funds that rise at a fairly steady pace, investing all your money at once should give the best returns. For higher-volatility funds, as shown in Tables 14-1 and 14-2, the greater number of shares bought during market lows usually means that dollar cost averaging will mean higher profits and better returns over time.

Dollar cost averaging can help the boomer who wants more safety in his or her portfolio. This strategy ensures that not all the money is invested at the market high. It also allows investors to profit from drops in the market; assuming that the market eventually moves higher, market dips help the investor, allowing him or her to buy more shares per investment. For the same reasons, if the market appears to be too high and a correction appears possible or likely, a dollar cost averaging approach yields more safety and higher returns. Conversely, if a market has been in a major correction or bear market and appears to be coming out of it, investing all your money at once should be much more profitable.

Mutual Fund Categories

When it comes to selecting a mutual fund to invest in, the average boomer today is overwhelmed with confusing choices and claims.

Most funds fall into one of the following broad categories: domestic stock, domestic bond, international stock, international bond, and specialty. Within each of these broad categories are a variety of subcategories, which can be very confusing. In addition, some funds span these categories, combining stocks and bonds, for instance.

The domestic stock category includes a multitude of subcategories. Magazines and companies that rank funds over specific periods of time have come up with definitions for these subcategories in an attempt to help investors. These include the following:[4]

- Aggressive growth funds trade stocks heavily to get maximum share price appreciation for the fund; many such funds replace their entire stock portfolio one to two times a year.

- Growth funds are the most common type of stock fund; they tend to buy stocks of large and midsize companies. Their

4. Source: *USA Today* research, Lipper Analytical Services, and *Barron's Dictionary of Finance and Investment Terms*.

main focus is on share price appreciation, and income from dividends is minimal. These funds can be core holdings if your goals are ten years or more in the future.

■ Growth and income funds are more conservative than growth funds; these types of funds invest in stocks of big, dividend-paying companies. These funds emphasize share price appreciation but also emphasize earning some income from dividends.

■ Equity income funds are the most conservative of all stock funds; these types of funds emphasize stocks with high, steady dividends, and many also invest some of their money in bonds.

■ Small company growth funds search for emerging companies with a high potential for price appreciation. These funds usually have more volatility than large company funds, sometimes allowing explosive returns but also having the potential for major losses.

Unfortunately, these subcategories can be confusing. One magazine or rating service may label a particular fund a growth fund, another calls it a growth and income fund, and a third calls it an aggressive growth fund. The validity of these definitions can be murky because they are based, in large part, on each mutual fund's own descriptions, and there is no standard by which to measure these descriptions.

Probably a better way to choose funds is to examine the average company size, based on the fund's portfolio, and the fund's investing style. Company size and investing style were discussed in Chapter 12; market leadership rotates among value and growth stocks as well as large-cap, mid-cap, and small-cap stocks. Certain management styles and company sizes fall in and out of favor. Funds that invest in large-cap value, for instance, will do reasonably well when those types of stocks are in favor, a variation on the idea that a rising tide raises all ships. Although the fund with the superior manager generally will perform better, much of the gain comes from the fund's market segment. A portfolio that includes large-cap growth, large-cap value, small-cap growth, and small-cap value mutual funds is a good way to spread risk while participating in the stock market's increases.

Bond mutual funds are pools of bonds with maturities longer than ninety days. Depending on the fund's objective, these pools can comprise corporate bonds, municipal bonds, government bonds, or international bonds of varying lengths or maturities. Generally the shorter the average maturity, the less uncertainty and the less volatile the fund, and the lower yield it has. A money market mutual fund specializes in bonds with a maturity of less than ninety days.[5] The money market mutual fund strives to keep the share price constant at $1.00 and pays out monthly dividends based on the mix of extremely short-term bonds.

As with stock funds, diversification is a major reason why investors choose bond funds rather than investing in individual bonds. With diversification comes lower risk; the fund manager is able to spread interest rate risk and credit risk over many bonds. Unlike with individual bonds, in a bond fund you are not assured of getting your principal back. Because bonds mature, new investor money flows in, and some investor money flows out, the portfolio of bonds in a mutual fund changes over time. If interest rates rise, the fund's net asset value (NAV)[6] falls, so an investor's shares are worth less money.

---

5. Many banks and credit unions have accounts called money market accounts. These are not the same as money market mutual funds.

6. The NAV equals the value of its portfolio divided by the number of shares outstanding.

Given changes in the portfolio, there is no assurance that the NAV will rise back to where it was if interest rates decline. This is in contrast to an individual bond; purchasing a $1,000 bond and holding it to maturity ensures getting the principal back unless the issuer defaults. Therefore, boomers and their parents who want to ensure that they will get their full principal back should invest in bonds rather than bond funds.

Time Periods

Seeing many advertisements and magazine covers touting the top-performing mutual fund, boomers tend to be drawn into trying to find the one investment that will make them rich. But is this wise? Is it wise to try to find such a hot ticket? In addition, is it wise to switch funds regularly, always looking for the fund that did the best over some recent period of time?

Many mutual funds take out ads in newspapers or magazines saying that they were rated number one by a certain rating service for a certain period of time in a particular mutual fund category or subcategory. Given how vague some of these definitions are, boomers should ignore these ads when deciding which funds to invest in. Similarly, the fact that a certain fund did well for one quarter should not be a major factor in deciding whether to invest in it; boomers should look at how well the fund did over a longer period of time and whether the fund fits their objectives. When investors flock to a fund whose performance stands out, all the extra money flooding into that fund tends to make it difficult for the manager to invest successfully.

Given how many funds there are, usually the only way a fund can rank very highly over a quarter or a year is to take unusual risks or, by luck or good fortune, invest in the exact right sectors. Taking big risks that always pay or always being in the right sector is not an exact science; this fund's manager could make incorrect selections over the next short-term period and do very poorly. As market sectors rotate in and out of favor, what has been hot is not necessarily what will be hot.[7] Often, just as a sector becomes popular in the press and with investors, market sentiment shifts to another sector, and funds that are heavily invested in the former favorite sector start to do poorly. So it is important not to chase the recent winners.[8]

Instead, it is better to look for consistent good performance. If a fund has consistently performed in the top quarter or, at the very least, in the top half of funds with the same style and objective over several years, this is a fund to consider. These funds can provide reliable returns over a period of time. In trying to judge consistent performance, it is important to compare your fund's performance with those of similar types of funds. If large-cap growth stocks have led the market and an investor has money in a small-cap value mutual fund, he or she should not get frustrated and compare the fund's performance to the market leaders. Instead, it is important to com-

---

7. Looking at how well eleven different market sectors did in three-year increments from 1982 to 1999 shows major market rotation. Technology, which led all sectors from 1994 to 1996 and from 1997 to 1999, was the worst from 1988 to 1990 and next to worst in the preceding three-year period. Health care, which did the best from 1988 to 1990 and second best from 1994 to 1996, did next to worst from 1991 to 1993. Consumer cyclicals did the best from 1982 to 1984 and the worst from 1994 to 1996. Source: "Diversification Deficit Plagues Many Investment Programs," *In the Vanguard*, Spring 2000, pp. 10–11.

8. Looking at the top-performing thirty funds for successive five-year segments starting in 1970 (i.e., 1970–1974, 1975–1979, etc.) shows that these funds underperformed the S&P 500 during each subsequent five-year period. For two of the time periods, they underperformed their peers in the subsequent five-year period as well. Source: William Bernstein, "The Grand Infatuation," *Efficient Frontier*, July 1999, www.efficient frontier.com.

pare that small-cap value fund's performance against similar funds. Many funds compare their performance to a broad market index, such as the S&P 500; this index is not a proper benchmark for many mutual funds, particularly small company funds, aggressive growth funds, and international funds.

Good managers have a definite investment philosophy and style. When investing in a fund, you are hiring the fund's managers and expressing confidence in their investment methods. Not every investment approach will do well in every market. If a manager has a small-cap growth approach and these types of stocks aren't doing well, investors should not be disappointed in that manager and immediately switch their money. It is important to give a manager time and not get out after one or two disappointing quarters. If that fund has done poorly as compared to other small-cap growth funds over a period of time, then it is time to do research and consider switching into a fund that is better positioned in that sector of the market. The next section describes what to look for in deciding whether to stay with your fund or switch to another.

Caution on Mutual Fund Information

An increasing number of magazines, newspapers, and radio and television programs provide information intended to help consumers pick through all the funds. Much of this information is aimed at baby boomers, often in the form of different portfolios based on different goals or life situations, such as imminent retirement, retirement in fifteen years, college tuition, and empty nesters; each portfolio is made up of several funds. This proliferation of information may confuse rather than help prospective mutual fund investors.

Some articles and programs clearly delineate what investors should and should not look for and then find funds that meet these criteria, but others use simplistic or faulty criteria that may harm overall investor performance. Thus, you should use such information as only one component in your own research and should not depend on any one article or recommendation as your only source. This section will help boomers understand what to look out for, and the next section discusses some good sources to use for investigating mutual funds.

It is important to look for the following:

- A long track record. In choosing a mutual fund, look for a fund with a manager who has experience, who has been managing money for a long time and through various market conditions. Don't be seduced by a fund that has done well over one quarter or even one year; comparing five-year track records is more meaningful. If a mutual fund has had a good track record but the manager has just left, then in most cases this wonderful long-term track record is meaningless.

- Good managers. In 1980, there were fewer than 1,000 mutual funds. The importance of finding a good manager becomes paramount when you consider how few good managers there can be for the more than 10,000 mutual funds; there has been a major dilution of talent. An oft-quoted statistic is that few managers beat the S&P 500 in the late 1990s; although the S&P 500 did well, there were too many managers who didn't have enough experience in running mutual funds. Consider the following analogy. Imagine if, over a twenty-year period, the number of baseball teams increased from 30 teams to 300 teams. Critics would bemoan the lack of talent in the big leagues because there would be so many mediocre players. Batting averages, home run records, and earned run averages would all go haywire; the few good hitters would feast on the poor pitching, and the few good pitchers would similarly dominate the poor hitters. So it is with mutual fund managers; some managers can add a lot of value to your portfolio, and you should concentrate on finding them.

■ No change in investing style. As defined earlier, *investing style* refers to whether the manager is a value or growth type of investor as well as the size of the companies he or she invests in. Boomers should watch out when a manager shifts his or her investment style from value to growth, or vice versa, simply because that segment of the market is hot and he or she wants the fund to look good. In most instances, a value manager won't do well investing in growth stocks, and a manager who specializes in small-cap stocks usually won't do well picking large-cap stocks. You should almost always avoid funds that have shifted strategies.

■ Specialized sector investing. Sometimes a fund does very well for a period of time because the manager has loaded up on stocks in one or two sectors, such as technology, financial services, or energy services. If those sectors do well, the fund does well and the manager looks like a genius. As the market rotates leadership and as different stocks shine at different times, a manager who constantly pursues a strategy of concentrating in sectors may sometimes guess wrong; at such times, the fund's performance will suffer. So before investing in a fund that has done well, if you find that it is heavily concentrated in one sector, don't invest unless you specifically want that type of investment strategy.

■ Large and sudden growth in assets. Money tends to flood into funds that have been doing well, leading to a lack of flexibility. Often as a fund grows in size, the excess cash forces the manager to start buying less preferable stocks and bonds or to keep a larger than normal cash balance, normally reducing the fund's performance.

In addition, watch out for a fund that started out as a small-cap fund but because of a rapid growth of assets is now investing primarily in mid- or large-cap funds. This is a common problem. Once a small-cap fund draws in too much money, its manager simply cannot find enough small stocks to invest in. The manager must begin to buy more mid- and large-cap stocks. However, his or her expertise may be only in small-cap stocks, and he or she will not do well in larger-cap stocks. In such cases, a small-cap fund that had done very well may start to perform poorly. Many unsuspecting investors, looking only at performance, will invest in a fund that had a good couple of years (as a small-cap fund) only to find that the performance starts to lag (when it has to invest in larger-cap stocks).

Mutual Fund Information Sources

Probably the best source for mutual fund information is Morningstar, Inc. Morningstar tracks most mutual funds and provides a lot of useful data. The facts for each fund are synopsized on one page, which is updated periodically. All of the information referred to in the previous section, along with other facts such as performance data, fund volatility, and the fund's largest holdings, can be found on this single page.

Morningstar provides these data to subscribers; the subscription is fairly expensive, but most major libraries have copies. Some of this information is available for free on their Web site (www.morningstar.com). Each major grouping of mutual funds is updated periodically. Along with each week's grouping comes a synopsis publication that summarizes the pertinent facts, as well as Morningstar's rating, for each fund.

It is this rating system for which Morningstar probably is best known. Mutual funds that have at least a three-year history are ranked from 1 to 5 stars, with 5 being the best. Funds that achieve the 5-star rating, or sometimes a 4-star rating, announce this fact prominently in display ads. The implication is that such funds have been ranked as the best or among the best. Unfortunately, many investors base their buy, hold, and sell decisions solely on the number of stars a mutual fund has earned recently.

There are several problems with making investment decisions based solely on this star system. The number of stars Morningstar awards a mutual fund is based on a proprietary formula that measures risk and reward, concentrating on volatility in down markets. This formula, although good, is not perfect, and other risk-to-reward formulas may be superior.

More important, this risk-to-reward formula is based on past performance. As every mutual fund prospectus cautions, past performance is no guarantee of future results. If the fund's sector has been hot, its performance probably will have been good, so the star rating will be high. In 1998 and 1999, funds that concentrated on large-cap growth stocks excelled, so these funds garnered the lion's share of 4- and 5-star rankings. Funds that concentrated on other parts of the market did not do as well and received lower rankings. Investors who concentrate on buying the highest-ranked funds often own funds investing in the same part of the market and thus are not very diversified. When the market shifts, these investors find themselves left out of the new leadership.[9] In addition, the star rank-

---

9. A good cautionary note was sounded by Nobel laureate William Sharpe: "Star ratings do not measure how good a fund competes in its asset class, but instead give good marks for any fund that happens to be in an

ings do not take into account changes in management as well as the other red flags mentioned in the previous section.

Value Line, Inc., also publishes a comprehensive review of mutual funds. Most of the pertinent information available from Morningstar is available from Value Line as well. Their timeliness and safety rankings (similar to what they do for their stock rankings) range from 1 to 5, with 1 being the best. Everything that was said about Morningstar's star rankings applies to Value Line's rankings also; they are a good starting place but are not a good ending place.

Mutual fund companies should be able to tell you whether there has been a management change, how much assets under management have grown (also available in each fund's prospectus), and whether the overall type of investments that they make have changed. They probably won't tell you that the fund manager's investing style has changed or that the fund manager is only mediocre.

Several popular investing magazines, such as *Forbes, Money, Mutual Funds Magazine, Smart Money,* and *Worth,* also group funds into categories, such as large- versus small-cap, growth versus value investing, and domestic versus international. The magazines, in the context of discussing these funds, often make note of other important facts that will help in fund selection. These magazines have useful Web sites, some totally free and some with only certain segments free; the Web sites are www.forbes.com, www.money.com, www.mfmag.com, www.smartmoney.com, and www.worth.com, respectively. Additional Web sites devoted to providing pertinent investing information related to mutual funds include www.armchairmillionaire.com, www.brill.com, www.cbs.marketwatch.

---

asset class in ascendance. The laws of reversion to the mean cause the star ratings to have little predictive value." Source: "Exclusive Interview with William Sharpe, Part II," www.indexfunds.com.

com, www.fundalarm.com, www.investmentdiscovery.com, www.indexfunds.com, www.infobeat.com, www.maxfunds. com, www.mfea.com, www.moneycentral.msn.com, www. micropal.com, www.personalfund.com, and www.quicken. com.

Mutual Fund Allocation

The previous sections in this chapter have described market leadership rotation among the different investing styles and the importance of giving each of these investment styles time to work for you. Let's suppose that you decide to put all your money into stock mutual funds and divide it so that 20 percent is put into each of the following categories: large-cap value, large-cap growth, small-cap value, small-cap growth, and international. You also decide to add money to each category in equal monthly amounts. After a period of time, you check to see how well your investments have done and discover that none of your category weightings are at exactly 20 percent any longer. How did this happen and what should you do?

This happened for several reasons, which include the following:

■ During that particular time period, some category areas performed better than others.

■ One of the fund managers has shifted his or her investment style to follow the hot areas and is not as proficient outside his or her area of expertise.

■ One of the fund managers left.

Let's look at these three reasons in order and map out your strategy.

■ Differences between categories are to be expected. Market preferences rotate, and in some years, certain sectors or categories are hot and others are not. It is important not to shift all your existing or new money to the hot areas because hot areas can cool off very quickly. In addition, some categories tend to outperform others; by the same token, some categories are riskier than others. By putting money into many different categories, you are spreading out your risk to maximize your performance. Some advisors advocate rebalancing the weightings in portfolios every six or twelve months to get back to the original weightings. Selling winners to buy out-of-favor stocks may not seem to make sense; however, it allows you to sell high and buy low and maximize your returns.[10] A disadvantage of this strategy is the potential tax consequences involved with selling holdings in a fund; this is not a concern in a tax-sheltered account such as an individual retirement account.

■ A shift in a fund manager's investment style should be seen as at least a yellow flag. Different managers have different expertise and excel in different parts of the market. If large value stocks are in vogue and the manager of your small growth stock fund is suddenly investing in large value stocks (to improve short-term performance), he or she probably won't do a good job. Phone calls to the mutual fund certainly are in order, as is investigating the possibility of switching funds.

---

10. Assume a portfolio made up of half large-cap stocks and half small-cap stocks. If you rebalanced to this ratio once a year from 1926 through 1998, your compound rate of return would have been 14.0 percent; if you never rebalanced, it would have been 11.9 percent. Source: Paul A. Merriman, "17 Steps to Improve Your 401(k) Returns," October 1999, as found at www.brill.com.

■ Fund managers leave from time to time. If the fund has underperformed because of a new manager, it is important to check out this new manager. If he or she had a good track record in a previous fund with similar objectives and is simply repositioning some of the stocks in the fund, and this is the cause for the underperformance, this is probably okay. However, if this manager is inexperienced, has a poor track record, or has experience managing a different type of mutual fund, it is probably time to look for another fund with the same original basic style and objectives.

Mutual Fund Fees

An area that confuses many people who are starting to invest has to do with the costs of and fees charged by mutual funds. Funds are sold either with no sales charges (known as a no-load fund) or with a sales charge (load). Buying a fund with a 5 percent load means that 95 percent of the money is invested in the fund, and the other 5 percent is the commission. Depending on the fund, the charge can be assessed when you buy the fund (front-end load) or when you sell the fund (back-end load). The charge on a load fund can be as high as 8.5 percent, but few are this high. To make things even more confusing, some no-load mutual fund families slap a low load (up to 3 percent) on some of their more popular funds. Some funds charge a load if you sell the fund within a certain time frame (such as less than six months).[11]

In addition, all funds charge a management fee. This fee goes to pay for the fund manager, research staff, and other

---

11. This is done to guard against rapid turnover and market-timing strategies.

related expenses necessary to run the fund and provide shareholders with services such as monthly or quarterly statements and toll-free numbers. Mutual fund shareholders should look into this fee carefully before investing because these expenses come off the top.[12] Money market and bond funds usually have the lowest fees, followed by domestic stock funds (because more research generally is needed for investing in stocks), and then international and sector funds, which often have additional research needs. Index funds typically have low management fees. An additional expense for many funds, both load and no-load, is known as a 12(b)-1 charge and is used for promotion and advertising.

Funds that carry a sales charge can be bought from a broker or directly from the mutual fund family, whereas no-load and almost all low-load funds generally are bought directly from the mutual fund family or mutual fund supermarket.[13] Some brokers and load fund families claim that load funds perform better than no-load funds or that load funds have lower management fees than no-load funds. Both of these claims are variations on the adage that you can't get something for nothing. There appears to be no correlation between having a sales charge and a fund's performance; there are good and bad load funds and good and bad no-load funds. In addition, comparing the management fees of load and no-load funds does not show lower fees for load funds.

In sum, you should buy a no-load or low-load fund if you feel comfortable doing the research. The only exception would be if a load fund in a particular category is clearly superior; it

---

12. A fund with a management fee of 1 percent whose stock portfolio increases 12 percent will return about 11 percent to its shareholders.

13. Normally, if you buy a no-load fund through a broker, you pay a transaction fee to purchase the shares. Mutual fund supermarkets, such as those run by Schwab and Fidelity, have several hundred no-load funds that charge no transaction fee.

is worth paying the load to invest in it. If you want the advice and support of a broker, then paying the load to get that advice and support is worth it.

Buying Mutual Funds at Banks

Investment lines are blurring. It all used to be so simple: You went to a bank (or savings and loan or credit union) to set up a savings or checking account, and you went to your local brokerage house to buy stocks, bonds, and mutual funds. Now brokerages and some banks offer cash management accounts, which combine access to your cash (in a money market fund) with access to your securities. One growing trend is the ability to purchase mutual funds from many sources. Unfortunately, some new investors buy their mutual funds from local banks.

Why unfortunately? Because in many cases the scenario goes like this: The novice investor goes into the bank, notices that mutual funds can be purchased at the bank, remembers having heard that mutual funds can make them money, and asks to speak to the mutual fund representative. This investor then meets with the mutual fund representative, who winds up selling the investor one or more funds.

What's wrong with this picture?

■ The investor might assume that because his or her savings and checking accounts are insured at the bank, mutual funds are equally safe. However, mutual funds, no matter where they are purchased, are not insured, and they can lose money.

■ The investor may not be aware that the funds he or she is buying are almost always load funds, so that a certain percentage of the investment goes to pay the mutual fund representative. The investor often is not told that if he or she sells the fund before a certain amount of time has elapsed, a penalty will be assessed. However, investors should be aware that the mutual fund representative earns his or her living in part from the commissions on the funds or on these penalties.

■ The conversation between the investor and the mutual fund representative generally is a short one; the representative might sell the investor what is hot or what has the biggest commission rather than what is appropriate for the investor. In this case, the investor often winds up with a fund that is inappropriate for his or her investment goals or temperament. This usually occurs because the representative doesn't take the time to get to know the investor and has only a limited stable of funds to sell.

In general, you should be very cautious before buying mutual funds or any investment based on a brief conversation with any salesperson. You would do much better to do your own research or seek the advice of a broker or a professional financial planner, who will take the time to get to know you better and who probably can make better recommendations.

Mutual Fund Alphabet Soup

A major reason why fund families charge loads is so that they can be sold by stockbrokers and gain a much wider audience. Many people, faced with the prospect of wading through and trying to choose among thousands of funds, throw up their hands and decide to pay someone to do the research for them. So they visit their local broker, who recommends a fund or funds based on their needs, and everyone lives happily ever after. Because brokers get commissions from load funds and don't get any from no-load funds, they obviously will sell their clients load funds.

One of the confusing aspects of buying load funds is the different classes, or shares, of funds. Almost all load funds have A shares, many also have B shares and C shares, and there are other variations. What do all these classes mean, and which one should an investor purchase?

Class A shares are front-end load funds. This means that the commission is taken out at the time of purchase and is deducted from the amount invested. For a fund with a 5 percent load, 95 cents goes into buying shares, and 5 cents goes to pay the commission. Class A shares also have breakpoints; if you invest a large sum of money, the load is reduced. For instance, for an investment of $50,000, the load may be reduced from 5 percent to 4 percent.

Class B shares are back-end load shares. These are also known as contingent deferred sales charge (CDSC), or deferred load. Nothing is paid at the time of purchase, but a deferred load is imposed if the shares are sold within six to eight years of purchase. Most B shares convert to A after the expiration of the CDSC. Many brokers try to steer their clients to class B shares, touting their lack of a front-end load.

Class C shares are also known as level load shares. Usually a 1 percent commission is advanced to the broker by the fund sponsor, with a 1 percent CDSC imposed on the investor for one year.

Which are the best to purchase? This question cannot be answered without also looking at the management fee charged for each of these share classes. Of these three classes, A shares have the lowest management fee, C shares have the highest, and B shares usually are somewhere in between or the same as C shares. This is an important distinction. Most boomers, while looking at the front-end load on A shares and comparing this to the declining back-end load on B shares and low back-end load on C shares, automatically assume that the A shares are to be avoided. But are they?

The higher management fee sometimes is called a sideways load, in that this higher amount is paid every year. The management fee difference between the A shares and the B shares often averages as much as 1 percent and between A shares and C shares is the same or higher. That means that every year you are in B or C shares, you are paying more in management fees. These higher management fees directly affect the fund's performance; you pay a fractional part of this fee daily because an amount is taken out of the fund's assets each day. Therefore, the A shares will do better than the B and C shares; a 1 percent difference in management fees roughly translates into a 1 percent increase in appreciation. Over the long run, these differences in appreciation add up.

Let's make some assumptions and analyze the results to flesh this out. Assume that the A shares have a front-end load of 5 percent; the B shares have a declining deferred load of 5 percent in the first and second years, 4 percent in the third year, and so on, and after six years they become A shares; and C shares have a deferred load of 1 percent just for the first year. Because of the difference in management fees, A shares appreciate 11 percent per year, B shares at 10 percent per year, and C shares at 9.75 percent per year. So which is the best buy?

The answer is based on how much money a shareholder would receive if he or she redeemed the shares at the end of any given year (in the first year for C shares and the first six years for B shares, investors don't get the full value of the fund). As shown in Table 14-3, for the first three years, the C shares are the best buy, and from the fourth year on the A shares are the best buy.

Table 14-3   Comparison of A, B, and C Shares on a
$10,000 Investment

	A Shares		B Shares			C Shares		
Year	Invest	Payout	Invest	Fund Growth	Payout	Invest	Fund Growth	Payout
1	$10,000	$10,545	$10,000	$11,000	$10,450	$10,000	$10,950	$10,841
2	0	11,705	0	12,100	11,495	0	11,990	11,990
3	0	12,992	0	13,310	12,778	0	13,129	12,129
4	0	14,422	0	14,641	14,202	0	14,377	14,377
5	0	16,008	0	16,105	15,783	0	15,742	15,742
6	0	17,769	0	17,716	17,538	0	17,238	17,238
7	0	19,724	0	19,664	19,664	0	18,876	18,876
8	0	21,893	0	21,827	21,827	0	20,669	20,669
9	0	24,301	0	24,228	24,228	0	22,632	22,632
10	0	26,974	0	26,894	26,894	0	24,782	24,782

The reason for this supposed anomaly is simple: If you pay the sales charge up front rather than deferring the load, the higher expenses on the deferred-load share classes won't drag down the fund's appreciation. A fund appreciating at 11 percent (class A) annually compounds that much faster than ones appreciating annually at 10 percent (class B) or 9.75 percent (class C). Therefore, for the long-term investor who wants to invest in a load fund, given a difference in management fees similar to those in this example, the A shares clearly are the best bargain. In situations where the fee structure is closer, the B or C shares may be the best buy; a careful investor will check these fees and make the calculations before investing.

Mutual Fund Distributions

Almost all funds make distributions at least once a year. These distributions can be in the form of dividends, short-term capital gains, or long-term capital gains. Most investors do not understand why this occurs and what the consequences are.

Over the course of a year, a mutual fund collects dividends on the securities it holds. Most bonds and some stocks pay quarterly dividends to shareholders—in this case, the mutual fund. These dividends help increase the value of the fund and thereby increase its NAV. Over the course of a year, a mutual fund will also sell securities that are in its portfolio, incurring profits or losses as capital gains or losses, respectively. When securities in the portfolio increase in value, they increase the value of the fund; selling them at a profit crystallizes this gain.

By law, a mutual fund company must pass through at least 90 percent of its dividends and capital gains to its shareholders. These distributions are paid to the shareholders anywhere from once a month to once a year. Most bond funds pay out dividends on a monthly basis and any capital gains once a year. Stock funds that emphasize paying income usually pay out these distributions two or four times a year, whereas stock funds that emphasize growth usually pay these out only once a year. If the fund has incurred a net capital loss, it can carry this over to future years to offset future capital gains, and there would be no distributions. Thus a fund might do very well but pay out no capital gains distribution in a particular year.

When the mutual fund pays this money out, its value goes down correspondingly. This makes sense: The dividend and capital gains boosted the fund's value, so paying out this dividend or capital gain to the fund's shareholders lowers its value, lowering the fund's NAV. The size of the distribution and this drop in the NAV vary from year to year.

This payout has tax consequences (except for dividends from municipal bond funds and funds in tax-deferred accounts). When a shareholder receives dividends or capital gains from a mutual fund, they are counted as part of the tax-payer's total income. Unfortunately, some people are not aware of this. Thinking that these payouts are free cash, people time their purchase of the fund to get these distributions. This strategy ensures that they will have an immediate tax conse-quence. In terms of increasing wealth, however, these payouts are a nonevent.

For example, before a distribution, investor A has 40 shares at $25 per share in XYZ Fund; the total value is $1,000. Suppose that XYZ Fund pays out a distribution of $0.61 per share; the fund's NAV would drop to $24.39 ($25.00 − $0.61). A would get a distribution of $24.40 (40 shares × $0.61/share), and his or her value in XYZ Fund would be $975.60 (40 shares × $24.39). Therefore, A still has $1,000 ($24.40 + $975.60).

Most shareholders reinvest their dividend and capital gain distributions. In this example, A would receive about one extra share ($24.40/$24.39) from XYZ Fund and would wind up with roughly 41 shares at $24.39 a share, which is about $1,000 (41 shares × $24.39). In both scenarios, A would be taxed on the $24.40.

Because mutual fund companies usually make their major distributions toward the end of the year, boomers who want to invest in mutual funds should be wary of making a major investment in a mutual fund or starting a mutual fund account late in the year. Mutual fund companies can tell you when their distributions will occur and the size of these distributions, and wise investors time their purchases accordingly.

Index Funds

Index mutual funds are funds that attempt to mimic the per-formance of a particular index, such as the S&P 500 or the

National Association of Security Dealers Automated Quotation (NASDAQ) index. These funds own all or a good representation of the stocks in this index; by investing in such a fund, an investor gains exposure to the stocks in this index and its performance. So rather than buying a representative number of stocks, an investor can make one purchase. Given their popularity and performance, an increasing number of boomers have been investing in them.

The most popular index funds are the ones that invest in the S&P 500; during much of the last half of the 1990s, the S&P 500 index funds have outperformed the vast majority of mutual funds. Largely because of this superior performance, leading to the perception that all index funds do well, index funds have become quite popular. They have lower expenses than actively managed funds; because all stock selection is based solely on what is in the index, there is little or no need for additional research, keeping management fees lower and boosting performance. An investor in these funds can never do worse than the segment of the market that that index makes up. And there is no bad manager to make a bad sector call or other miscalculation. Therefore, everyone has heard of them and they are doing well, and this popularity feeds on itself.

Why have S&P 500 index funds outpaced nonindex funds in many recent years? It is important to remember that different sectors of the market lead at different times. In much of the second half of the 1990s, large-cap stocks have been hot. Because the S&P 500 is an index of the largest 500 companies, it is only natural that this index has done well. During this time period, the primary direction of the S&P 500 was up, so an index fund made up exclusively of these stocks would have appreciated significantly. Funds made up primarily of mid-cap or small-cap stocks would not have done as well.

Even funds made up primarily of large-cap stocks probably would not have done as well for several reasons:

- These funds almost always need to keep some of their money in cash to handle redemptions, so they cannot be 100 percent invested.

- These funds may not have had enough money invested in the large-cap stocks that appreciated the most.

- In many cases, these funds have some money invested in some smaller company or international stocks.

- These funds have higher management fees than a non–actively managed index fund, eating into appreciation.

For these reasons, it would have taken superior management, superior stock-picking skill, and some luck to beat the S&P 500 index funds.

Should you invest only in index funds? This question is addressed in the next section.

Problems with Index Funds

The previous section discussed some of the reasons why boomers should invest in index funds. However, there are problems with investing only in index funds:

- Just because an index, such as the S&P 500 index, has done so well over the last few years is no assurance that it will continue to outshine all other investment options. People tend to believe that what has worked in the recent past will continue to work. From an investment point of view, this simply does not work. The S&P 500 has done well recently because large-cap stocks have led the market. Yet large-cap stocks have not always led the market. Because of inflation, gold was the recommended investment choice in the mid- to late 1970s. In the early 1980s, commercial real estate was the hot investment because it was a great inflation hedge, had tax benefits, and allowed investors to profit from leverage. As inflation declined, both gold and real estate lost out to bonds. But bonds have not done well in the 1990s. No investment stays hot forever; large-cap stocks will not always lead the market, so it is important to diversify.[14]

■ What makes up an index and who makes these determinations? Indexes are not sacrosanct; a committee decides which securities will be included or replaced in a particular index. In recent years, the committee that determines the makeup of the S&P 500 index has replaced an average of thirty companies a year to supplant those that have merged or gone out of business.[15]

■ Except for a few bad decisions, the Dow Jones Industrial Average (DJIA) would be much higher. For example, IBM was originally put into the index in 1932 but was delisted and replaced by AT&T in 1939. IBM did not return to the DJIA for forty years, during which time it rose more than 21,000 per-

14. Looking at five asset classes, real estate, and international and domestic large- and small-cap stocks from 1972 to 1998, each had years in which it either led or lagged the others. Over this time period, domestic large-cap stocks did not do as well as an equally weighted portfolio of these five asset classes. Source: David Bugen, "Why Diversify," February 26, 1999, www.morningstar.com. In addition, looking at returns from 1970 to 1999, the following asset classes did better than the S&P 500: U.S. large-value, U.S. small-value, and the smallest 20 percent of stocks on the New York Stock Exchange, as well as both large and small international stocks. Source: Paul A. Merriman, "The Best Buy-and-Hold Strategy We Know," May 1999, www.fundadvice.com.
15. Source: Louis Braham, "The Shifting S&P," October 19, 1999, www.smartmoney.com.

cent. Meanwhile, during this same time period AT&T rose about 100 percent. Had the committee that determined the makeup of the DJIA included IBM for that entire forty-year period, the index would be about 90 percent higher today.

■ The most efficient part of the stock market is that which contains the large-cap stocks; the stocks of large corporations are the most researched, so the chances of major surprises are fairly slim. However, the mid- and particularly the small-cap portions of the domestic market as well as the international markets are less efficient; there is more potential for undiscovered value here. Given this potential for such surprises, index funds for these areas of the market have a better chance of underperforming an actively managed mutual fund with similar market objectives.

Each small-cap index fund must buy a representative share of the companies in the index; an index fund cannot buy shares in all the thousands of companies that make up a typical small-cap index. Not only would the transaction costs be too high, but many small stocks are illiquid, so the fund buying (or selling) the requisite number of shares would affect the stock's price. So the managers must buy only a certain number of these companies, and the percentage of shares in the fund must replicate its percentage share of the total market capitalization of that index. So not only are the managers constrained into guessing which would be the representative companies, but they must buy them regardless of what these companies' prospects are. In a nonindex fund, the manager can choose among all the companies; given how little information is known about some of these small companies, a good manager can ferret out companies with exciting potential.[16] In

---

16. Over a trailing ten-year period, 74 percent of small-cap growth funds and 55 percent of small-cap blend funds beat their respective in-

addition, unlike large-cap and total market index funds, small-cap index funds are not very tax-efficient. For example, an index fund that tracks the Russell 2000 must sell every stock that has become too large or too small for that index.[17]

- If the index's sector of the market is flat or declining, this index fund will necessarily have poor performance. In an actively managed fund, the manager can shift to a high percentage of cash, shift to another part of the market, or concentrate on a carefully selected number of stocks. In the 1973–1974 bear market, the S&P 500 index dropped more than 40 percent. In such a situation, the fact that an index fund cannot diversify or move into cash can act like a straitjacket.

- The U.S. stock market is among the most developed in the world, so there is more consistency in the indexes used for these markets than in many international indexes. There are numerous international indexes, and there is more subjectivity in constructing these indexes and in what stocks are used in them. In addition to the Europe, Australasia, and the Far East (EAFE) index, there are indexes for Asia, the Pacific Rim (both of these with and without Japan), Europe, Latin America, and developing markets. It is not always clear which index is the appropriate one to invest in or to measure a fund against. International indexes must presuppose which countries qualify

---

dexes. (A mutual fund manager's investing style that does not fall strictly into a growth or value regimen often is called a blend.) Source: Russell Kinnel, "A Great Four Months for Active Management," May 15, 2000, www.morningstar.com.

17. The Russell 2000 is reconstituted every year as some of the larger stocks are elevated to the Russell 1000 and some of the smaller stocks drop out. Therefore, the Vanguard Small-Cap Index, which tracks this index, lost 20.4 percent of its return to taxes over the past three years. The fund's tax efficiency level ranks 127th out of 240 small-cap funds with three-year records. Source: Lewis Braham, "The Taxing Side of Funds," September 28, 1999, www.smartmoney.com.

for a particular index, what percentage each selected country will be of the whole index, and what stocks within that country will be included in the index. In other words, the people who construct the index must be right in all three instances for the index to be successful.

Index funds can be a useful and well-performing part of a portfolio. However, when you invest in an index fund, it is important to remember that these investments are not devoid of subjectivity and opinion; they simply allow a different manager to decide what to invest in. With an actively managed fund, you can find out who the manager is and what his or her investment philosophy is and can hold him or her accountable; with an index fund, it is rare that anyone knows who is making the decisions and what their selection criteria are. Therefore, the advantage of such funds is their low management fees and tax efficiency, not the elimination of human input.

Chapter 15

INTERNATIONAL INVESTING

In 1970, the United States produced nearly half of the world's output, but by 1998 it produced only about one-third. Thirty years ago, more than 65 percent of the valuation of the world's stocks was traded in the United States,[1] but today, two-thirds of the world's stocks are traded abroad.[2] Should boomers looking to increase their wealth consider investing abroad?

There are potentially greater rewards and greater risks in investing outside the United States. First the rewards. The economies of some foreign countries are growing faster than the U.S. economy, and many countries have the potential to grow faster in the future; such growth can translate into major stock market advances. As of 1998, five of the ten largest banks, eight of the ten largest automobile companies, and nine

---

1. Source: Morgan Stanley Capital International, as referenced in "International Investing," www.troweprice.com, 1998.
2. "Pros Say Act Globally When Investing," March 5, 1997, www.usatoday.com.

of the ten largest steel companies could be found in foreign countries.[3] Therefore, by investing only in the United States, many boomers miss attractive investment opportunities. Stock market returns in foreign countries often are higher than those of the U.S. market, on both an individual year and a multiyear basis.[4] In addition, if a country's currency rises against the U.S. dollar, the value of stocks in that country will rise for an American investor.

However, it pays to be cautious because there are also risks in investing abroad. Most foreign stock markets are not as well established or regulated as the U.S. stock market, so the possibilities of fraud or market price inefficiencies may be greater. Accounting practices are not as well established in some countries, so companies and their future prospects cannot be analyzed as well. In many developing countries, the industrial infrastructure is not firmly entrenched, thus causing production bottlenecks, which could hurt a company's profitability. Political uncertainties are also a factor in many newly developing countries; companies could be nationalized, the stock market could be shut down, or a capitalist system could be overthrown. And there is always the risk of currency fluc-

---

3. "International Investing," www.troweprice.com, 1998.
4. Looking at the ten major markets from 1980 to 1998, the U.S. market performed best in only one year, 1982. Historically, returns from foreign stocks, as measured by the Europe, Australasia, and the Far East (EAFE) index, have exceeded those achieved by U.S. stocks, as measured by Standard & Poor's (S&P) 500, over the long term. Comparing these returns over rolling ten-year holding periods from 1979 through 1998 shows that foreign stocks outperformed U.S. stocks in sixteen of the last twenty ten-year periods. Because the four periods of foreign stock underperformance occurred recently, some analysts have questioned the wisdom of international investing. However, historically, every few years a shift has occurred between superior U.S. performance and superior foreign performance. In addition, the EAFE includes Japan, which had negative returns in the 1990s, thus dragging down this index. Source: "International Investing," www.troweprice.com, 1998.

tuation; if a country's currency value falls relative to the U.S. dollar, the value of a stock, expressed in U.S. dollars, will also fall. Clearly, you should not invest all or most of your money in foreign countries.

Market studies have shown that a portfolio made up of 20 to 30 percent foreign stocks and 70 to 80 percent American stocks is safer and generates higher returns than a portfolio made up exclusively of American stocks.[5] For this reason and because international markets do not always move in tandem with U.S. markets,[6] many financial planners recommend that investors have a portion of their portfolio in international investments. In a year when the United States is experiencing a bear market, some foreign countries might be experiencing bull markets. Therefore, investing in foreign markets helps to moderate losses and generate better overall portfolio growth.

Most boomers, whether they know it or not, have been participating in foreign markets. Many domestic stock and bond mutual funds currently have some percentage of foreign securities in their portfolios. Many domestic companies derive

---

5. These percentages are based on an application of modern portfolio theory, looking at the maximum rate of return for every level of risk. When the historical returns of different percentages of U.S. stocks, as represented by the S&P 500, and foreign stocks, as represented by the EAFE, were plotted on a graph, the point representing the lowest risk occurred between a 20 percent and a 30 percent weighting of the EAFE. This point also has a higher return than a portfolio of only U.S. stocks. Source: Frank Armstrong, "Improving a Portfolio: Adding International Equities," October 3, 1997, www.morningstar.com. In addition, in sixteen out of the last twenty ten-year rolling periods, a portfolio comprising 20 percent international stocks and 80 percent U.S. stocks equaled or outperformed one invested exclusively in U.S. stocks. Source: "International Investing," www.troweprice. com, 1998.

6. Comparing the monthly returns of the S&P with those of the EAFE from 1976 through 1998 showed a correlation of 0.47. Source: William Bernstein, "The Gospel According to Ibbotson," *Efficient Frontier*, February 1999, as found at www.brill.com.

some of their revenues and earnings by selling products and services abroad. And most consumers, whether they know it or not, are already purchasing products from foreign companies; many companies that were started in the United States have been bought by or merged into foreign-owned companies.

The rest of this section discusses how to invest internationally using individual stocks and bonds, and the next section focuses on investing internationally using mutual funds. Possibly the easiest way to introduce international exposure into your portfolio is to invest in a multinational corporation (MNC) or a mutual fund that is made up, in large part, of MNCs. Such companies, many of which are based in the United States, derive a quantity of their revenues from sales abroad. Given the increased emphasis on competing in the global economy, an increasing number of American companies export their goods. If you want to go this route, key things to look for include an increasing commitment to expand overseas and increasing revenue and profitability from overseas operations.

Many foreign stocks can be purchased directly in the different U.S. stock exchanges. They are sold as American depository receipts (ADRs) and can be bought and sold in dollars. Many mutual funds do some of their international investing using ADRs. Some of the problems of investing directly in a foreign country's stock exchange, such as different regulatory practices, do not apply to ADRs. In addition, these companies are well known, they have been analyzed in detail, and their stocks have good liquidity. Different stock rating and evaluation services appraise most ADRs sold in America. Therefore, you can easily compare these stocks to domestic stocks. Still, there is always the risk of foreign currency volatility; if that country's currency falls against the dollar, the value of that stock will fall.

You can also set up accounts in foreign countries for the

purpose of purchasing stocks and bonds. Potential problems with investing this way include finding reputable brokers, navigating language barriers, understanding local trading customs, and finding reliable information on specific stocks. In many foreign countries, there is little trading activity on some stocks and bonds, making it hard to buy or sell at an acceptable price. In newly developing countries, there are additional problems, including the possibility of the stock or bond market being closed down. Still, an investor can find good stocks and bonds abroad that are not yet well known and have high profit potential.

Web sites with information on international investing include www.adr.com, www.adrbny.com, www.cbsmarketwatch.com, www.ft.com, www.intltrader.com, www.megastories.com, www.micropal.com, www.wn.com, www.wisi.com, and www.worldlyinvestor.com.

Investing in International Funds

As was discussed in Chapter 14, there are areas of the market in which the average investor cannot develop the knowledge necessary for prudent investing. International investing certainly qualifies as one of these areas. Most boomers do not have the time or expertise to understand and follow the markets in one or many other countries, so it might be best to use mutual funds.

If you want to invest internationally by using mutual funds, it is probably safer to start out by purchasing shares in a global fund or a foreign fund. The former can invest anywhere in the world, and the latter is limited only by not being allowed to invest in the United States. Both options give the manager a lot of latitude, providing the investor with broad exposure.

Given a good manager, a global fund may have the better chance of doing well because the manager is unfettered in his or her search for good securities. Because each manager's style and outlook are different, investing in more than one global or foreign fund should give an investor better safety and diversification. In addition, given the number of stocks and investing opportunities that exist abroad, entrusting all investing decisions to one mutual fund manager in one mutual fund probably will not maximize potential returns.

After investing in one or more global or foreign funds, you might consider an emerging or developing markets fund. Although these funds are riskier, at times some of these countries' economies have grown faster than the economies in the United States, western Europe, and Japan. Accordingly, over time, their markets have the potential to do better and at times have done better. The key words here are "over time": These markets are very volatile, so it is very important to have a long time horizon when investing in such funds. Given the very different mindset that existed in former Communist countries, such as those of eastern Europe, in terms of product quality, profits, and savings for the future, investors should also be cautious about putting much money into this area because it will take time for an understanding of the free enterprise system to develop.

Only when you have already invested in global, foreign, and emerging or developing markets funds should you consider a regional or single-country fund. These probably are the riskiest because the manager is limited to investing only in that region or that country and cannot invest money elsewhere. Such a fund will do poorly if the markets in that country or region fall.[7] Regional funds usually have higher management

---

7. For example, the five-year annualized return for Pacific/Asia funds was only 6.93 percent, whereas the average foreign fund returned 15.54 percent per year. Source: Hap Bryant, "Around the World with 80 Funds," May 8, 2000, www.morningstar.com.

fees than broad-based foreign funds.[8] In general, you might be better off trusting the judgment of a fund manager to choose between different countries in seeking good investments. However, if you have good information about a particular region or country and feel comfortable with the risk, such funds can have great profit potential.

As with foreign stocks, currency risk applies to global and foreign mutual funds as well as regional and single-country funds. These funds' performances are based both on how well that stock or bond does in the country of origin and on how that country's currency does against the U.S. dollar. Baby boomers who decide to invest abroad should understand this risk because it can either penalize or reward the investor. The effects of currency fluctuations are explored in the rest of this chapter.

Introduction to Foreign Exchange

One day, we hear that the dollar is up, and the next, we hear that the dollar is down. What does this mean? Is this something you need to be concerned about? What does any of this have to do with your investments?

Why do different currencies exist? Because the laws of each country differ and because the ability to transact business differs, each country needs its own currency, which allows its residents to purchase goods, make transactions, and save and invest within the laws of that country. Why do exchange rates between these different currencies fluctuate? These movements reflect the relative strength of the different economies. Given changes in factors such as productivity and inflation, the

---

8. Most Latin American and Pacific funds charge at least 2.75 percent in fees, whereas the average foreign fund charges 1.71 percent. Source: Bryant, "Around the World with 80 Funds."

actual and perceived strengths of each country's economy differ, leading to changes in exchange rates.

Exchange rates also move up and down for other reasons. Many currencies can be bought and sold on the open market; this is what American tourists do when they exchange U.S. dollars for local currency. The prices of these currencies can move up or down for technical and fundamental reasons as well as emotional reasons. Strong feelings about the perceived strength or weakness of a foreign economy can translate into large banks going on major buying or selling sprees, radically changing exchange rates. Investment companies also buy and sell currencies, either to hedge the performance of international mutual funds or to profit from the perceived direction of a currency's movement.

In mid-1995, less than 90 Japanese yen would have purchased $1 U.S., but less than two years later, $1 U.S. would purchase more than 120 yen. Did the U.S. economy change that much relative to the Japanese economy over this time span? In the first half of 1997, the U.S. economy was seen as strong and growing, with both inflation and unemployment low, whereas the Japanese economy had been stagnating for a number of years. So part of the rise in the value of the dollar can be traced to the perception of a stronger U.S. economy as compared with the Japanese economy. In addition, part of this increase resulted from the fact that, for numerous reasons, the value of the U.S. dollar had been declining since the mid-1980s and may have been too low. Therefore, the exchange rate prevalent in mid-1995 probably underrepresented the true value of the dollar.

What do these changes in exchange rate mean for the average consumer? Let's look at a hypothetical example with the dollar at two different exchange rates: $1 = 90 yen and $1 = 120 yen. Let's suppose that a TV made in Japan costs

36,000 yen. At the former exchange rate, it would cost an American consumer $400 (36,000/90), and at the latter exchange rate, it would cost $300. As the value of the dollar rises, Japanese goods become cheaper in the United States, helping American consumers (who are able to buy cheaper goods) and Japanese firms that manufacture goods for export while potentially hurting U.S. firms that manufacture the same or similar goods. Conversely, suppose that a computer made in the United States costs $2,000. At the former exchange rate, it would cost 180,000 yen (2,000 × 90), and at the latter, it would cost 240,000 yen. As the value of the dollar rises, U.S. goods are more expensive in Japan, hurting the overseas sales of U.S. firms and helping Japanese firms that manufacture the same or similar goods. However, U.S. firms that import goods or raw materials can cut costs because they can buy more of that country's local currency per dollar.

Therefore, a cheaper currency can help domestic consumers, and an expensive currency can hurt domestic consumers. Depending on the mix of a company's imports and exports, the strength of a currency can either help or hurt portions of the domestic economy. It is ironic that governments seem to feel that it is important to have a strong, more expensive currency, equating a strong currency with national pride.

How Changes in Foreign Exchange Affect Stock Investments

Is there a correlation between the strength of a currency and how well investments do? The U.S. stock market has gone up and down when the value of the dollar has been both rising and falling, so at first glance there does not appear to be a direct correlation. When the dollar is declining, firms that export goods overseas should be able to export more and increase their earnings, thus driving up the price of their stock. Conversely, when the dollar is strengthening, firms that import a lot of goods or raw materials find the costs of these imported goods decreasing, which increases their profitability.

Strengthening and weakening currencies affect the value of foreign investments. If your international mutual fund rises 15 percent over a period of time as the dollar weakens, part of this 15 percent rise would be attributable to the increasing value of the underlying securities, and the remainder would be attributable to the weakening dollar; a weakening dollar drives up the values of securities when they are converted to dollars. On the other hand, if the dollar is getting stronger (making the foreign currencies worth less), this tends to counteract some portion of the increases in foreign stocks and bonds.

For example, suppose that on a certain date, the exchange rate between American dollars and Japanese yen is $1 = 100 yen. Further assume that on that date, your international mutual fund purchases shares of a Japanese firm, XYZ, Inc., at 1,000 yen per share, or $10 U.S. per share. Later, the share price of XYZ, Inc., moves up to 1,800 yen per share, for an 80 percent gain. However, suppose that during this time period, the exchange rate changed to $1 = 120 yen instead. In American dollars, this company would be worth $15 per share (1,800/120). An American investor would have made a 50 percent gain on this stock; the rising value of the dollar wiped out 30 percentage points of the gain in the Japanese market of that stock. On the other hand, if the exchange rate had moved to $1 = 90 yen, in American dollars, this stock would be worth $20 per share (1,800/90), so the American investor would have made a 100 percent gain on this stock. In this case, the falling value of the dollar would have augmented the gain in the Japanese market.

Mutual fund managers sometimes try to rectify this situation by hedging a portion of their funds. For instance, if they believe that the dollar is gaining strength, which would depress the value of their portfolio in dollar terms, they could enter the currency futures market to try to make up part or all of this expected loss. (The mechanics of this are complicated and are not explained here.) The strategy of hedging tends to be risky; it reduces the amount of capital that can be invested in securities, which tends to reduce any potential portfolio gains. If the currency futures market behaves in a way contrary to the expected result, losses occur.

Obviously, currency risk works in reverse for foreign investors. If the foreign currency is gaining strength relative to the dollar, any investment made in the U.S. stock market would lose some of its potential gain. For much of the late 1980s and early 1990s, as the dollar lost value, there was less incentive for foreign investors to invest in the U.S. stock market, no matter how well the U.S. market performed. Conversely, in the mid- to late 1990s, the dollar strengthened and attracted foreign money into the U.S. market. This increasing cash inflow increased demand for stocks, leading to a higher U.S. stock market.

How Changes in Foreign Exchange Affect Bond Investments

The interaction of increases and decreases in the strength of the U.S. dollar relative to foreign currencies is the same for bonds as it is for stocks. Therefore, if a bond in a foreign country pays 10 percent per year, and over the first year that currency loses 4 percent of its value compared with the U.S. dollar, an American investor will net 6 percent.

In some foreign countries, particularly developing countries, interest rates are higher (sometimes much higher) than those in the United States for at least two reasons. Because investing in a developing country is riskier than investing in a developed country, banks need to promote a higher interest rate to reward investors for taking this larger risk. In addition, these higher rates are an incentive for local residents to keep their money in that country and invest it in the local banks (to help investments in that country) rather than sending it abroad to a safer banking system or keeping it under the mattress. American investors, looking for a higher yield on their money, should take this currency risk into account, along with other risks, before deciding to invest in foreign-denominated bonds. A supposedly generous interest rate return could shrivel rapidly if that country's currency suddenly loses value. For example, in December 1994 the Mexican peso was suddenly devalued, so peso-denominated bonds lost value in dollar terms. The value of the currencies in many neighboring countries also dropped.

There is another interplay between interest rates and exchange rates. Often, the higher a country's interest rate, compared to another country's interest rate, the more foreign money it attracts. This increased demand can help drive up the value of that host country's currency.

In November 1999, the yield on a ten-year U.S. Treasury bond was around 6 percent, whereas in Japan it was closer to 2 percent. Not surprisingly, a fair number of investors in U.S. Treasuries were Japanese. The wider this gap, the more attractive U.S. bonds appear to the Japanese, thus increasing demand. As demand increases, the demand for dollars to buy these bonds increases, thus increasing the value of the U.S. dollar relative to the Japanese yen.

At times, different countries' central banks buy or sell different currencies to try to affect, in one way or another, the exchange rates. Through the first part of the 1990s, as the value of the U.S. dollar was falling, other countries' central banks sold their currency to buy dollars in an attempt to shore up the falling dollar. Unfortunately, most of the time, such efforts don't have much of an effect because the market tends to define appropriate exchange rate levels.

These central banks also play a large role in determining the interest rates in their countries. One major consequence is a change in the relative value of their country's exchange rate. If the Fed raises interest rates, for example, this makes U.S. bonds more attractive to foreigners, thus increasing the demand for dollars and driving up the value of the U.S. dollar against other currencies. This increase in the value of the U.S. dollar, in turn, can make U.S. goods more expensive for foreigners and foreign goods less expensive for U.S. consumers. This is an additional variable that the Fed must take into account when weighing interest rate increases and decreases.

Chapter 16

INVESTMENT STRATEGIES

Along with the explosion in financial information has come an explosion in investment strategies. Newsletters, magazine articles, and Internet Web sites abound with "surefire" strategies, and an increasing number of radio call-in shows are catering to this growing appetite for ways to increase wealth. Because so many boomers have not been investing seriously and are trying to make up for lost time, most seem to be searching for the Holy Grail, the plan that will make them wealthy overnight; however, many such strategies will wind up hurting them much more than helping them. Lost in all this turmoil are ideas and strategies that have proven their worth.

Think about it: If there were successful get-rich-quick strategies, wouldn't they be known by now? And if someone has come up with such a plan, would he or she be willing to sell it to you for $99, $299, or $499? In addition, wouldn't there be mutual funds designed to increase people's wealth through such ideas?

This chapter defines some of the characteristics of ideas that have been successful for many people over many years. It is not a map to instant riches but rather a collection of investing approaches that are designed to help you build wealth over time and reduce risk. All investing is a balance between risk and reward; high-risk strategies, which have the potential to build wealth rapidly, also have the potential to lose wealth rapidly. And this is an important point. In an effort to make up for lost time, some baby boomers may throw caution to the wind and use some high-risk strategies. Such action can push them further behind, causing them to lose a large percentage of their current net worth and forcing them to delay retirement even longer or limiting their ability to help their children or parents financially.

To help baby boomers reach their goals, this book has emphasized the following steps:

- Establish clear, concise, achievable financial goals.

- Pay off all credit card bills.

- Maintain three to six months' worth of living expenses in an easy-to-access savings account or money market mutual fund.

- Save and invest at least 10 percent of your gross income.

- Fully fund your 401(k) plan and IRAs.

- Dollar cost average into one or more mutual funds regularly.

- Review your investment selections at least twice a year, shifting money when appropriate.

- Educate yourself every month about finance and investing.

If you take these steps consistently, you can accumulate large sums of money.

These steps are one of many fine strategies for building wealth. Many Web sites give good financial planning and strategy information; some of these are free, and others charge. These include www.directadvice.com, www.estrong.com, www.fidelity.com, www.financialengines.com, www.fplanauditors.com, www.investorama.com, www.kickassets.com, www.morningstar.com, www.personalwealth.com, www.quicken.com, www.smartmoney.com, www.troweprice.com, www.vanguard.com, and www.wallstreetcity.com. Many of these emphasize investing in stocks as the best way to build long-term wealth.[1]

Whichever strategy you choose, it is important to trust it, give it time, and stick with it rather than letting your emotions cloud your investment logic. Although it is important to review and possibly fine-tune your strategy over time, it is equally important not to make frequent large-scale modifications. The worst thing you can do is to keep changing your focus. Changing your focus too frequently negates the advantages of time and compounding and gets you out of the habit of saving and investing regularly.

Don't Be a Market Timer or a Trader

The idea that an investor can time the market is seductive. Such a strategy seems to be an ideal way to maximize profits

---

1. Examining portfolios of different mixes of stocks, bonds, and cash over the last seventy-four years shows the superiority of stocks. For any time period of at least eighteen years, bonds would weigh down the portfolio's performance, and for any period of at least fifteen years, cash would do the same. Source: "Building a Better 401(k) Strategy," www.smartmoney.com.

and minimize losses. Who wouldn't like to pick the exact market tops and bottoms, getting out at the top and back in at the bottom?

Trying to time the market is a key reason why many boomers do not make much money investing. People who try to time the market use any number of indicators to determine the market tops and bottoms. Several newsletters and market timing services are available to help boomers try to maximize profits by timing the market.

It is almost impossible to time the market. As discussed in Chapter 11, during most market advances, much of the upward movement occurs during just a few trading days. A majority of the time, the market moves up or down within a broad trading range. Usually something such as an unexpected piece of news triggers the market to move broadly higher or lower. Someone who is out of the market, waiting for the right time to invest, will miss such sudden explosions. These sudden gains are where the bulk of the money is made.[2]

Some models purport to predict market moves using formulas based on an index's price-to-dividend ratio or the number of months since the last 10 percent decline. As discussed in Chapter 10, the problem with such formulas is that they are static and that some of their underlying assumptions make no sense. Because markets are not static, boomers who decide to use any of these models need to examine the inherent assumptions very closely.

Some investors, both novice and professional, believe that the way to get wealthy is by trading stocks. A trader is one who

---

2. For example, two-thirds of the stock market increase in 1991 came in a twenty-one-day trading period starting on January 16, right after the start of the Persian Gulf War. Source: Alan R. Feld, "Market Timing Is Harder Than It Looks," *The CPA Journal Online,* February 1995, www.cpa journal.com.

buys and then sells the same stocks within a short period of time, whereas an investor buys a stock with the idea of holding it for a long period of time. The trader moves in and out of the different stocks, looking for fairly rapid price swings in which to make a profit, but an investor ignores the fairly rapid price swings in favor of long-term rises in the stock's price.

Why do people trade stocks? Traders believe that they can identify stocks of specific companies that have the potential to rise in a short period of time. This belief can come from the following:

■ Knowledge of a specific industry, such as the oil services or food manufacturing industry.

■ Knowledge of market dynamics, such as noticing that a certain segment of the market has been beaten down and is selling for less than traditional measures say it should. An example is the pharmaceutical industry: In 1993 and 1994, the prices of drug stocks fell because of fears of major declines in profit.

■ Technical analysis, which involves charting and then examining the price of the stock (and its moving averages) over a period of time. Technical analysis purports to be able to determine resistance points (prices at which there is resistance to the stock falling), entry points (good prices at which to purchase the stock), and sell prices.

There are several drawbacks to being a trader, which include the following:

■ Paying higher commissions for more frequent trades

■ Paying higher taxes because most trades do not qualify for preferential long-term capital gains

- Not fully understanding the ins and outs of technical analysis and thus buying and selling at incorrect times

- Missing out on sudden price surges by being out of the market while waiting for the next trading opportunity.

Boomers who trade stocks believe that they can find pockets of opportunity for quick profit; by doing this enough, they assume that they can parlay a lot of quick gains into a highly profitable operation. A lot of quick 10 percent gains here and 15 percent gains there can add up nicely, and some traders can do this quite well. However, history shows that, on average, most traders don't do so well.

In a follow-up study by Dalbar, Inc., to the one referenced in Chapter 11, Dalbar said that some investors "switch in and out of funds trying to time the market. By not remaining invested for the entire period, they do not benefit from the majority of the equity market appreciation."[3] The study concluded, "Individual investors lose out because of their frequent, irrational buying and selling."[4] Although irrationality, like beauty, may be in the eye of the beholder, it is clear that any advantages gained from these frequent trades were offset by choosing stocks poorly, paying high trading commissions, and missing some of the more favorable price moves.

Another study looked at the trading activity of 78,000 households that used one large discount broker between February 1991 and December 1996. The study broke 78,000 households into quintiles based on how frequently they turned over their portfolios. The low-turnover group averaged just a

---

3. Jeff Troutner, "Do-It-Yourself Investors Face a Hard Reality," www.indexfunds.com, 1999.
4. Hayley Green, "Fund Timing: An Inalienable Right?" May 3, 2000, www.smartmoney.com.

1.44 percent turnover per year, and the high-turnover group averaged a 283 percent average annual turnover rate. The average portfolio in the high-turnover group produced a 10 percent annualized net return whereas the group with the lowest turnover had a 17.5 percent net return on average. The study's conclusion was that "trading is hazardous to your wealth."[5] The percentage gains do not include consideration of capital gains taxes, which put traders at a further disadvantage.

In most cases, baby boomers wanting to build wealth are better off investing in rather than trading in stocks.

Investing Defensively

With the stock market having hit new highs for much of the 1990s, and with the more than 20 percent returns it has provided in the latter half of the 1990s, why should anyone think about investing defensively? Given all the money flowing in from the baby boomers who are investing for retirement, won't the market simply continue to rise?

There is no guarantee that the stock market will continue to rise, hence the need to invest defensively. Investing defensively means, while striving to be a successful investor, trying to minimize losses rather than maximize gains. This may seem counterintuitive, but trying to maximize gains often can maximize losses.

In addition to market timing and trading, some boomers try to maximize their gains by chasing the latest hot trend. There is no guarantee that the sectors that have been hot will

---

5. Brad Barber and Terrance Odean, "The Common Stock Investment Performance of Individual Investors," *The Journal of Finance*, Volume 55, No. 2, April 2000, pp. 773–806.

remain hot.[6] Leadership in the market rotates between economic sectors and investing styles. Therefore, buying last year's or last quarter's winners often guarantees owning tomorrow's losers.

It is easy to lose sight of the fact that going for the big gain usually means taking big chances that increase the possibility of greater losses. To make up for a 20 percent decline, the investment has to gain 25 percent.[7] Similarly, a 100 percent increase is needed to offset a 50 percent decline. In other words, going up is steeper than coming down.

There are several ways to help prevent such major losses. One way to reduce major losses is to find investments with a low beta. Beta is a statistical gauge that measures volatility against a specific index, often the Standard & Poor's (S&P) 500. By definition, the S&P 500 has a beta of 1.0. A fund that has a beta of 1.2 is 20 percent more volatile than the S&P 500; if the S&P 500 goes up (or down) 10 percent, all else being equal, this fund will tend to go up (or down) by 12 percent. Conversely, a fund with a beta of less than 1.0 is less volatile than the index. Again, when an investment declines, it needs a larger percentage rise to return to par. With low-beta stocks and funds, the upward incline to make up lost ground usually is less steep than with high-beta funds. Another strategy to help prevent losses is to have investments that do not move together in the same direction or by the same magnitude. When investing in equities, spread out risk by making sure that you

---

6. A good example of how hot segments of the market can cool off rapidly involves the National Association of Security Dealers Automated Quotation (NASDAQ) index. This index rose steadily from market lows in October 1998 and gained more than 80 percent in 1999. The NASDAQ peaked on March 10, 2000, close to 5,100 and, in about a month, dropped by more than 35 percent, including a 25 percent drop in just one week.

7. A 20 percent decline from $1,000 is to $800. A 25 percent increase from $800 is needed to get back to $1,000.

have successfully diversified among both large- and small-cap stocks (or funds) as well as stocks (or funds) that represent both the growth and value styles of investing. These investment types rarely decline at the same time or to the same degree. Therefore, your entire portfolio will not decline during a market downturn or bear market.

By increasing your diversification, you will add layers of protection.[8] REITs have good dividend yields, which also helps to cushion market corrections. REITs and certain specialty areas, such as natural resources, often move differently from the stock market in general and technology stocks in particular. Additional layers of protection, such as investing in companies with large international exposure, foreign companies, or global or international funds, help ameliorate risk because international markets often do not move in tandem with U.S. markets. Bonds, which are sensitive to both current and projected interest rates and inflation rates, often perform well in markets in which stocks do not perform well.[9] Convertible bonds have the advantage of rising in a rising stock market, but their guaranteed yield generally cushions market corrections.

Certain investments are riskier than others. If you need to raise cash unexpectedly in the middle of a market downturn, a diversified portfolio, which allows you to sell your less volatile investments that have not fallen as much, will ensure that your net worth won't suffer as big a loss.

Another way to invest defensively is to emphasize value

---

8. A look at selected four-year time periods since 1975 shows rotating leadership: International small stocks did the best from 1975 to 1978, real estate from 1981 to 1984, international large stocks from 1983 to 1986, U.S. small stocks from 1991 to 1994, and U.S. large stocks from 1995 to 1998. Source: David Bugen, "Why Diversify," February 26, 1999, www.morningstar.com.

9. Jeremy Siegel, *Stocks for the Long Run* (New York: McGraw-Hill, 1998), pp. 33–34.

investing. As discussed in Chapter 12, value stocks are those that are temporarily out of favor. Thus, their share price has been beaten down and they can be purchased at a good price. This strategy is discussed further in the next section.

Value Stocks

Stocks appreciating at an average of 11 percent per year means that, on average, your money will double in about 6½ years. But do all stocks do this well? How can you find stocks that have the potential to exceed this historical average? And what stocks should you buy when the market deviates from its upward bias and either goes down or doesn't grow?

Baby boomers looking for stocks with these attributes should consider value stocks; these stocks generally have relatively low price-to-earnings (P/E) ratios. Many have been beaten down in price. Some value companies operate in industries currently out of favor with investors. One of the cornerstones of fundamental analysis is to look for stocks of companies selling below what they "should" be selling for, that is, what they would sell for if all the information about that stock were correctly understood.[10] If they are good companies, investing in them can be an excellent way to increase your net worth.

As discussed in Chapter 12, the major alternative to value stocks is growth stocks; these are stocks of companies whose earnings have the potential to grow faster than the stock market but whose P/E usually is higher than that of the market. Although growth stocks did much better than value stocks in

---

10. Fundamental analysis involves looking at a company's financial conditions, which can include cash flow, competitive position, debt service, earnings, and sales.

1998 and 1999, the historical average shows just the opposite. Not only have value stocks done better over time than growth stocks, but they have done so with less risk.[11] All else being equal, a low-P/E stock has greater upside potential and lower downside risk than a high-P/E stock.[12] Investors often frantically get rid of companies with temporary problems, so the stocks of these companies become bargains. Thus, when the stock market declines, value stocks do not decline as much because their stock price has already been discounted by investors. Therefore, value stocks' limited downside can help protect your portfolio.

A company with a P/E of 10 usually has more growth potential than a company with a P/E of 50. Why? A P/E of 50 is harder to maintain. This ratio is high by historical standards. For the stock price to rise, either the company's earnings must increase dramatically (to support this high P/E) or the multiple would have to go higher than 50. The P/E of 10 could increase much more readily (because 10 usually is less than the market average); in addition, the stock's earnings would not have to increase as fast for its price to move up.

There are other reasons why investing in low-P/E stocks often has the edge over investing in high-P/E stocks. When the companies associated with these stocks turn around, they

---

11. From July 1963 through March 1999, large-cap value stocks outperformed large-cap growth stocks by 29 percent with 10 percent less risk. Over the same time period, small-cap value stocks outperformed small-cap growth stocks by 70 percent with 20 percent less risk. Source: William Bernstein, "Value Stocks: Hidden Risk or Free Lunch," *Efficient Frontier,* September 1999, www.efficientfrontier.com.

12. Data from 1978 to 1993 show that that the cheapest 20 percent of stocks, based on P/E or price-to–book value, have beaten the market by about 10 percentage points. Source: "Tweedy Browne American Value Fund Annual Report," March 31, 2000, p. 12. See also James K. Glassman, "A Contrarian View: Stocks' Risk Is Low," *The Washington Post,* May 10, 1998, p. H1.

often produce better-than-average gains as investors realize their potential. This is in part because the prices of these companies have already been depressed because they have been out of favor; therefore, they have further to rise. One analogy is to compare this rise to the explosion potential in a coiled spring; because the stock price is low, it can shoot up very rapidly. Some analysts stop following companies once they fall out of favor with investors; this creates investment opportunities when these companies suddenly become popular and are followed by more stock analysts.

Large price increases can occur when an undervalued company reports earnings that exceed analysts' estimates. Investors tend to overreact and sell quickly when a promising company reports disappointing earnings results; they tend to overreact and buy wildly when an undervalued company releases better-than-expected earnings. This overreaction can create a sudden, rapid rise in the stock price.

Earnings projections tend to be an inaccurate measure of what a company's actual earnings will be. Earnings estimates generally are unreliable in a rising market and are usually even more suspect in a volatile market. Because many earnings projections are inaccurate and high-P/E stocks have further to fall, low-P/E stocks can help cushion a portfolio.

Closed-End Funds

Attractive profit potential exists in using closed-end mutual funds. Unfortunately, many boomers do not know about such funds. This section defines them and then discusses some of their uses.

The funds with which most investors are familiar are known as open-ended funds. These funds stand ready to sell and redeem shares directly to new and existing shareholders. No-load funds sell their shares at net asset value (NAV), and load funds sell their shares at NAV plus the sales charge. Sometimes, when a fund becomes too popular and too much money comes in, the fund closes to new investors; too much money can force a manager to buy securities that he or she does not like or keep a large cash position. In addition, fund managers always need to keep some money in cash; given a sudden rush of redemptions, managers often have to sell securities to raise money to honor these redemptions. Therefore, cash flow problems can constrain a manager's performance.

These problems do not occur in closed-end mutual funds, which are made up of a fixed number of shares. An investment company sells these shares in an initial offering. However, once all the shares have been sold, the only way to purchase shares is on a stock exchange; they can be bought and sold like shares of individual stock. Thus, the major difference between open-end and closed-end funds is the way in which shares are bought and sold. Because no money is redeemed from the fund itself, it does not have cash flow problems.

Because they sell on the stock exchange, closed-end funds actually have two prices: the NAV and the price shareholders are willing to pay. Because both prices can fluctuate, closed-end funds sell above or below their NAVs. This is also known as selling at a premium or a discount, respectively.

Most closed-end funds sell at a discount to their NAVs. Because the amount of this discount can fluctuate, investors can garner additional profits. For instance, assume that a closed-end fund normally sells at a 10 percent discount. If investor sentiment suddenly turns negative on the stock market or if the particular market in which that fund invests loses popularity, more people will want to sell the fund than buy it. Consequently, its market price will drop, and its discount can increase, maybe to 15 or 20 percent. An astute investor can purchase this fund at this larger discount and, when it returns close to its normal discount, sell it for a profit. Or if that fund or market in which it invests becomes popular, demand could rise and both the market price and the NAV could increase; the discount could narrow and even turn into a premium, which would mean an even larger gain.

Closed-end funds occasionally change into open-ended funds or liquidate at a certain date; the former occurs when the shareholders vote for it to happen, and the latter occurs as defined in the prospectus. When either happens, shareholders automatically receive the fund's NAV. If the fund had been selling at a discount, the investor gets an immediate profit.

Closed-end bond funds have some additional major advantages over open-end bond funds. Unlike with stock mutual funds, where a good manager can make a huge difference in performance, bond fund performance does not vary much from fund to fund within the same type of bond category; bond fund managers have the same pool of bonds to choose from. A good manager may be able to ferret out bonds that have been overlooked, boosting the yield or total return of the fund. But this extra yield or total return generally is measured in fractions of a percentage point or just a few percentage points, not dozens of percentage points, as a superior stock fund can earn. So it is important to look at the impact of the following factors:

- Most closed-end bond funds sell at a discount to their NAV. This gives an added boost to the yield. If the composite yield of a fund is 8 percent and it is selling for a 10 percent discount to its NAV, the actual yield is around 8.8 percent. Thus, you tend to get a higher yield for the same quality of bonds in a closed-end fund than in an open-end fund.

■ The manager of an open-end bond fund has no control over the money that flows in and out of the fund. Therefore, when rates increase, driving down the NAV, shareholders often redeem their shares, causing the fund manager to sell many of the holdings at a loss. These redemptions tend to outweigh any new money looking to take advantage of higher rates. Without additional money, the manager cannot purchase any of the higher-yielding bonds. Thus, even when rates come down, the NAV will not rise to where it was before the rate increase; at a lower NAV, your principal is worth less.

■ This scenario does not happen with closed-end bond funds. Because these funds are traded on the exchanges, the fund manager never has to worry about redemptions. The portfolio of bonds in which he or she is invested remains intact. Even if the NAV drops because of a rate increase, it will return to where it was originally when rates return to where they were originally.

■ Because of money flow problems and bond redemptions, fewer bonds mature in an open-end fund, causing them to appreciate less than in a closed-end fund.

Finding good closed-end funds is more difficult than finding good open-end funds. This is a function of the much larger number of open-end funds and the paucity of information on closed-end funds. A stock broker or brokerage firm can easily recommend open-end funds, and most mutual fund companies have a stable of open-end funds for your perusal. Mutual fund rating and evaluation services tend to devote most of their resources to covering open-end funds. However, information on closed-end funds is available from brokerages, Morningstar, and S&P, as well as on the Internet (www.icefi.com and www.morningstar.com).

In sum, once you become comfortable investing, closed-end funds are an area worth investigating.

Growing Dividends

Retirees tend to put a greater importance on dividends than do nonretirees because of their need for a steady stream of income in retirement. One way to obtain a steadily increasing stream of dividends is by purchasing stock. This may seem counterintuitive because people tend to buy bonds for dividends and stocks for capital growth. This section explains this strategy.

Investors make money on their stock investments in two ways. The most obvious one is through the increase in their price. If you buy a stock at $20 per share and it rises to $30 per share before you sell it, you have made a capital gain of $10 per share. If your original purchase was for 100 shares, your profit would be $1,000, minus commissions and taxes. The other way to make money on stocks is through dividends.

Not all companies pay dividends. For those that do, dividends can range from a minuscule dividend for growth companies to dividends of 5 percent and higher for utilities and REITs. The money to pay the dividend usually comes from profits. When a company makes a profit, it can use it in one of several ways: to buy competitors, to fund research and development, to repurchase stock, or to give shareholders dividends.

Companies often pay dividends to help to stabilize or boost the price of their stock. A major determinant of stock price is the current and projected earnings. If a company's earnings fall below expectations, if these earnings dip precipitously, or if it appears that projected earnings will not increase, the stock price usually falls as investors perceive that that company's prospects do not look good. However, if this company also regularly pays a dividend, demand for (and consequently the price of) this stock generally does not fall as much on bad news; people are buying the stock for both its earnings potential and its current dividend. In other words, for companies that pay a dividend, the stock price is supported by both its current and projected earnings and its dividend; the stock prices of companies that do not pay dividends lack this buoyancy.

Unlike fixed-debt instruments, such as bonds and certificates of deposit, the yields on stocks are not fixed. If a stock priced at $30 pays a $1 annual dividend, its dividend yield is 3.33 percent ($1/$30). However, if that stock rises to $40, this $1 dividend yield drops to 2.5 percent, and if the stock falls to $25, the dividend yield rises to 4.0 percent. Stock dividends do not move in tandem with stock prices; they are increased (or decreased) occasionally by the corporation, often once a year. It is this increase that can lead to a superb dividend strategy with stocks.

Assume that you buy 100 shares of XYZ Corp. at $40 per share and that XYZ Corp. pays a dividend of $1 per share; therefore, the dividend yield is 2.5 percent. With an investment of $4,000, you can buy 100 shares and are entitled to an annual dividend of $100. Assume that XYZ Corp. grows at 9 percent a year and is committed to keeping its annual dividend yield at 2.5 percent. At a 9 percent growth rate, the stock price doubles in eight years to $80. The dividend also doubles to $2 per share. Your investment is now worth $8,000 and you get an annual dividend of $200. Even though the current yield remains at 2.5 percent, you are earning 5 percent on your original investment ($200/$4,000).

Moving forward another eight years, your investment is

now worth $16,000 and you receive an annual dividend of $400. Once again, even though the current yield is still at 2.5 percent, you are earning a 10 percent yield on your original investment ($400/$4,000).

Let's look at what is happening here. As this company's share price rises and the dollar amount of the dividend payout increases, the return on your original investment rises. This is different from what happens with bonds, which promise only a fixed stream of constant dividend payments. In this example, you are being rewarded in two ways: through an increase in the value of your stock and through an increase in the dividend yield on your original investment.

This strategy carries more risk than investing in bonds for their yield; the assumptions in this example (that both the stock's price and its dividend will rise over time) may not hold for every stock. And it is a long-term strategy because you must invest in the stocks now for this dramatic increase in the stock's dividend yield to manifest itself. But it is a good strategy to consider if you are interested in securing both capital appreciation and a rising dividend stream.

Internet-Related Investing Trends

Wayne Gretzky, considered by many to be the best hockey player ever, was once asked the secret to his success. In effect, he said, "I don't skate to where the puck is, I skate to where I know it will be."

The same principle applies to successful investing. Don't invest in what's popular, what everyone wants now. Invest in what feeds this popularity and in what will be popular, where the demand will be tomorrow. Invest in companies that will profit from today's and tomorrow's demands. Look for long-term trends, and invest in them.

By blindly following what's popular, you don't know whether you are getting in at the bottom, the top, or somewhere in between. In addition, you don't know when to sell. By figuring out what will be popular before it has become popular, you will get in at or near the bottom. This is tough to do because you may be sitting on "dead" money for a while. It takes more discipline. But it can be more financially rewarding in the long run.

Too many baby boomers, hoping to make fast money, yearn to invest in companies that are in the news and whose stocks are soaring. However, many have no idea how mercurial these companies can be.

The important thing is to discern the important long-term trends and invest there. Two such trends involve the Internet and the changing needs of baby boomers; the former is covered in this section and the latter is covered in the next section.

Today's hot stocks include Internet stocks, stocks of companies whose services or merchandise sell directly over the Internet. The ways in which the Internet will change our lives cannot yet be imagined. Internet companies are springing up like mushrooms after a spring rainstorm, and investors are flocking to them. The problem with such stocks is that nobody knows what the demand for their products will be tomorrow. There are few barriers to entry for such companies; the Web company that is hot today may be a has-been in six months.

The sudden explosion in Internet-related companies replicates the pattern of a classic investment bubble. This has happened many times before: A new technology becomes viable, a lot of companies quickly spring up to take advantage of this new technology, vigorous competition establishes industry-wide standards and begins to winnow the field down, and increasing numbers of mergers occur, leading to a much smaller number of survivors. In their own day, telegraph, railroads, telephone, and hard disk companies were thought of as the exciting new technology, certain to change the way people lived. However, in each of these industries, the number of viable companies has dropped precipitously. The number of telegraph companies has gone from 50 in 1850 to 1 today, the number of railroad companies peaked at nearly 1,400 in 1900 and shrank to 30 today, the number of telephone companies fell from more than 1,000 in the 1890s to less than 600 today, and the number of hard disk manufacturers dropped from 52 in 1980 to 12 today.[13] Who knows which of the thousands of Internet companies will still be around 10 years from now?

There is money to be made from the Internet; it just takes some work and ingenuity. However, rather than investing directly in one of the online sites, consider investing in companies that should prosper no matter which online merchants still exist a few years from now. Such companies are called Internet enablers. A good analogy is that these companies are similar to the people who sold equipment to the gold miners who went to California in the 1800s; they prospered no matter who found gold. And what types of companies fit the description of these Internet enablers? Here are a few examples that baby boomers should consider:

- Transportation companies, which will transport the goods sold over the Web

- Cable and networking companies, which keep Internet services flowing to customers

13. Hal Varian, "5 Habits of Highly Effective Revolution," *ASAP*, February 21, 2000, www.forbes.com.

■ Bandwidth companies, which supply the chips and other equipment to expand the Internet bandwidth

■ Data-processing companies, which process the credit card and bank transfer data that result from Internet sales

■ Credit card companies, which will see increased volume with increasing Internet sales

■ Financial service companies, which deal in stocks, mutual funds, and other types of financial services and should flourish from the increase in online stock transactions

■ Established companies with solid, established product lines that have diversified into the Internet, where this diversification complements their existing business

With each of these types of companies, you do not have to choose which Internet-based company will flourish. By investing in these Internet enablers, or in a mutual fund that invests in these enablers, you will add more stability to your portfolio than if you tried to pick the few Internet winners.

Baby Boomer–Related Investing Trends

One sure way to have gotten rich over the last 50 years is to have invested in what the leading edge of baby boomers needed or wanted. As the demand for products to satisfy boomers increased, the stock prices of the companies producing these goods exploded. Investors buy stocks based on anticipated earnings increases; the demands of this leading edge of boomers determined which industries and which companies have seen increased earnings.

In the past, the following events were important in the lives of boomers and spelled great profit potential:

■ When boomers were young, companies manufacturing items such as diapers, baby food, and cameras and film (for baby and family pictures) successfully met growing demands.

■ When boomers were in grade school and college, companies able to build schools and produce textbooks saw major increases in business.

■ When boomers bought their first houses, real estate boomed, driving up the prices of houses, condominiums, and rental units. This helped to define the real estate boom of the late 1970s and the 1980s.[14] Companies able to supply products for these houses also did well.

■ When boomers began to have discretionary income in the late 1980s and the 1990s, companies able to supply goods such as technological wonders (computers, VCRs, compact disc players) did well. In addition, as some of this discretionary income went into investing, so mutual fund and stock brokerage firms did well.

What does this mean for the future? What are baby boomers most concerned about today? Many have already purchased their homes, cars, and computers. Immediate concerns for many include putting their children through college and caring for their parents. Future concerns include retirement and the quality of health care. Baby boomers clearly should use their own needs as investment opportunities.

---

14. The real estate bust of much of the 1990s can be explained, in part, by the fact that most boomers had already bought their homes, so demand waned.

The widespread interest in paying for college, helping parents, and saving for retirement translates into an increased need to accumulate wealth. The current perception, right or wrong, is that the stock market is the only place for anyone to make the double-digit returns necessary to make money grow quickly enough. Therefore, the demand for stock has been rising; as shown in Chapter 11, all else remaining equal, this will also lead to an increase in prices and an increase in the value of the stock market. Therefore, as baby boomers are getting more serious about investing in stocks, you should ride this trend upward.

In addition, demand for financial service companies should also increase. Given the increasing need to save and invest for the future, companies that cater to these needs should profit from the increase in the demand for their services. This includes banks, savings and loans, brokerage houses, mutual fund companies, and insurance companies. Thus, baby boomers are creating good investment vehicles for themselves.

Baby boomers also are realizing that they and their parents will have increasing health care needs. So what companies will benefit from increasing health care demands? They include pharmaceutical companies, biotechnology firms, and companies that supply pharmacies and hospitals. Given baby boomers' desire to fight aging, companies producing health food and herbal supplements might also do well. The growing demand for long-term care facilities also suggests investment opportunities. Insurance companies that sell health-related insurance, such as overall health insurance, dental insurance, and long-term care insurance, probably will see an increase in their business and might see their profits rise. On the other hand, health maintenance organizations, because of recent bad publicity and the perception that they are more interested in profits than in people, may not be a good investment. As with financial service companies, baby boomers, with their increasing health-related needs, are creating good investment vehicles for themselves.

Boomers who want to profit from these trends should not blindly invest in the areas suggested here but should do their own research to find the industries and companies that could profit.

INDEX